# Persian Heritage Series
Editor: Ehsan Yarshater

## No. 31

## Iskandarnamah
*A Persian Medieval Alexander-Romance*

# Persian Heritage Series

The Persian Heritage Series aims at making the best of Persian classics, historical and scientific texts, and folklore available in the major Western languages. The translations in the series are intended not only to satisfy the needs of the students of Persian history and culture, but also to respond to the demands of the intelligent reader who seeks to broaden his intellectual and artistic horizon through an acquaintance with major world literatures.

*General Editor*
Ehsan Yarshater (Columbia University)

*Advisory Council*
I. Gershevitch (Cambridge University)
G. Lazard (University of Paris)
B. Morgenstierne (Emeritus, University of Oslo)
B. Spuler (University of Hamburg)
G. Tucci (University of Rome)

*Late Members*
A. J. Arberry (Cambridge University)
W. B. Henning (University of California)
H. Masse (University of Paris)
T. C. Young (Princeton University)

## UNESCO Collection of Representative Works
This volume is jointly sponsored by Unesco,
The Royal Institute of Translation and Publication,
and the Iranian Ministry of Arts and Culture.

A complete list of volumes published in the Persian Heritage Series appears on pages 239–42.

# Iskandarnamah

## A Persian Medieval Alexander-Romance

TRANSLATED BY
Minoo S. Southgate

New York
COLUMBIA UNIVERSITY PRESS
1978

Library of Congress Cataloging in Publication Data

Anonymous
    Iskandarnamah.

    (Persian heritage series)
    Translation from the Persian text edited by Ī. Afshār published in 1964 under title: Iskandar-nāmah.
    Bibliography: p.
    Includes index.
    1. Alexander The Great, 356–323 B.C.—Romances.
I. Southgate, Minoo S. II. Afshār, Īraj.
III. Title. IV. Series: UNESCO collection of representative works: Persian heritage series.
PK6451.C32H513    891'.55'32    77-27047
ISBN 0-231-04416-X

Columbia University Press
New York   Guildford, Surrey
Copyright © 1978 Columbia University Press
All rights reserved
Printed in the United States of America

*To Lillian Herlands Hornstein*

# Acknowledgments

*I wish to thank Professors Lillian Herlands Hornstein, John Hurt Fisher, Peter J. Chelkowski, Patrick J. Leach, Maurice Wohlgelernter, and Dale Bishop for their assistance.*

# Contents

| | |
|---|---:|
| Introduction | 1 |
| **Iskandarnamah: A Translation** | |
| The Birth of Alexander | 9 |
| The Expedition of King Alexander the Dhul-Qarnain to Iran to Fight Darab the Son of Darab | 11 |
| Alexander's Arrival at Oman and What Happened between Him and the King of Oman | 15 |
| How Alexander Went to Porus Disguised as a Messenger and What Happened between Them | 17 |
| Alexander's Journey to Kashmir and What Happened between Him and Azadbakht, the King of Kashmir, and His Daughter, Mahafarin | 22 |
| The Story of Azadbakht, the King of Kashmir, and Porus's Daughter, Who Was Alexander's Wife | 30 |
| Alexander's Journey to Cylon and What Occurred between Him and Kayd, the King of India | 30 |
| Alexander's Pilgrimage to the Tomb of Adam and His Journey from There to the Land of Gold | 30 |
| Alexander and the Davalpayan, and the War between Them | 36 |
| Alexander's Arrival at Mecca and the House of the Prophet, and What Happened between Him and the People of Mecca | 39 |
| Alexander's Arrival at Yemen, and What Happened between Him and the King of Yemen | 40 |
| How the King of Egypt, Disguised as a Messenger, Went to Alexander upon His Arrival in Egypt, and What Happened between Them | 44 |

| | |
|---|---:|
| How King Alexander Asked the Chief of Egypt to Tell Him Stories, and the Chief Did So | 44 |
| How Alexander, Disguised as a Messenger, Visited Candace, the Queen of Andalusia, and What Happened between Them | 48 |
| Alexander's Journey to the Land of Darkness and What Occurred There | 56 |
| The Story of the Scorpion, the Snake, the Youth Who Was Sleeping in the Garden, and the Wonder That the King Saw | 60 |
| Alexander's Arrival in Turkistan by Way of the Akhzar Sea, and What Happened between Him and the King of That Region | 65 |
| The Story of the Barrel of Wheat Found in the King's Treasure House and the Life Story of Bahram, His Father, and Their Wives | 65 |
| The Story of the Hermits and the King's Daughter, and What Occurred | 66 |
| Alexander's Arrival at Siyavushgard and What Occurred between Him and the King of That Land | 66 |
| Alexander's Arrival at China, the Wonders He Saw There, and What Occurred between Him and the King of That Land | 66 |
| How Alexander Went to the Emperor of China as a Messenger and What Occurred between Them | 67 |
| How Alexander's Aunt Contrived a Plan to Murder Him and What Occurred | 73 |
| How the Son of the Emperor of China Contrived a Plan to Poison Alexander through His Concubine, and How the King Discovered That by Sagacity | 74 |
| How Alexander Arrived in Taghmaj and Visited the King of That Land as a Messenger | 74 |
| Alexander's Arrival in the Land of the Giants and the Cannibal Zangis, and His Battle against Them | 75 |
| Alexander's Arrival at the Well, the Story of the Maiden, and What Occurred between Alexander and the Zangis | 75 |
| Alexander's Arrival at the Hermit's Cloister on the Mountaintop and What Occurred | 76 |

CONTENTS                                                                xi

| | |
|---|---|
| Alexander's Arrival in the Fairyland, His Meeting with Araqit, the Fairy Queen, and What Occurred | 76 |
| How Alexander Invaded Araqit's Territory and Araqit's Uncle Came to Her Aid | 94 |
| The Arrival of Araqit's Uncle and His Fairies at the Camping-ground and What Occurred between Him and King Alexander | 94 |
| Alexander's Arrival in Russia, What Happened between Him and the Russians, and the Dream He Had in That Land | 100 |
| Alexander's Arrival at the Fortress of Qatil, the Zangi, the Seizure of the Fort, and What Happened between the King and the Zangis | 106 |
| How Qatil the Zangi Sent 2,000 Men to Seek the Bride, and Alexander Made a Surprise Attack on Them | 112 |
| How Rafi' the Zangi Came to the Aid of His Brother and They Fought Alexander | 112 |
| How 'Anbar Received Qatil's Letter, Gathered an Army, and Went to the Aid of His Uncle, and What Happened between Them and King Alexander | 112 |
| How 'Anbar Descended from the Fort with 2,000 Men, and the Battle between the Zangis and the King | 114 |
| [Scribe's Commentary] | 114 |
| How Buqraquz, Shahmalik's Son, Made a Surprise Attack on Alexander's Army, and What Occurred between Him and the King | 116 |
| Alexander's Battle against Qatil the Zangi and What Occurred between Them | 119 |
| How the King of Zangis, Mankus, Came to Shahmalik with the Zangis, the Battle between Shahmalik and Alexander, and What Occurred | 120 |
| How Shahmalik Seduced Araqit for His Son, Tafqaj, and What Occurred | 122 |
| How the Cupbearer's Wife Deceived Tafqaj and Surrendered Him to King Alexander | 126 |

| | |
|---|---:|
| How Tafqaj's Letter to Araqit Was Discovered by Alexander | 130 |
| How Araqit Pursued Tafqaj and the Zangis and Fought Them | 131 |
| How Shahmalik's Daughter Tried to Poison Alexander, How the King Discovered Her Intention, and What Occurred | 133 |
| How the Cupbearer's Wife Deceived Shahmalik and Surrendered Him to Alexander | 134 |
| How Shahmalik Was Taken Captive by Alexander, and How Arsalankhan Became King in His Place | 134 |
| How Arsalankhan Became King and What Occurred between Him and King Alexander | 136 |
| How Araqit and the Sage Were Informed of King Alexander's Captivity and Contrived a Plan to Rescue Him | 137 |
| The Return of Alexander to His Camping-Ground and the End of His Story with Arsalankhan | 147 |
| How Tarzak, Prince Qaymun, Qaymaz, and Ayaz Fared after They Accepted the Faith | 147 |
| The Arrival of Jundul the Zangi, What Occurred between Him and Alexander, and Shahmalik's Escape to the Zangis | 147 |
| How Araqit and the Fairies Attacked Shahmalik's Army and Captured Shahmalik | 148 |
| Alexander's Battle with the Elephant-Ears and Arsalankhan, His Displeasure with Araqit, and How He Cast Her Away | 151 |
| Araqit's Sojourn at Zubaydah's Cloister and What Occurred between Her and King Alexander and Arsalankhan | 155 |
| How Alexander Was Captured by Arsalankhan, and How Araqit and the Army Rescued Him | 157 |
| How Arsalankhan Was Captured and Killed by Araqit, and the City Conquered | 158 |
| The Events Concerning Araqit, King Alexander, Yaqutmalik, and the Fairies | 160 |
| A Glossary of Characters' Names | 165 |
| Appendix I Persian Alexander-Romances | 167 |
| Appendix II Alexander in Pahlavi Literature | 186 |

| | |
|---|---|
| Appendix III Alexander in the Works of Persian and Arab Historians of the Islamic Era | *190* |
| Afterword | *203* |
| Notes | *205* |
| Bibliography | *225* |
| Index | *229* |

# Introduction

## Alexander-Romances

No HISTORIC or mythic figure captured the imagination of the Middle Ages like Alexander the Great. Kings of legendary stature, Arthur and Charlemagne, are mere local heroes compared to Alexander, who dominated the literature, legendry, and iconography of the East as well as the West.

The Middle Ages learned about Alexander through historical works derived from the tradition of Quintus Curtius, Justin, and Orosius—fabulous accounts that had little basis in fact—and the Pseudo-Callisthenes, a Greek prose biography of Alexander, written between 200 B.C. and A.D. 200, which combined fiction with some fact.[1] Eastern and Western romances of Alexander go back to this anonymous romance, which owes its name to the false identification of its author as Callisthenes in one manuscript. The work of a native of Alexandria, the romance makes Alexander the son of an Egyptian sorcerer-king, Nectanebus, who, disguised as the god Ammon, sleeps with Philip's wife, Olympias, and fathers Alexander. According to a prophecy, Alexander would free Egypt from subjugation to the Persians. The accounts of Alexander's birth, his childhood and youth, his early martial adventures in Macedonia, and his expedition to Persia and India, present Alexander as a hero of mythic proportions. The romance embodies current legends of Alexander while retaining a good deal of historic truth. The Pseudo-Callisthenes appealed to the medieval audience in two ways: its hero, in his attributes and achievements, embodied medieval man's conscious and unconscious ambitions, and its account of the marvels of India captured his imagination. In the East, the authors of Syriac, Ethiopic, and Persian romances added new wonders to those in the Greek original.

The Pseudo-Callisthenes was translated into Latin first by Julius Valerius (c.300 A.D.)[2] and later by Leo, Archpresbyter of Naples (c. 950 A.D.).[3] These Latin versions and their derivatives became the source of most romances of Alexander written in the vernaculars of Western Europe.

In the East, the *δ recension (one of four branches of the original Pseudo-Callisthenes) became the source of Pahlavi, Syriac, Arabic, Ethiopic, and Persian romances.[4] The Pahlavi translation is now lost, but the sixth-century Syriac translation of it indicates that it followed the Greek manuscript closely. The Syriac romance was translated into Arabic in the ninth century. The Arabic, now lost, became the source of the fourteenth to sixteenth-century Ethiopic version.

Persian romances belong to this group of texts, but they are not direct translations of the Pseudo-Callisthenes, the Syriac, or the Ethiopic versions, and, although they belong to the *δ Pseudo-Callisthenes, they vary greatly in their fidelity to this version. Firdawsī's romance of Alexander, for example, in spite of the influence of Persian and Islamic material, is close to the Pseudo-Callisthenes; whereas Ṭarsūsī's *Dārābnāmah* and the anonymous *Iskandarnāmah*, though based ultimately on the Pseudo-Callisthenes, are so remote from it that they should be classified as fabulous romances.

The Pseudo-Callisthenes tradition has been the subject of numerous studies. The fabulous romances, on the other hand, have received little attention so far. Studies by L. Donath, I. Lévi, M. Gaster, I. Kazis, and R. Reich attempt to identify elements in the Pseudo-Callisthenes that were derived from the fabulous accounts of Alexander and folklore and legendry.[5] None of these authors, however, deals with the Persian Alexander-romances. In the appendices, therefore, I have provided summaries of the Persian romances and demonstrated the relationship of these romances to the Pseudo-Callisthenes and the influence of non-Alexander materials on their contents.

## Iskandarnāmah

*Iskandarnāmah* (The Book of Alexander) is an anonymous twelfth to fourteenth-century Persian prose romance of Alexander belonging to the fabulous tradition.[6] A written version of *Iskandarnāmah* remains in

# INTRODUCTION

a manuscript in the private library of Saʿid Nafisi in Tehran.[7] The manuscript has 264 leaves. One or two leaves are missing from the beginning of the manuscript and the story breaks at the bottom of 264b. For this reason, the name of the author or compiler, usually given in the beginning or at the end of a manuscript, is unknown. Since at the end of the manuscript the conclusion of the story is nowhere within sight, a considerable number of pages must be missing, if we assume that the work was ever completed.

Information provided by the scribe indicates that his source was not the original but rather a manuscript copied by ʿAbd al-Raḥmān ibn Abī al-Barakāt, another scribe, who had access to several other copies of the text, among them the original manuscript, and was able to compare his source against them for accuracy (see pp. 114–15).

The Persian text was printed for the first time in 1964. The editor of this edition, Iraj Afshar, believes that the romance was written some time between the twelfth and fourteenth centuries A.D.[8] The reference to Sulṭan Maḥmūd, who died A.D. 1030, with the phrase "May God have mercy upon him," sets the earliest possible date for the romance, if we assume that this phrase existed in the original romance and was not a later addition. Judging by the scribe's handwriting and the type of paper used in the manuscript, Afshar concludes that the manuscript could not have been copied later than the beginning of the fifteenth century.[9] Among Persian scholars, M. T. Bahar and Z. Safa[10] set the date of the romance as the eleventh century. Bahar's judgment is based on the linguistic evidence of the text.

The unornamented, simple style of the romance and the infrequency of Arabic words in its vocabulary suggest that the author or compiler intended the romance for a general audience. The romance tells the story of Alexander, identifying him with the Dhul-Qarnain of the Koran. It also Persianizes Alexander, making him the brother of Dārā (Darius), and details his adventures in Iran, India, Hijaz, Yemen, Egypt, Andalusia, the Land of Darkness, Turkistan, China, the land of the fairies, the giants, the Zinj, and the dominion of the Gog and Magog. In its interest in marvels of foreign lands, the romance resembles a medieval travel book. The author exploits the wonder motif and revels in description of fantastic objects and places: his Alexander is as much interested in seeing the world as he is in conquering it.

The loose structure of *Iskandarnāmah* provides room for heterogeneous materials. In addition to Alexander's wars, love affairs, and domestic problems engendered by jealous wives, it includes Islamic religious lore, legends of the prophets, and stories of Persian kings. At points, *Iskandarnāmah* resembles a frame collection, containing stories told to Alexander, or stories related to the events in the romance.

Internal evidence indicates that *Iskandarnāmah* is an abridgment of a much longer original. The author of the present romance at points informs the reader that he is omitting some sections because otherwise his book would grow too long. As a rule, he has apparently omitted stories found in Firdawsī's epic, the *Shāhnāmah*, as he expects his readers to be familiar with that work. He has also omitted accounts recorded in the collection of the legends of prophets, *Qiṣaṣ al-anbiyā'*, because they are not directly related to the story of Alexander. Some stories were omitted simply because he found them uninteresting.

In general, my translation of *Iskandarnāmah* is as close to the original as the linguistic differences between English and Persian permit. In a few instances, however, I have had to resort to a free translation in order to convey the meaning of the text.

In the Persian text, third-person pronouns are frequently used when the antecedent is grammatically unclear and may be determined from the context only. Again, in dialogues direct discourse usually follows the phrase "he said," for both parties. In these cases I have generally substituted proper names for the pronouns to avoid confusion. Frequently the author uses phrases like "Alexander ordered them to return" without identifying those addressed. Whenever the "them" referred to can be identified from the context, I have substituted the antecedent for the pronoun, e.g., "Alexander ordered his attendants . . ." and so on. For stylistic reasons, conjunctions "and" and "then," used too frequently in the original, are used more sparingly in the translation. Pious expressions after God and the prophets have also been omitted.

There is no punctuation in the manuscript except for the division of the text into chapters with the chapter headings in larger hand inside parallel lines. The editor of the printed edition has subdivided chapters into paragraphs, and has introduced internal punctuation into the text. The paragraphs in my translation do not always correspond with those in the printed edition.

# INTRODUCTION

Proper names have been transliterated except when familiar in English, in which case the original form is given when it is mentioned for the first time, followed by the familiar form in parenthesis. The familiar form is substituted thereafter. In the case of *Dārāb*, however, I have preferred to use the Persian form rather than the familiar form *Darius*, for Dārāb, the last of the legendary Kiyānīd dynasty, is not identical with Darius III, the Achaemenid king who was defeated by Alexander. Many historical elements entered Dārāb's life story so that he was later identified with Darius III.

The bulk of the work (770 pages in the printed edition) made a complete translation almost impossible. I have therefore studied the complete text and made selections for translation so as to present fully the characteristic styles and incidents of the work as a whole. The repetitive nature of the romance made selection easy. For example, certain patterns of action recur throughout: Alexander arrives in a country and goes to its king disguised as a messenger, demanding tribute. On several occasions his identity is discovered, but he escapes before his host can do him any harm. Depending on whether Alexander's demand for tribute is accepted or not, a battle or a peace treaty follows. Once given a few such episodes in their entirety, the reader cannot lose much when subsequent similar accounts are summarized.

Parts of the text, although interesting in themselves, are only remotely connected with the tale of Alexander. Such are stories told to Alexander in China and Egypt, and legends of David and Solomon narrated by hermits whom Alexander meets on his expedition. These also have been summarized. Summary passages are italicized.

A TRANSLATION

*Iskandarnamah*

# The Birth of Alexander

. . .DARAB[1] son of Darab was a descendant of Bahman, and many have told his story. Darab was king of Iran, brother of Dhul-Qarnain,[2] and the kingdom of Iran had been under his rule for fourteen years. He had also subjugated Rum[3] and there his decrees were obeyed. Every year he would receive 500 golden eggs, weighing 100 *misqals* each, with other rare and precious gifts as tribute from Rum.

Filqus [Philip], the Caesar of Rum, who obeyed Darab, gave his daughter in marriage to him, sending with her a magnificent dowry and great riches, hoping that the enmity between the two kingdoms might come to an end. When the maiden and all the riches and goods were brought to Pars, where the king of Iran held his court, King Darab rejoiced greatly. He ordered everyone to celebrate and welcome Caesar's representatives. He married Caesar's daughter, showing her great honor and respect, and he favored her above all women in his harem.

The maiden was exceedingly fair and Darab was very fond of her. For the love he bore her he freed Rum from paying tribute, and he sent precious gifts from his treasure house to Caesar every year. A year later, one night as she was sleeping beside the King an unpleasant odor came from her mouth. The King noticed it; his heart was turned away from her, and he no longer admitted her to his bed. He ordered his physicians to cure her. Skillful physicians, summoned from all parts of the realm, cured the maiden. But the King could not be won back, and Caesar's daughter lost all hope of regaining his favor. When some time had passed since the separation, the King ordered that the dowry and the riches that she had brought from Rum be returned doubled, with again as much from his treasure house. They placed Caesar's daughter in a *howdah* and sent her back to Rum. Now, it so happened that she was pregnant, but King Darab did not know of it.

When she went back to her father Philip, he was overcome by sorrow; for a month he did not sit on the throne, and abstained from all that gives man pleasure. He ordered his daughter to remain in her quarters, thus concealing from all what had happened to her. Caesar considered it a disgrace that people should know his daughter had come back pregnant; therefore, he ordered that her childbirth be concealed from all. She lay down her burden, bearing a boy like the moon. The news spread that a son had been born to Philip by a concubine. The event brought celebration and rejoicing.

Then astrologers summoned by Caesar cast the horoscope of the boy and studied it with great care. They sent word to Caesar, saying, "This boy shall rule over the East and the West. He shall go round the world and subjugate all the kings of the earth to his rule. No king shall withstand him, and all shall pay tribute to him."

Having heard the words of the astrologers, Philip concealed the true parentage of the child from all and pretended that it was his own son, giving orders for the boy's upbringing. Philip called him Iskandar [Alexander], and ordered that he be taught all that befits a king. Alexander surpassed his peers in manliness, horsemanship, polo, and the art of war. And the whole world thought him to be the son of Philip. (This story is being related here so that you may know who the Dhul-Qarnain was, what his life and the manner of his birth were like, and why he was known as Dhul-Qarnain. Much has been said concerning this name, and explanations of it are found in many reliable books. But it cannot be clarified unless we tell the story from the start.) Alexander grew to young manhood before his grandfather died. Philip, who had made Alexander his heir, commanded his subjects to follow and obey him. When Philip died, they all chose Alexander as their king and ruler. No one knew that he was the son of Philip's daughter; everybody thought that he was Philip's son.

Alexander became the king of Rum. He ascended the throne and he conquered the world through justice. He established good laws, suppressed heresy, and put an end to all that caused injustice. Mankind was gladdened by his justice and equity, which brought peace to the world. Kings sent him their good wishes through messengers and rejoiced in him.

Alexander the Dhul-Qarnain knew that he was King Darab's son, for his mother had told him of his true parentage. But he kept the truth concealed.

When the kingdom of Rum was firmly under Alexander's rule, Darab son of Bahman, who was the King of Iran, passed away. His son, Darab [Darius], born of the daughter of the king of India, became king. After his kingship was firmly established, Darab sent a messenger to his brother and asked for tribute; whereas his father, from the time he sent Alexander's mother back to Rum, had never demanded tribute. Alexander was therefore angered by the message. He answered the letter, saying, "I pay no tribute; prepare for war." And King Alexander, who knew that King Darab was his own brother, concealed the truth and kept it secret.

## The Expedition of King Alexander the Dhul-Qarnain to Iran to Fight Darab the Son of Darab

Having prepared an army, Alexander left Rum to make war against Darab. On his way he conquered many kingdoms of which he became King. When Alexander was close to Pars, King Darab prepared an army and left the city. Now, in Pars there is a city called Darabgard. And when Alexander heard this word, he wept to hear the name of his father and sent a messenger to his brother, saying, "I have not come to win your kingdom. You demanded tribute from me whereas your father Darab, who was greater than you, had freed Rum from paying tribute. It was you who started this hostility. There is kinship between you and me. I do not want enmity to start between us, to lead the world to confusion, and to cause the loss of lives, for which you and I shall carry the blame. Beware! Do not poison the pleasures of kingship and the kingdom given you by your father. Listen to me and take counsel, for the world is fleeting and stays not with us. Nothing befits the memory of a king better than a good name. Come to an accord and cease seeking war. Follow in the footsteps of your father, who was a prosperous king, for I have not come to deprive you of the kingdom of Iran. I wish to go round the world, to establish proper laws wherever I go, to induce kings to righteousness and leniency toward their subjects, to leave a good name wherever I pass, and to protect my subjects from injustice and tyranny.

For the conduct that best befits a king is to shelter his subjects from injustice and tyranny, and to let the benefits of his justice and equity reach his equals. If you start this hostility and war, you will suffer the evil results, and the outcome will be grievous. Set not your mind upon quarrel and hostility, and observe the rules of friendship and righteousness. Do not seek to fight me, so that the world may remain in peace and Iran, given you by your father, may stay in your hand. I shall be your guest for a month and we shall enjoy each other's company. Then I shall depart in peace, and leave the kingdom of Iran to you."

The messenger came to Darab the son of Darab to deliver King Alexander's message. He presented Darab with what Alexander, through friendship and harmony, had proposed. Darab made answer in anger and unkindness, saying, "Between us only the sword shall speak; I shall not hear Alexander's nonsense. Return and say to Alexander, 'Leave this kingdom alone, for I will not make peace with you. Nor will I free Rum from paying tribute or give you leave to stay in this land. Prepare for war.'"

The messenger returned and made the circumstances known to Alexander. It was hard for King Alexander, whose mother had told him the truth about his parentage, to bring himself to fight his own brother. But he prepared for battle, and they fought for four successive days. On the fourth day, Darab was defeated and fled from Kerman. King Alexander went to Istakhr [Persepolis]. He won the kingdom of Iran and ascended Iran's throne. The elders and the nobility came to salute him as King. Some of them knew that he was King Darab's son. They said to him, "May you enjoy your father's throne." Alexander bowed his head and his eyes filled with tears. Meanwhile Darab's flight to Kerman had left his home, his wife, and his children in the hands of Alexander. Alexander sent a messenger to them and revealed the secret. He called Darab's wife and children to himself, saying, "I will be to you as Darab was. Be at ease and remain where you are in peace. None will disturb you." They all prayed for him, and Alexander stayed in Iran for a year.

Darab's wife wrote a letter to King Darab, saying, "This king treats us kindly and he says, 'If King Darab returns, I will give him back his kingdom and leave.'" But when King Darab received the letter he said,

"I would sooner die than be ruled by the Rumis." King Darab did not know that King Alexander was his own brother.

After a year, Darab prepared a great army in Kerman and started for Pars. When Alexander was informed of this he left Istakhr and camped before Darab. He sent messengers to Darab again, saying, "Do not bring harm upon yourself. Come and sit upon your throne—the kingdom is yours—and I will go to Bahrein." But King Darab answered, "It shames me to be subservient to the Rumis. I shall win back my throne by the sword." Thus Alexander's efforts were fruitless; they prepared for war again and much blood was shed on both sides. Darab was nearly defeated, for Alexander was strong.

Darab had two ministers (according to some, two chamberlains), Mahyar and Janusibar.[4] They conspired together, saying, "Darab will not remain king, and his defeat will endanger our lives. We must kill him and go to Alexander, for thus we will win his favor." After contriving this plan, they went to Darab, who was in his tent, and said to him, "Order everyone to leave; we have a secret to reveal to you." When Darab did as they said, they suddenly drew their daggers and stabbed him. As he fell, they left the tent and went to Alexander. They bowed before him and they said, "Rejoice, O King, for your enemy is dead." "Who are you, and what enemy?" inquired Alexander. "We slew Darab; we were both his ministers," they replied. The King was angered, but he concealed his wrath. "Where is the slain enemy? Take me to him," he said. He mounted his horse and they came to Darab's camping-ground. Darab's soldiers had fled and his army had dispersed.

Entering Darab's tent Alexander saw Darab, who was still alive, and his heart was moved. He wept, placing Darab's head on his knee. "O brother," he said, "more than once I sent to you and declared that I did not seek to win Iran's kingship, that the kingship was yours, and that I would leave it to you and depart. But you did not listen. I am your brother; I am not Philip's son. Darab, the son of Bahman, was my father. Arise if you can and mount your horse. Iran and Rum shall both be yours." Thus Darab realized that Alexander was his brother. And when he saw that his case was beyond hope, for the wound was mortal, he said to Alexander, "Know, my brother, that this was my fate and the will of God. One cannot question His will. There are my children and my wives to think of. One wife is the daughter of the King of the Indians; another is pregnant. I do not know what she will bear. Her name is Rushanak [Roxana][5] and she is of noble birth, a descendant of Gudarz of Isfahan. If she bears a son, give him your daughter in marriage, and call him Bahman. If she bears a girl, call her Humay and give her to whomever you wish, that the name of Isfandiyar may remain.[6] The daughter of the King of India is six months pregnant. Her homeland is near, for I brought her from Ceylon. Dispatch her to India with her dowry that they may give her to some other bridegroom, for she is young; or ask her hand yourself, if you wish."

Alexander replied, weeping, "I will do as you have said in all things except in this. God forbid that I should want your wife, for I have four wives who are free women and forty concubines, some from here and some from Rum." Darab was moved. He took Alexander's hand and held it. And before Darab was dead, Alexander called the ministers before him. First he had their hands and feet cut off, and then he had them hanged. And he had heralds proclaim, "He who is treacherous to his king will be thus rewarded." Then Darab, who was still alive, was carried to the city. Alexander went before him on foot. They took Darab to the women's quarters and placed him in a bed. Alexander sat beside him. Then Darab's mother came. She was a noble and learned woman, the daughter of the King of Kashmir. She bowed before Alexander, then she placed her face on her son's face, and he gave up the ghost. His mother tore her hair. As a sign of mourning the saddles of Darab's horses were overturned. Alexander ordered his attendants to prepare a vault. They placed Darab in a golden coffin in the vault.

Alexander stayed in Iran for five months, until all was settled. He sent the daughter of the King of India back to her homeland with all her dowry. Roxana, the wife who was pregnant, gave birth to a girl, but died herself.[7] Then Alexander went toward Isfahan, taking along Darab's household. He gave them the area between Pars and Isfahan, and he appointed a deputy to settle their affairs. He then went toward Kerman and from there to Oman. Ten thousand mules carried his belongings, and he was accompanied by a cavalry of 70,000 worthy warriors. After he left Isfahan he visited and crossed many lands. Monarchs who paid

Alexander homage and sent him provisions were allowed to remain king; but those who disobeyed him were imprisoned and replaced by Alexander's deputies. And Alexander came to be known as "the Conqueror of Countries."

He marched on in this manner till he reached the sea, where his army stayed four months and built ships and equipped them for the voyage. Then Alexander embarked for Oman with a great quantity of provisions and equipment.

## Alexander's Arrival at Oman and What Happened between Him and the King of Oman

The story goes that when Alexander came near Oman he said to his men, "I will go to the King of Oman as a messenger, for he is said to be a just and equitable monarch." When news reached Oman that Alexander, the Conqueror of Countries, had arrived, all were afraid. The King of Oman summoned the nobility and said to them, "Alexander has arrived from the sea and is heading toward our land. What is to be done?" His men all replied, "The King knows best." Then the King said, "I have a plan. I will prepare rich gifts and provisions and send them to Alexander. Then I will go to his presence myself, for we ought to be very thankful if he passes our land without doing any harm." At his command, a great quantity of provisions was prepared and sent to Alexander. He also instructed a messenger to make apologies to Alexander and to invite him to stay and rest in the land for a month, if he found the place worthy of him.

The message pleased Alexander. He said to the messenger, "It is hot. We will stay here for a few days, if it pleases your King to come to me that I may see him and know his mind."

The messenger returned and conveyed this message to the King of Oman, Kasandar. He obeyed Alexander's command, and with many presents and rare gifts came to salute him. Alexander treated him kindly and gave him the seat of honor. "I am your slave," said the King of Oman to Alexander. "You have received much trouble from our expedition," said Alexander. "His Majesty's command is binding," said the

King of Oman. Then Alexander ordered his attendants to show him the presents that the King of Oman had brought. There was gold, aloeswood, camphor, rarities from lands beyond the sea, and great riches. Alexander accepted the gifts and wrote the charter of Oman's sovereignty in Kasandar's name.

Then the King of Oman asked Alexander to stay there for a few days to allow his men to rest, for it was the hot season. "We shall stay here for some ten days," said Alexander. Then the King of Oman returned and during the ten days that Alexander stayed there, he sent provisions to Alexander's camp.

Then Fur [Porus] sent a messenger to the King of Oman with a letter, saying, "We have learned that Alexander has arrived from the sea. Why did you allow him to come ashore, for he will deprive us of our kingship. He will start with you and our turn will come next. Have you not heard what he has done to other kings on his way from Rum to this region, and what he did to Darab, who was the King of Kings? Now that he has already come ashore, fight with him; and if you need assistance, ask for it, and it shall be given you. If you are not his equal in war, invite him to your house and capture him, and thus you will win yourself a great name in the world."

When the King of Oman read this letter he grew fearful. He summoned his ministers and said to them, "These circumstances will not remain hidden from Alexander. The secret will come to light, Alexander will become displeased and angry with us, and his wrath will bring all to waste." The ministers said, "The King himself knows the remedy to this." Then the King of Oman took the letter as it was to King Alexander. When Alexander saw the letter he marveled at the King of Oman's truthfulness and treated him kindly. "The King of Kings, Darab, was my brother," he said, "and I did not kill him. His own ministers stabbed him, and on that same day I had them slain as an example for the others. On my way to this land I treated all as I treated you. Those who came to our presence and expressed obedience received no harm. But those who quarreled with us lost their lives. And this shall be our policy hereafter wherever we go. Our aim is to go around the world. You will hear the news when I cross Porus's land."

And when the ten days were passed, Alexander left Oman. The King of Oman gave him ten elephants. Alexander and his soldiers had never seen elephants before, as there are no elephants in Rum. Then Alexander set out toward the land of Porus.

And Porus had been the King of all of India before Kayd brought India under his rule. Among his royal possessions Porus owned 70,000 elephants; what else he had can be judged from this. His soldiers were innumerable. He held his court at Ceylon, the capital of India. But according to some, his court was at Kashmir, the home of the white Indians.

Alexander camped near the kingdom of Porus, and Porus ordered his men to shut the gates firmly and block those passages that led to the city. Alexander said to himself, "This man is not being honest with us and has no intention of making peace. I will go to him as a messenger myself, learn the circumstances, and discover the extent of his wealth."

## How Alexander Went to Porus Disguised as a Messenger, and What Happened between Them

The story goes that Alexander came to the gate of the city dressed as a messenger and accompanied by some horsemen. When the Indians saw him they asked who he was and what he wanted there. "I am a messenger," he replied, "and I come from Alexander, the Conqueror of Countries, to the King of India."

When they brought the news to Porus he commanded that the city squares be decorated and that the elephants and lions be arrayed. Gold-belted slaves stood there in line. Then he asked his attendants to bring the messenger to him. They took the messenger by the hand and led him to the King. Alexander bowed after the manner of messengers. They brought him a golden chair on which he sat, and they asked him to deliver the message. He said, "The King of the Earth, Alexander, the Conqueror of Countries, says thus: 'Prepare provisions for my army, for we shall stay here a few days. Come to our presence and visit us, if you want us to pass through your land in peace. Otherwise, be prepared for war.'"

Porus was angered. He said, "Who is Alexander to speak to me thus? I will set the elephants to trample his camp." Alexander turned red in anger, but said nothing. Porus, who was observing him carefully, became suspicious and thought, "This man could be Alexander. I will seize him and free the world from his nuisance." He said to Alexander, "Stay here tonight, that we may consider the message, and tomorrow morning you shall have our answer." Alexander bowed and said, "The King is to be obeyed." Then Porus told his attendants to take Alexander to the messengers' quarters. He honored the messenger and sent him food and drink, as kings are accustomed to do.

But King Alexander through wisdom and divine inspiration perceived that Porus had discovered his identity. He said to a chamberlain who had accompanied him, "Make haste and find a strategy, or else my life will not be worth two grains of barley. Porus knows that I am Alexander." "What is to be done?" asked the chamberlain. "Bring me a woman's veil and a pair of boots and help me escape," said Alexander. The chamberlain gave much gold to a woman in return for the veil and the boots. Alexander put them on and left through the gate, protected by the dark. He rode until he reached his camping-ground, and offered many thanks to God.

Now Porus did nothing when he guessed at the messenger's identity, thinking to himself, "Things should be done in the proper way." He sent for the merchants and the nobles and said to them, "Answer what I ask in truth, for, I swear, you shall pay dearly if you lie." "We will say what we know," they answered. "Have you seen the messenger who has come from Alexander?" asked Porus. "Yes," they replied, "we saw him after he left your presence." "Do you know who he is?" he asked. "Yes, we know him," they replied. "He is Alexander." "How did you recognize him and where had you seen him before?" Porus asked. The merchants answered, "We saw him in Oman, where for ten days he was the guest of our king." "Do you see now that I was right in my suspicion?" said Porus to his ministers. Then he ordered his men to surprise Alexander and put him in chains. "A wonderful deed has been accomplished at my hand, for I will avenge the blood of Darab and other kings," said Porus, his heart pounding for joy.

But when the soldiers went to the messenger's room to capture Alexander, they found it empty. They returned and told Porus that Alexander had made his escape and saved his life. "Alas, all is lost," said Porus, shaking his head. "When one neglects the opportunity, one comes to nothing but regret. Now this has come to pass and I do not know how it will end."

The next morning Alexander ordered his men to beat the battle drums. Twelve thousand cavalry armed themselves, and, led by Alexander, set out for the city gates. When Porus was informed of this, he put his army in order and drove out the elephants, 1,000 in number, each as big as a mountain. In addition, he recruited 70,000 cavalry and infantry from the city and the country.

When Alexander saw Porus's army and the elephants, those awesome mountains of iron, he was alarmed, for neither he nor his men had ever seen so many elephants in one place. His men complained, "We cannot battle elephants; and we have no power against mountains of iron." Alexander replied, "Be not dismayed, for God is on our side. Have courage. They shall be defeated in no time." He then summoned the people of Pars. Five thousand men who had accompanied him from Pars came to his presence, all dexterous marksmen. He ordered them to build boxes; and he chose 2,000 of them to carry out his plan. He ordered 1,000 young, strong camels to be smeared with tar and he had the boxes placed upon the blackened camels, each box manned by an archer with his bows and arrows. He then summoned all the Arabs in the army, and two dark Arabs mounted every camel. They set for the lines of elephants with bottles of naphtha and with fire. And Alexander positioned his troops, giving the right wing to the Indians and the left to the Rumis, while he and the nobles stood in the center of the troops.

When Porus's army arrived before that of Alexander, Porus said to the elephant drivers, "Wait until you see how we fare in the battle. If, God forbid, we are defeated, use the elephants."

When the armies started the attack, Alexander's men charged at the elephants with the blackened camels. They beat the drums while the Arabs on the back of the camels cried, "*Allah Akbar*,"[8] and threw the bottles of flaming naphtha at the elephants, who, terror-stricken, turned to flee. But the marksmen continued shooting at them from the boxes, killing more than 400 elephants, and putting the rest to flight. When Alexander saw that the Arabs and the men from Pars had defeated the Indians, he rejoiced. He attacked the enemy with all his men and broke their lines. The King of the Indians, who did not know that the elephants had been defeated, persevered in battle, thinking that the elephants would soon join the battle and trample Alexander's army under their feet. But when he saw the elephants, some dead, some fleeing, he said, "Alas, all is lost. It was a mistake to save the elephants for the end; we should have attacked them with the elephants first. Now all is lost and my life is at the mercy of this horse. At such a time it is wise to escape." But, turning his horse, Porus could find no way to escape, for his men were all dispersed and Alexander's army had surrounded him and his treasury.

Fearful, Porus took a gold idol from his breast, placed it on the saddle and bowed to it, saying, "Oh, god, deliver me from Alexander!" Alexander saw that, and, spurred by religious ardor, shouted, "Charge! For these are infidels, and if we kill them we will be *ghazis*."[9] The men attacked; Porus was taken prisoner, and his men who were put to flight went to Ceylon to join Kayd. Alexander and his men seized the booty.

Then King Alexander entered the city and told his men to plunder it for three days. He said to his men, "These are idol worshippers. It is permissible to take their property." But when the three days were over, he sent heralds to the city, ordering his men to harm the people no more.

Then he had Porus brought to his presence in shackles. "What now?" said Alexander, when Porus came before his throne. "It was my fault to let you escape that night," said Porus. "I had to find out about your army, see how you fared, and how strong your army was," said Alexander. "All you relied on were the elephants. Did you see what I did to them?" "That was not your doing, but the King of Oman's, who allowed you to come ashore," said Porus. This was humiliating to Alexander, but he wanted to seize Porus's treasures before slaying him. He said to Porus, "Bloodshed is not our policy. You brought this upon yourself, for we passed through Oman and did no harm. You did not obey me. Now you are in my power. If you want to regain your kingdom and your sovereignty, fulfill these conditions. First, renounce idolatry, turn to the Creator of heaven and earth and say, 'There is but one God in the seven spheres and he has no wife or child, and no partner.' Second, you have great treasures and hoards of buried riches. Bring them before me. I will take what I want, and give you back the rest. Third, go with me to Ceylon and call Kayd to surrender, and, if he resists, make war against him. If you fulfill these conditions, I will return your land to you."

When Porus heard this he replied, "Of the three I can accept one easily, but the other two are impossible. First, I cannot renounce my religion, for this is the religion of Jamshid and from the days of Jamshid this has been the religion of India.[10] Second, I will not fight Kayd, for he is my master. But I will bring the treasure house and the buried treasures all before you." "Bring us the treasures," Alexander ordered. And it took four days before Porus had uncovered and sent all his hidden treasures to the King.

King Alexander marveled at all the riches and had the rarities stored in a safe place. That night he sent Porus back to prison. The next day, Alexander's men said to him, "Porus's wives and daughters are beautiful as the moon." But the King said, "God forbid that I allow such a thing. We will leave his women's quarters alone." And that night Alexander sent a slave girl with a messenger to those women. "Do not worry," he said, "and stay in your home in peace. Be not afraid, for no one will do you any harm. If Porus obeys my commands, he will regain his sovereignty. And if he does not, we shall think of something for you."

When the women heard the King's message, they were relieved. They remained happy and at peace, and praising Alexander they said, "This is what befits a king." Then they sent someone to the prison to Porus, informed him how nobly Alexander had treated them, and advised him, saying, "Obey Alexander, so that you may regain your kingship and your kingdom." Porus refused; "He has demanded that I renounce my religion," he replied.

The next day Alexander called Porus to his presence. Again he urged Porus to turn to God, but Porus would not obey him. Then Alexander said to him, "Take upon yourself to pay tribute and head tax, and I will give you back your kingdom." But Porus refused. "Then prepare for death," Alexander threatened. "Better dead, than alive before one such as you," replied Porus. Thus provoked, Alexander had Porus beheaded.[11] When Alexander had done with Porus, he had heralds proclaim that all was safe and tell the people to remain where they were and live their lives as usual. He then sat on his throne, summoned the guides before him and inquired about the land. "Where do the roads lead from here?" "To Kashmir," they replied. "And it takes two days to Kashmir, and fifteen days to Ceylon. When you cross this land you will arrive in a region where God, most high, has created gold."

Alexander appointed one of India's rulers as King of Porus's country. After marrying Porus's daughter, Alexander took along as much as he could from Porus's treasures and riches. What he could not take, he left behind. Alexander used to take two men with him whenever he went to hide his treasures. And after they had buried the treasure, he would kill them so that they might not reveal the place. He thought he would live forever, and he buried those treasures, planning to take them along when he returned. But he left treasures in many places to which he never returned.

Alexander married Porus's daughter. She was an exceedingly fair maiden called Nahid, and he loved her dearly. He stayed in India for forty days until he had restored order in that land. Then he started for Kashmir. And it is said that 30,000 camels carried his belongings, and 170,000 warriors accompanied him. Seventy thousand mules carried his treasury and his gold. No king has ever possessed such riches.

The way to Kashmir was shorter by water than it was by land. But Alexander chose to go by land because it was difficult to go by water. He set out toward Kashmir with all his magnificence.

## Alexander's Journey to Kashmir and What Happened between Him and Azadbakht, the King of Kashmir, and His Daughter, Mahafarin

*Hearing the news of Alexander's arrival, Azadbakht sent a messenger to him, expressing his obedience and promising to send Alexander whatever he wanted if he consented to leave Kashmir. Otherwise, he would fight against him. Alexander answered that he would stay there for a month and asked for provisions. Azadbakht decided to deceive him.*

He sent a second messenger with a large amount of provisions, saying, "We are Alexander's servants, and we shall do as he says. Let the King stay as long as he wishes. His decrees shall be obeyed." Hearing these words, Alexander suspected Azadbakht of duplicity, and cautioned his men. "Be watchful during the night, and be not without vanguards and watchmen, lest we receive injury, for the enemy is numerous." (And Alexander's camp stretched for four parasangs.[12]) The men replied, "Your will shall be obeyed." The next day Azadbakht chose rich, rare gifts and went to Alexander's presence. Alexander was sitting on his throne as was his custom. The King of Kashmir was young and God had given him a comely face. And in India there are none so handsome, clean, sweet-smelling, and fair as the people of Kashmir; and there is kinship between them and the Turks, who have dark skin and are descendants of Kashmir people.

When Alexander saw Azadbakht's face, he marveled. "Praised be God," he said, "who creates such a face from a drop of water." And when he looked at those who accompanied Azadbakht, he found each surpassing the other in beauty. He thought, "Their men are so comely, how much more beautiful their women must be. If this King has a daughter or a sister, I will ask her hand in marriage." He asked Azadbakht to be seated, treating him kindly and accepting the presents he had brought, for he was pleased to see him.

Then the King of Kashmir said to Alexander, "In the whole world there is no land more pleasant than ours. Would it please the King to stay here for a month while he prepares for the expedition; and would it please him to come into the city, for it is more pleasant there than in the fields." "Let it be as you say," King Alexander replied. Azadbakht returned into the city and every day he expressed his obedience to Alexander and sent him all the provisions his army needed.

The people of Kashmir were mostly cow worshippers, but some of them worshipped the stars. King Azadbakht was a star worshipper, but the citizens considered the cow their deity.

When a few days had passed, Azadbakht prepared to receive Alexander. Kashmir is a vast city, with twelve gates, deep woods, and a temperate climate. Alexander entered the city, meaning to ask Azadbakht's daughter in marriage. Therefore he told his men to find out from the citizens whether their King had a daughter. They made inquiries and were told that he had a daughter, and that in the whole world there was none to rival her beauty. They asked who her mother was, and they were told that her mother was the daughter of Kayd, the King of India.

When they told Alexander what they had learned, he sent a messenger to Azadbakht, saying, "I have heard that you have a daughter worthy of my harem. Give her to me in marriage according to my faith and send her to me. May it please God to give me a son, that my name may remain in the world."

When the messenger came to Azadbakht and rendered this message, Azadbakht was perplexed and did not know what to answer. He said to the messenger, "Be it so. But in India it is customary to acquire the maiden's consent. If the King is agreeable to wait until tomorrow, I will speak to the mother and daughter and get their consent. Tomorrow, early in the morning, I will give King Alexander my answer." The messenger returned to the just monarch with these words. Alexander realized that Azadbakht meant to deceive him.

When the King's messenger left his court, Azadbakht summoned the chief men of the army and the city and said to them, "King Alexander wants to marry my daughter, whereas I have been planning to slay him. How can I give him my daughter?" "How could you possibly kill Alexander?" they asked. "I will invite him as a guest, and I will slay him," he replied. "You cannot do this," they said. "You cannot kill him except by poison. We are unable to withstand his army. They will play havoc with our city and ourselves." "You are right," said Azadbakht. "What is to be done?" The wise among them replied, "If you are determined to slay him, it is advisable to leave your daughter with him for a month. She will find an opportunity to poison him." "Be it so," replied Azadbakht. "There is no harm in this, but that our daughter will cease to be a virgin, and that is a great shame." Then one of the Indian Brahmans (who are learned men and are called "ruhban" in Rum, "ahbar" by the Jews, and " 'ulama" by the Muslims[13]), and to the King, "Do not fear; give him your daughter, for I will make him impotent with her and she will remain a sealed virgin." Azadbakht was pleased. "Be it so," he said, and they dispersed.

The next day Alexander's messenger returned and Azadbakht gave his answer, saying, "I would not even dream that the King of the East and the West would want my daughter in marriage. His will is to be done."

Then the King sent Arastatalis [Aristotle], who was the most learned man in Rum and whose counsel the King followed, to sign the marriage contract according to the rules of the pure faith of God. When the contract was signed, Azadbakht ordered his attendants to prepare his daughter according to custom, and he sent her to Alexander with great riches and many servants and slave girls.

The name of the maiden was Mahafarin and when Alexander saw her he fell in love with her with a thousand hearts, for he had never seen a face like hers. Little did he know that they had made him impotent with her. But the maiden knew what her father had done, and what else he meant to do. Her father had said to her, "Be at ease. We will not let this King take you away. Stay there a month, for we have contrived a plan." And that maiden knew all this.

And when the maiden went to bed with King Alexander, Alexander wanted to lie with her but he could not take her virginity. He waited that night. The next night he tried again, but still failed. He was embarrassed before the maiden, yet he said nothing of the fact that in Rum he had taken the seal off forty maidens in one night. Now it so happened that Azadbakht's daughter fell in love with Alexander and her heart became tender toward him. She said to herself, "Where will I find a better husband in the whole world? I will reveal the secret to him." "Are you dismayed?" she asked the King. "If you swear to choose me above all women, both here and in Rum, and favor me above Porus's daughter, and make me your Queen, I will reveal a secret to you." Alexander took an oath and gave Mahafarin his word. Then she told him all that she knew, saying, "My father is not honest with you. He means to murder you, and he has made you impotent with me." "Who made me impotent with you?" he asked. "The King's Brahman," she replied. "How is he going to kill me?" asked Alexander. But the maiden knew nothing about the poison. "They instructed me to stay here for a month and see how the events develop," she said.

When Alexander heard these words from Mahafarin, his love for her increased. That very night he went to other women, and, seeing that he was not impotent with any of them, he was assured that Mahafarin had spoken truthfully. The next day he said to her, "Do you know where the Brahman who made me impotent lives?" She answered, "There is a cloister outside the city. The Brahman is there and the cows there are our deity." When Alexander heard her mention the cow deity, he said to himself, "It is more important to convert this maiden to Islam. Otherwise, where can I take her? If she refuses Islam, I will destroy the city, capture the King, and go away." Then he said to the maiden, "What is your religion?" She said, "I believe in my father's religion, not the Brahman's." "What is your father's religion?" he asked. "He worships the planet Saturn, and the Brahman and the citizens worship the cow," she replied. The King said, "I will not and cannot have any concern for you unless you renounce heathenism, and turn to the God of the heaven and earth." Mahafarin bowed and said, "I turn to the God of the heaven and earth, and renounce the worship of the cow or the planet Saturn." Alexander was pleased. He said, "Now it rests on me to find a solution for this."

Now, Alexander and the nobles were in the city; but Alexander's army was outside the city, and it was four parasangs from the city to where he had camped. Alexander went to his camping-ground and summoned his attendants. "I have heard that on this mountain lives a Brahman," he said. "I ought to see this man. You must bring him to me without the Indians' knowledge. Before you speak to him, keep watch over his cloister, but do nothing until night comes. Then put him in chains and bring him before me." Two attendants went after the Brahman and found him, the cursed devil of an old man. They said to him, "Pray for us." "With all my heart," he replied. "Are you always here alone?" they inquired. "Yes," he replied, "whenever King Azadbakht is in trouble, they take me to the city." When they had found out these facts they left. Upon returning that evening, they found him completely drunk. They put him in chains, placed him in a sack, and brought him to the King.

"Are you drunk?" asked the King. "Drunk!" the old man replied. The King told his men to lock him in a room by himself until the next day. When daylight came, the King asked everyone to leave, and summoned the Brahman to his presence. "What is your name?" he asked. "Mankus," replied the old man. "What are you?" asked Alexander. "A Brahman," he replied. "I want you to do something for me," said the King. "Your will is to be obeyed," he replied. "There is a man to be made impotent with a woman and 1,000 dinars to be gained." "What man and which woman?" asked the Brahman. "That man is I, and that woman

Azadbakht's daughter," replied Alexander. The Brahman trembled with fear, for he realized that the King knew his secret. "Your Majesty! This is beyond my power," he said. "Call the executioner to behead this man," Alexander told his men. "What have I done, O King?" he asked. "You know full well what you have done," said the King. The Brahman trembled with fear and said, "Promise to spare my life, and I will tell the truth. The King of Kashmir ordered me to make you impotent." "Then make me potent again," the King said. "I fear him," the Brahman replied. "You villain!" cried Alexander, "do you not fear me?" "I will make you potent tonight," the Brahman said. "If you want to stay alive, make me potent at once. Return to your cloister and never say a word of all this to anybody," said Alexander. "Your will is to be obeyed," said the Brahman. And when night came, he said, "O King, send me to my cloister for only there can I make you potent." Alexander trusted his words and set him free, with the condition that he would make him potent that night. But when the Brahman went away, he made the King impotent with all the women in the world and himself hid in the mountains.

That night Alexander called the maiden to himself, but he was more impotent then ever before. Then he went to Porus's daughter, and found himself impotent with her also. Then he went to his concubines; again he was impotent. He was perplexed. In the morning he sent the two attendants to seek the Brahman, but they could not find him. By this they knew that he had deceived them. Then the King left the city and went to his camp, downhearted. He looked pale, and he was ashamed to speak of what had happened to him to the nobles in the army.

Aristotle suspected that something had gone wrong in the King's relations with women. He said to himself, "I must find out what it is or else the kingdom will fall to destruction; for he who is impotent with women is not fit for kingship." Therefore he went to the King and asked why he was so downhearted. Alexander told him what had happened to him. Aristotle was relieved. "Be not dismayed on this account," he said, "I will make you potent this minute. For this practice started in Rum, and it was the Rumis themselves who invented it." And that instant he made the King potent. When night came, Alexander went to the daughter of the King of Kashmir. He broke her seal, and they were very joyful.

It so happened that the next day the King of Kashmir came to King Alexander's presence and asked to be allowed to see his daughter. The King gave him leave. When Azadbakht went to his daughter, he found her wearing a crown, happily sitting on the throne, with 400 Rumi and Turkish slave girls standing before her. King Azadbakht was puzzled; he said to himself, "My plans must have gone wrong, for my daughter is happy with Alexander. What is to be done?"

When he came before his daughter, she rose and bowed to him, and she kissed him on the face. "How is it with you?" he asked. "Wonderful," she replied. Then he asked her in the Indian language, "Are you resolved that he shall be your husband?" "Yes, I am resolved," she replied. "What of my instructions to you?" he asked. "Where can I find a husband better than Alexander, who is the King of Kings, and who believes in the right faith while you are all infidels?" she said. Her father made no reply for fear of Alexander. He congratulated her, saying, "We want nothing but your happiness. What we said to you were lies to give you consolation. I will go to the Brahman this moment, make the matter known to him, and order him to make the King potent, since you are happy here." "Praised be God," she said to her father, "Alexander is potent already. It would be strange if he who has conquered Iran, Turan, Pars, Kerman, and India were unable to make this conquest.[14]

When Azadbakht heard this from his daughter, he was afraid. "My dear child," he said to her, "forgive your father and have pity, for if you say these words to King Alexander, your parents' blood will not be worth two grains of barley. Then to our household will come what came to Porus's, and we will be exiled from our home." Then Mahafarin said to him, "If you cannot withstand him, why do you deal with him with cunning?" As they were talking, Alexander entered. Mahafarin descended the throne, ran to the King, kissed his hand, and bowed before him. Alexander sat upon the throne and she stood before him. The King of Kashmir rose and bowed before Alexander. Alexander made him sit and treated him kindly. He said, "We have stayed here too long and caused much inconvenience to you." Azadbakht bowed to him and said, "Your decrees are obeyed by us and by our subjects." Then he rose and went away. Mahafarin told Alexander all that she had said to her father, and what her father had said to her. "I called them infidels," she boasted. "I told my father of my conversion, and I asked how Alexander, who has conquered the world, could fail to make a conquest of me." Alexander marveled at Mahafarin's affection and her kindness. He abstained from other women, did not sleep with any of his wives and concubines, and gave his whole heart to the daughter of the King of Kashmir.

Then the other women became jealous and said, "Let us devise a plan to make the King lose interest in this woman." Therefore they contrived a scheme and they went to Nahid, Porus's daughter, for help, because she knew more about that land than they did. She said, "There is an old peddler-woman. Bring her to me." They brought the woman to her, and Nahid gave her a few precious articles, saying, "Go to the King's quarters and show these to his wife." The woman did as she was told, and Mahafarin bought all that the old woman had brought. And when the King came, she showed him what she had bought. The peddler-woman, who was a witch, came to frequent the King's quarters.

One day she said to Mahafarin, "Your hair is ugly. I will show you a remedy for it."[15] (The other women had told her to find a way to make Alexander lose interest in Mahafarin, and she was biding her time to fulfill their command.) Therefore when Mahafarin, who did not suspect the woman's treachery, asked her for a remedy, the witch gave her a dagger made of bright steel, saying, "You must keep this under your pillow every night when you lie with the King, and you must clean your forehead with it twice a day, for this makes your forehead beautiful." Mahafarin placed the dagger under her pillow. Now it so happened that Alexander went to Porus's daughter, who had grown wild with jealousy, and she said to him, "O King, keep away from Mahafarin." "Why?" asked the King. "Father and daughter have conspired to murder you," said Nahid. "If you do not believe me, look where you sleep. There is a poisoned dagger under your pillow." Alexander did not believe her. He thought envy had goaded her to speak thus. But then he thought to himself, "Perhaps she speaks the truth, for women are softhearted and unstable. Perhaps Mahafarin's father has deceived her a second time, for women are half-witted." With these thoughts, he went to Mahafarin.

Now Mahafarin was very forward with Alexander. She bowed to him and said, "Does my forehead look prettier than it looked yesterday?" "What have you done today?" asked the King. She rose, lifted the pillow, and brought out the dagger, saying, "I bought this for cleaning my forehead." By this the King knew that the other women had lied to him and that they envied her.

As the Prophet has said, he who digs a pit for others, will fall into it himself.

## The Story of Azadbakht, the King of Kashmir, and Porus's Daughter, Who Was Alexander's Wife

*Azadbakht seduced Alexander's wife and tried to poison Alexander through her. But the plot was discovered, and, in revenge, Alexander ordered his men to plunder the city and ravish any women they found. Azadbakht was dethroned and replaced by his brother, Farrukhbakht. Alexander called the people of Kashmir to accept Islam; those who refused were put to death.*

## Alexander's Journey to Ceylon and What Occurred between Him and Kayd, the King of India

*Alexander went to King Kayd in disguise, won his confidence, and married his daughter. After a series of adventures, he took Kayd prisoner. Kayd accepted Islam and was restored to his rule. Alexander went to the pilgrimage to Adam's tomb.*

## Alexander's Pilgrimage to the Tomb of Adam and His Journey from There to the Land of Gold

The story goes that after staying with Kayd as his guest for three days, King Alexander went on a pilgrimage to the tomb of Adam.[16] He gave gold and rich gowns to the Indians who were guardians of Adam's tomb, and they showed him all the wonders of that land. On the mountain, Alexander saw a vast site from which light emanated; and close to that he saw a spot where, even in full daylight, darkness and smoke issued forth. He asked the Indian guardians what the dark and the light spots were.

The Indian guardians replied, "O King, when God commanded Adam, Satan, and the serpent to go to earth and be one another's enemies, they landed in this place. Adam touched the ground on the spot where light emanates. Eve landed in Jidda, and the serpent in Qum. As regards Satan opinions differ; some say he landed in Pars, and some say he landed in Isfahan and believe that for that reason Dajjal[17] will arise from there. Others contend that he landed in Babylon. And this light emanates from Adam's footsteps."

Then Alexander found thousands of different herbs growing on that mountain in Ceylon, some sweet and pleasant, some bitter and unpleasant. King Alexander asked the Indians what the different herbs were and why some tasted sweet and some tasted bitter.

They said, "The dark and unpleasant herbs grew from the tears of Adam, who for many years wept over his sin, and they can all be used as medicine and cures.[18] And those herbs that are fresh and pleasant, and when looked at fill the heart with joy, grew from the tears of Adam when, as it is written in the glorious Koran, 'God accepted him, so he repented and achieved salvation.' Adam wept for joy, and these herbs grew from tears of joy." The King marveled at what he heard, and he felt a joy and exuberance the like of which he had never experienced before.

Then he asked what the dark spot was. They said, "In that spot Cain slew Abel, and since that time darkness issues from it." The King stayed there for a day and saw these wonders. Then he provided himself with guides and went on board his ship. They prepared thousands of ships, and more boats than could be numbered. And since God created the waters, never so many creatures crossed the sea as on that day.

Alexander steered the ships and they sailed the seas day and night for a month. The winds were favorable, and the ships advanced as he wished. When a month had passed, Alexander asked Aristotle what provisions were left for the army. Aristotle replied, "O King, the provisions are nearly all gone." Alexander grew sad. He said, "The sea is dangerous, the water salty and stale, and we have no food for 200,000 men and many thousands of beasts of burden. What will become of us?" "O King! The shore is nowhere within sight," said Aristotle. "What is to be done?" "We must turn to God," the King replied. But prostrating himself in prayer and weeping, his heart was instantly filled with hope. He ordered his men to pull the anchors, and the vessels moved on swiftly. When one more day had passed, a huge mountain appeared in the middle of the water. The men cried, " *Allah Akbar,*" and praised God. Then Alexander told one of his men to climb the mountain and see what was behind it. One of the Indians climbed that huge mountain, finding behind it a world of God-made ingots. He did not know what they were. He returned to the King, saying, "Behind this mountain the land is covered with plants like millet. The field must lead to inhabited land. There must be people here, and this is their farm." Alexander realized immediately that this was the Mountain of Gold, and the Land of Gold created by God.[19] But he said nothing. The next day when they went ashore and camped, his men fell upon that land, gathering gold, for it was dawn and the sun had not yet risen high. They collected as much gold as they could, bringing it to the King, who added it to his treasure house. But when the sun rose and the day grew hot, for every bar of gold an animal came out of a hole. Together, they swarmed over the land of gold and when they saw the men they started toward them, killing those who still remained in the Land of Gold.

Alexander was sorrowful. He said, "Gold is so highly prized because God created such danger in this region, so that those who come after gold may not leave the land alive. Were it not for this, gold would be abundant." Then he ordered his men to shoot at those animals with their arrows, and they slew many of them. And these creatures are called gold bees, each being the size of a dog. Now, as the day progressed, so did the bees increase until for every man in that army there were ten gold bees and more. But when the time for evening prayer came and it turned cold, the bees grew faint, for they had no power against cold. Then the King told his men to shoot at them with their arrows.

That night, a group of people appeared from the sea and came to the presence of the King. They bowed to him and offered him presents. The King asked them who they were. They said, "O King, we are human beings and this is our birthplace and our home. We have left our houses behind because of the bees. During the day, we remain on an island, for the bees cannot cross the water to do us harm. When night comes, and they escape from the cold, we come ashore." "What do the bees feed upon?" asked the King. "They feed upon grass," they replied. "But they can scent human beings and they tear them apart and devour them. They have devoured many of our children." "How big is the Land of Gold?" asked the King. "God knows best," they replied. "What is your number?" inquired the King. "There are 1,000 of us on this island," they replied. "Is the gold there all the time?" asked the King. "O King, it is only once in a lifetime that a stranger is saved from this perilous sea to land here. For fifty, forty, or thirty years may pass without anyone arriving here; except, perhaps, for an unfortunate merchant whose ship has sunk in the sea and who is thrown upon this land. In this sea there is a spot called 'Ayn al-Sha'ab, and when the ship sinks there, the waves bring the passengers ashore here." The King asked, "Has any King ever set foot here?" "O King," they replied, "our fathers have told us that a king passed this land, whose name was Zahhak, and that he ruled 1,000 years."[20] "Where did your fathers learn about him?" asked the King. "We found this in chronicles, where we read that another king will arrive with many thousand men and he shall conquer the water and the land. The name of this king is Dhul-Qarnain. He will come ashore during the night, and on the same night he will win the Land of Gold and take as much gold as he wants." "What else did you read?" asked the King. "We read that Zahhak ruled for 1,000 years," they said, "and the other king who will reach this land will rule for fourteen years, during which he will go around the world and into the Land of Darkness, and many kings will be slain at his hand."

Alexander was saddened, for of the fourteen years, six had already passed. But he said nothing, and they did not know that he was the king mentioned in their chronicles. Then the King asked them, "Are there any other people beside you in this land?" "No," they replied. "I must free you from the nuisance of these creatures," said the King. And he asked them where those creatures lived. They said, "The mountain in the middle of the sea is full of holes, and they come from those holes." Then the King said to his men, "Tomorrow, let the Iranian soldiers wear annulated armor and remain on the shore." Then he ordered that the horses be taken on board the vessels. When this was done, they dropped the anchors and thus the animals were safe: The next morning, twice as many bees as there had been before came from the holes. And when they smelled human flesh, they came to the seashore, discovering the men and the beasts on board the vessels. They wanted to enter the sea, but they could not. The King ordered his men to shoot them with arrows from the sea and many of those creatures were thus slain. But the rest went inland and stood at a distance where arrows would not reach them.

When the sun set and it was time for evening prayer, it grew cold and the men were cold at sea. The King chose 5,000 of the Iranians and the men from Pars. These were the most courageous men in his army. He ordered them to put on cuirasses quilted with silk, to arm themselves with bows and arrows, and to go to the mountain to prevent the creatures from returning to their holes. After sunset, the gold bees, who were numb with cold, started to return to their holes, but the men shot at them with their arrows and killed them all. And when night came, the soldiers went ashore, pitched their tents, and stayed there. The inhabitants of that land praised Alexander, saying, "O King, it is 5,000 years since Zahhak reached this land and punished these creatures. Then you came and freed us from their nuisance." Then the King asked, "Are any of them left alive?" "O King, their chief has not yet come forth," they said. "How did Zahhak destroy them?" asked the King. "O King, we have read that he was a sorcerer. He cast a spell upon the sea, so that it seemed like the land. Then he went on board the ship. The gold bees, chasing him and his army, entered the sea, thinking it was dry land, and were drowned. Those that remained went to their holes and multiplied. Now their chief is still in the hole and has not yet appeared."

"Zahhak did that through sorcery," said the King, "We know no sorcery; what we do is accomplished in the name of God and through our strength."

When day came and the sun was high, the King ordered his men to carry the tents into the ship. Then as many bees as there had been the first time appeared from the holes, and their chief was as big as a donkey. They moved toward the camp and they caught and devoured two or three of the men. The King was alarmed. Meanwhile the men armed themselves and began to shoot their arrows at the bees from the sea. But the bees did not retreat, and their chief came to the edge of the water with the rest. When King Alexander saw their prevalence, he prostrated himself in prayer, saying, "O God, you have given your servant all that he ever desired, and you have made him dominant over all nations. Grant him victory over these enemies of mankind, for from the gnat unto the elephant all are in your command." Then he rose from prayer, put on his armor and his helmet, took an iron spear, and went to the shore on foot. None of these creatures dared approach the King as he went toward them in the name of God. And it is said that Alexander carried with him thirty of the names of God. These names were called *tamkhisa* and will, may it please God, be described in their proper place.[21] Every conquest Alexander made was by virtue of those names, which are in Hebrew. He kept those names, which have great virtues, encased in gold in his treasure house. And on that day, bearing the names in his hand, he roared like a lion, attacking those creatures with his spear. Now, by God's decree it so happened that when the bees, who were over 100,000 in number, saw the light [?], they were frightened and even their chief turned to flee. The chief did not succeed, however, for Alexander's men barred his way, crying "*Allah Akbar.*" And when the bees began to flee, the King left the camp and ordered his men to block their holes. They approached the holes armed with bows and arrows. The King, who also had a bow and arrow in his hand, shot a long arrow that struck the chief to the ground. The rest, who had grown faint (for the day had reached its end), had no power against the arrows. They were all slain, except for the few who had remained in the holes. And King Alexander remained there for four more days; and, for fear of the King, those creatures never left their holes until the King had departed.

Then the King took much gold from the land but he knew that he would not live long. He showed much kindness to the inhabitants of that land, then went on board and departed, thinking day and night of his approaching death. Then he said to himself, "The Land of Darkness is not far from this region. I will go and search for the Water of Life." They steered the vessels until they reached a mountain in the middle of the sea. Alexander ordered his men to climb the mountain and find out what was behind it. They discovered a meadow full of fruit trees, gay as the Garden of Eden and so vast that none knew its length and breadth, except God. They stayed there that night, and when morning came the King went to that mountain. In a thicket he saw a shepherd with many sheep. The King told his men to bring the shepherd to him, and they did so. "Who are you, and whose sheep are these?" the King asked the shepherd, who marveled to see all the ships and the army, for he had never seen the like of them on that island. He replied, "I am a merchant, and there were ten more with me when we happened upon this place. We were all from Kerman, and we had gone to sea for trade. It was God's will that we be shipwrecked. Each one of us tied himself to a board and we were borne by the current for one month. Our food and drink was nothing but seawater, except for times when we happened to reach a mountain where we could find edible herbs or fruits. Then we were driven to this land, which is inhabited by Davalpayan, who are the children of Adam.[22] They are fair-skinned, clean, and beautiful. Their land is fertile and full of orchards and fruit trees, and they feed upon fruit. They have many sheep, but they do not know the use of the knife or the sword, and they have never seen fire. They tear the throat of the sheep with their teeth, and devour them. Their teeth are like the lion's; and they are called Davalpayan, for they have no bone in their shanks. When they see us, they cling to us and tear our flesh with their teeth. They sit on our necks, using us as beasts of burden, and they make us their shepherds. There are 170 of us in their hands, driven to this land over a period of time. The daughters of these reptiles are as beautiful as the moon and the sun. They hang from our necks and force us to lie with them so that they may become pregnant and give birth to sons who have shank bones and use them as their steeds. We are their captives." The King was sorry for him and marveled at what he had heard.

## Alexander and the Davalpayan, and the War between Them

The story goes that when Alexander learned about the predicament of these prisoners, he was distressed, for they were Muslims. He said to them, "Be happy and fear not, for I will free you from their tyranny. I will play havoc among them this instant." Then he asked, "How many are they?" "God knows best," they replied. Alexander said, "Go and tell them, 'Alexander the Dhul-Qarnain has come. You must go to his presence if you wish him to do you no harm.'" The men rejoiced. The captives, 170 in number, were all observant Muslims. Each had stumbled there from a different land. When the shepherd gave them the glad tidings, they said, "May God rescue us from these Davalpayan, and may He end our suffering." Then the shepherds went to the chief of the Davalpayan and warned him, saying, "The King of the World, Alexander the Conqueror of Countries, has come to this land. He slew all monarchs on his way and subdued them all. He has conquered the whole world. Now he is here, and he has summoned you to his presence." Hearing this, the chief of the Davalpayan and a number from his army mounted their captives and went to Alexander. When Alexander saw them thus riding their captives, he was enraged. None had ever seen Alexander so angry. He commanded a prince, who happened to be standing before his throne with a drawn sword, to strike. The Davalpayan were twenty in number. The prince raised his sword and struck their heads off. And in his anger the King ordered part of the troops to arm themselves and to take bottles of naphtha and set the thicket on fire. The Davalpayan were frightened, and they took refuge on a high mountain in the middle of the sea. Only God knows their number. But their females were unable to escape and they were very beautiful. Alexander's men ravished many of them, for they had been away from home for many years without having seen any women. When they returned to the King they said, "We slew whom we could; the rest have taken refuge in those high mountains." Then the King freed the 170 captives, and he took them to his camp. "Our aim was to set these merchants free," he said. "Now we can leave." Then he asked the merchants how long they had been captive there. Some said ten, some said twenty years. Then he asked them to answer truthfully what their capital had been. They all answered truly. From his treasury Alexander gave each his lost capital. He told them to be of good cheer, saying, "I will take you back to Oman, and from there each shall return to his own home and family." All praised the King. Some of the merchants were from Rum.

Once more Alexander prepared for the sea, went on board, and set sail. After a short time he reached India. When he went ashore, he thought, "Our journey has taken long. From the fourteen years, seven have already passed and I have not yet seen half the world. I fear that before my wishes are fulfilled the exalted and holy Lord will summon me to Him." But although he feared death in his heart, he had not given up hope and continued to search for the Water of Life and for a wise man who could tell him of the Arab Zahhak, who had been king for 1,000 years. Having failed to find someone who could tell him of these things, he said to Aristotle, "What is to be done? Our expedition has taken many years, and we have not yet seen the world. The kingdoms of Iran and Rum have been left unsupervised. Our enemies could attack from Turkistan and win Iran and Rum, for the Turks and the descendants of Afrasiyab seek to take vengeance on Iran and Rum, and the soldiers there are too few in number to withstand them."[23] Aristotle said, "The King is to be obeyed; what he says is right." "We shall go round the world and soon return home," said the King. "But God forbid that on our return we find the enemy thriving, for then we shall have nothing but trouble." "It is as the King says," replied Aristotle. "What is to be done?"

Then the King came ashore and visited the tomb of Adam a second time. And King Kayd prepared provisions and sent them to Alexander and went to welcome him with all his army. When he saw Alexander, he descended from the elephant and bowed to him. Alexander showed him generosity and straightaway entered the city and the palace of Kayd. Kayd scattered 100,000 dinars in Alexander's honor.

Alexander was pleased. "You did justice," he said to Kayd. "Go to the harem and visit your daughter." In the harem, Kayd's daughter welcomed him courteously.

Alexander stayed in Ceylon for five days. Then he bade Kayd farewell, saying, "I do not know whether we shall ever meet again." He went on board the ship and sailed for Kashmir. When the news of Alexander's return from the pilgrimage to Adam's tomb and from the journey to the Land of Gold and the Land of Davalpayan reached Farrukhbakht, the King of Kashmir, he ordered his men to decorate Kashmir. They went to welcome Alexander with thousands of elephants bedecked with fineries and carrying musicians on their backs. Alexander entered Kashmir with splendor and magnificence such as none had ever seen before.

He remained in Kashmir for ten days, and he gave his mother-in-law, who was Azadbakht's wife and Kayd's daughter, to Farrukhbakht in marriage and they celebrated the event.

One day, as the King was riding, he saw a man who had no limbs and no eyes begging by the road. He inquired who the man was and learned that he was Azadbakht. Alexander felt pity for him. He ordered his attendants to take him to the palace and asked Azadbakht's brother to give him lodging and provide him with all that he needed until the day of his death. All will die, the slave and the free man; only God is immortal. And Farrukhbakht said to Alexander, "O King, it was for fear of you that I did not take care of him before. Now that you command I am bound to obey, and I will not fail in my duty."

Then Alexander moved from that land. The size of his army was beyond measure. All the elephants were loaded with gold, and only God knows the amount of the gold that Alexander brought to Oman from India and from the Land of Gold.

When the King of Oman heard of Alexander's arrival, he ordered that the city be decorated. He prepared three days' provisions for Alexander's army, and with many presents went to welcome him. He offered thanks to God for the safe return of Alexander.

Alexander stayed in Oman for a week, and then gave the merchants permission to return to their own lands. Having bid the King of Oman farewell, he started by sea for the House of God. He came ashore at Mecca and the news of his arrival was brought to the people of that land.

# Alexander's Arrival at Mecca and the House of the Prophet, and What Happened between Him and the People of Mecca

The story goes that when Alexander reached Mecca, the news of his arrival was brought to the inhabitants of that shrine and its chiefs.[24] They were alarmed and did not know what Alexander would want with them. At that time, the chiefs were the descendants of Ilyas; and the chief of Mecca was Ilyas the son of Khara, the descendants of Ishmael having been deprived of their position. And Ilyas said, "Let us go to his presence before he comes to us." Therefore all the descendants of the Prophet came to Alexander, who had camped with his vast army of soldiers, horses, and elephants within four parasangs of Mecca.

The chiefs of Mecca, who had never seen such a vast camp, marveled at the size of Alexander's army. Alexander was informed that the chiefs of Mecca had arrived, and he admitted them to his presence. As they entered, the King saw in them a holiness that moved his heart. He had never seen Arabs before. He looked at them closely and asked who their chief was. "This is our chief," they said, pointing to Ilyas, the son of Muzar.[25] Alexander honored Ilyas and told the chiefs of Mecca that he regarded them highly. Then he gave them leave to return.

The next day, Alexander and all his men came to visit Mecca and the house of God. The King entered the House of God, and performed the circumambulation, weeping and imploring God to forgive him. He stayed in Mecca for fifteen days, and he visited Mina and Muzdalifah and the 'Arafat.[26] He drank from Zamzam, and said his prayers at Maqam-i Ibrahim.[27]

When he was through with the religious rites, he sat in the House and ordered his men to decorate it with fine silk. And the amount of gold he spent there is known to no one but God. Then he summoned the chiefs of Mecca to his presence. And the blessed and exalted Lord had given Abraham's light to Ishmael and from Ishmael, generation after generation, to his sons.[28] In the time of Alexander the light was on the forehead of Nasr, the son of Qabit.

*Praying in the Ka'bah, Alexander saw a young man, a light emanating from his forehead. This was the true heir. He had been deprived of his position as chief of Mecca because of his poverty. Alexander restored him to his position and left for Yemen.*[29]

## Alexander's Arrival at Yemen, and What Happened between Him and the King of Yemen

The story goes that when Alexander came near Yemen, he camped and decided to go to the king of Yemen as messenger. Aristotle said to him, "Beware O King, for Mecca is never without Yemenites, or Yemen without people from Mecca. They have seen you and they know you. I fear that they will do you some harm."

Alexander dispatched his wives and his concubines to Rum in the company of Aristotle's son, Filinus, a virtuous, devout, wise, and learned man. The King commanded him to go to Rum, and he sent with him a letter to his mother. Azadbakht's daughter was then pregnant, and so were Kayd's daughter and eight concubines. Alexander sent them all to Rum with tons of valuables and an abundance of gold. And he sent 20,000 worthy horsemen with them. The King ordered them to go to Babil and from there to Rum. And Babil is today called Baghdad.

In his letter, Alexander said to his mother, "It is seven years since I left Rum. It will take a book to describe all the wonders I have seen. From the time I left my brother, the King of Kings, Darab the son of Darab, wherever I went, I found nothing but victory and all my desires were fulfilled. In seven years, I won half of the world, and I am now in the middle of the world. But, Mother, I fear that my death will come unexpectedly.

"Of the gold and riches I have sent you, distribute 100,000 dinars among the poor every month, and be charitable to the needy. Among the women I am sending to you ten are pregnant; two are daughters of kings and eight are concubines. Take good care of the kings' daughters, and respect above all Mahafarin, Azadbakht's daughter, for she is the Queen of Rum and Iran, and all the women there shall obey her.

"If she bears a son, call him Darab, and call the other wife's son Philip. And if they give birth to girls, call them what you will. And beware! Do nothing by day or night but pray to God to give me more years to live."

*Alexander entrusted the management of his army to Aristotle and went to the King of Yemen, disguised as a messenger. In Alexander's absence, Aristotle was to pretend that he was Alexander. Alexander demanded provisions from the King of Yemen.*

*The King of Yemen's daughter, Suhayl, was a brave fighter, equal to 100 men in battle. She had seen Alexander in a dream and had fallen in love with him. When Alexander came to her father as a messenger, she recognized him and when night came went to his chamber.*

. . . When the evening had proceeded in its course and it was time for rest and sleep, the maiden rose, covered her face with a veil, tied a dagger to her waist, took a candle, and all alone came to Alexander's bed. Now, whenever Alexander went somewhere as a messenger, he would not go to sleep, but would stay awake all night. He was sitting with his sword unsheathed before him, when he saw the candle. He seized the sword and stood. The maiden said, "Be not afraid." Alexander realized by her voice that she was a woman, and he felt secure. And Alexander was very fond of women and his companions were all asleep. Then the maiden unveiled her face and said, "Do not be afraid." When Alexander saw her beauty, strength departed from his limbs, for in that region he had never seen a woman as beautiful as she.

"Who are you?" he asked. "I am Suhayl of Yemen, and the daughter of King Munzar," she replied. "When I ride, I can unhorse 100 men with my spear and cast them to the ground." "What brings you to the messenger of Alexander in the middle of the night? For if we are discovered, I will be slandered and your reputation will suffer." "My reputation is safe," she replied, "and among the Arabs this is not considered wrong." Then the King asked, "What is your pleasure?" If you have a request I will impart it to the King of the Earth when I go to his presence." "Say no more of this," she replied, sitting at a distance from him, "for you yourself are the King of the Earth, Alexander. I have seen you in a dream, and I am in love with you. If you do not betray me and ask me in marriage from my father, I will conceal your secret; otherwise, I will spill your blood." Alexander turned pale, and thus she was assured that he was the King himself. Then he said, "That dream was from a demon. I am not Alexander, but a servant of his." The maiden replied, "Stop this nonsense and have pity upon your youth. For if you do not betray me I swear to the Creator of Heaven and Earth that I will not reveal your secret."

Then the King said to himself, "This is no place for meekness; it is time for manliness." He pitilessly took the maiden, cast her down, and tied her hands. She said to him, "I am content with what comes to me from you. If you take me with you thus in chains, I will be content and will not reveal your secret." Alexander was puzzled and did not know what to do. He decided to leave the maiden as she was and go to the

King. Therefore, he left her in the room with ten men to guard her, and he came to King Munzar, saying, "O King, Alexander had ordered me not to stay here over two days. It is three days already since I came to you, and he is hot-tempered and taxing." King Munzar replied, "I was preparing for your departure all night. I will dispatch you this moment."

*After returning to his camping-ground, Alexander sent word to the ten men who were guarding the Yemenite princess, Suhayl, to untie her chains and return to him. The next day, the King of Yemen went to Alexander with the Arab nobles and Suhayl accompanied him disguised as a man. She saw Alexander and recognized him as the messenger. Munzar, too, recognized Alexander and was afraid.*

*Alexander demanded that Munzar renounce idolatry. He asked also that the King of Yemen send for someone who could tell him about Zahhak. Munzar did so.*

*Alexander proposed a friendly joust between ten horsemen from his army and ten from Munzar's. Suhayl participated in the events, disguised as a man.*

The maiden's adversary was the son of the King of Mukran. When she entered the field, she displayed great dexterity with the lance, and the King of the Earth, Alexander, looked at her beauty, her deftness, and horsemanship, and he was moved with love. Then suddenly she hit her adversary on the head with her spear and cast him from the horse. Having done so, she dismounted, ran to Alexander, and kissed the ground before him. Alexander was riding a horse bedecked with gold trappings. He dismounted and sat on another steed, giving his horse with its trappings to Munzar's daughter.

*Later, Alexander told Munzar that among his cavalry there was only one good horseman, and that a woman not a man. Munzar denied this charge, claiming the horseman to be his son. Alexander was angered by this. He plundered Munzar's camp, and he ordered his servants to dress Suhayl in a veil and forbade women to ride horses. "For the woman's place is in the seclusion of the house." He left for Egypt, but later sent Aristotle to Munzar to ask his daughter's hand in marriage. Munzar imprisoned Aristotle, but Alexander married Suhayl after rescuing Aristotle.*

*Alexander then reached Palestine and marched toward Egypt.*

## How the King of Egypt, Disguised as a Messenger, Went to Alexander upon His Arrival in Egypt, and What Happened between Them

*The King of Egypt went to Alexander's camping-ground disguised as a messenger. He told Alexander to leave the land in peace, or else prepare for war. Alexander promised to send his answer the next day. That night the Chief of Egypt came to Alexander to complain against the King of Egypt, who had ravished 1,000 maidens, among them the daughter of the Chief of Egypt himself. He saw the messenger and revealed his identity to Alexander.*

*Alexander and the King of Egypt did combat. The latter was defeated and subsequently surrendered to his people who took him to the market-place, cut him to pieces, and fed him to dogs.*

*Alexander took possession of the gold and silver belonging to the King of Egypt. Later, Aristotle was sent to Rum with all that riches and with a letter to Alexander's mother.*

*Alexander married Sitarah, the daughter of the King of Egypt. She and her sister decided to kill Alexander, but their plot was discovered and they were surrendered to a minister who was instructed to kill them in secret. The minister, however, became infatuated with Sitarah and he lay with her. He hid the sisters in his house and continued to live in sin with Sitarah.*

## How King Alexander Asked the Chief of Egypt to Tell Him Stories, and the Chief Did So

*The Chief told Alexander the story of his own daughter, who was ravished by the King of Egypt on her way to her cousin's house, where she was to be married to her cousin. She returned to her father in shame. A year later, her cousin sent for her and married her in spite of what had happened. She lived with him for twenty-five years and bore him a son. On her deathbed she said to him, "O my husband, in the twenty-five years that I have been in your house, I never suffered at your hand, and you always treated me well. Never did you taunt me for the shame that* was done to me, either in the day of peace or in quarrel. May God reward you for this. In return, I will give you some advice. Beware! If you take a wife, do not marry one who as a maiden has belonged to another. For it is twenty-five years since that incident happened, and I have not yet forgotten the pleasure of that first night when that tyrant ravished me." The husband never married again.

Alexander told the Chief of Egypt that since he had attained manhood he had taken seventy-two wives who were all virgins. He said that God commanded men to marry in order that they may prosper. The Chief proposed to tell a story on that theme. He said: "A scholar who had decided to take a wife told his master of his intention and sought his approval. The master said to him, 'All, half, none.' The scholar did not understand his meaning, but he was shy and therefore did not ask for an explanation. Some time later he asked for the teacher's approval again. The teacher repeated what he had said before and explained that if the student married a virgin, she would be all his. If he married one who had had a husband but no child, she would be half his, and half the first husband's. And if he married a woman who had had both husband and child, she would belong half to her husband and half to her child, and none to him."

Alexander was pleased to hear these stories about women and he asked the Chief of Egypt to tell him stories every night.

Alexander suspected that the minister had kept the daughters of the King of Egypt rather than slaying them. He spoke to the Chief of Egypt of this matter, and the latter told him a story on this theme:

"The King of Yemen, who was a believer, fought an Arab King who was an idolater, slew him, and later married his daughter. The son of the Arab King, who had succeeded his father, sent poison to his sister and asked her to poison her husband. She agreed to do so, but her intention was discovered and the King delivered her to his minister to slay her.

"The woman told the minister that she was pregnant, and asked that her life be spared until she had delivered. The minister informed the King of this. But the King did not want a child born of her, and he ordered that she be killed. The minister, however, hid her in his house. He castrated himself and put his organ in a vessel which he gave to the King, asking him to put his seal on it, record the date, and place the vessel in his treasure house. The King did so.

"The woman gave birth to a son, and a long time went by. One day the

King told the minister that he was unhappy because he had no son to inherit the kingdom. The minister ordered the attendants to bring the vessel to the King and show the contents to him. The King asked him why he had emasculated himself. The minister explained that he did not deem it wise to kill a pregnant woman, and that he emasculated himself to protect the King from slander.

"The son, then seven years old, was brought to the King who rewarded the minister generously and forgave his wife. . . ."[30]

Alexander said to the Chief of Egypt, "Old man, my life story will become a science in this world. It will be written and studied, and the kings of the earth will rejoice to hear it. They will read and write and study my life story until Resurrection Day. But alas that I will not live long. If I lived long enough, I would discover so many wonders in the world that a mule would be needed to carry Iskandarnamah [The Book of Alexander].[31]

Alexander discovered the treachery of his minister and the unchaste daughter of the King of Egypt and put them to death. Then he said to the Chief of Egypt, "Most women are unchaste and wicked." The Chief replied, "There have been many good women in the world, and women who have ruled." He told the following story on this theme:[32]

"The King of Yemen, Tahtaj, asked a merchant who had come to his land whether he knew of any chaste and beautiful maiden whom he could marry, for he had no children by his wives. The merchant told him about the King of Syria and his daughter. But the King of Yemen was Christian, and the King of Syria, who was a Jew, refused to give him his daughter unless he gave him all the gold he demanded. Tahtaj sent all his gold and riches to Syria. As a result, he became poor and his army deserted him. He went to Syria, where the King gave him his daughter, with nothing more than the dress she wore. They went to live in a village and Tahtaj became a porter.

"Some time passed after this. Two sons were born to Tahtaj, and his fortune improved. It came to pass that a Jewish merchant he had invited to his house fell in love with his wife. He gave Tahtaj 100 dinars, asking him to send his wife to the ship to help his concubine who was in labor. The wife refused to go and when her husband insisted, she warned him against selling for a handful of gold what he had bought for a kingdom. But Tahtaj forced her to go. And when she went on board the ship, the Jew pulled anchor and sailed away. The next morning, Tahtaj found the ship missing. He took his sons and set on the way, searching for his wife. Some time later, his sons were stolen by a Kurdish tribe. Hungry and exhausted, Tahtaj lay down in a wilderness and went to sleep.

"He was awakened by 100 horsemen who, seeking an heir to their dead monarch, had decided to make the first man they came upon in the desert their king. Thus Tahtaj became the king of that land and he adopted two slave boys as his sons. One day a ship came to that land. Tahtaj invited its owner, a merchant, and sent the two slaves he had adopted to the ship to guard the merchandise while the merchant remained in the palace.

"The slave boys decided to tell each other their life stories in order to stay awake. Doing so, they discovered that they were brothers and the sons of the King of Yemen, who had bought their mother for a kingdom and later lost his wife and his sons. Then from a chest in the ship they heard a woman's voice, saying that she was their mother. She had been a prisoner on the ship for twenty-five years, but had remained chaste. They all went to the palace to beg the King to punish the Jew. There, the woman discovered that the King was none other than her own husband. The Jew was punished, and they were happily reunited."

Alexander asked that the story be recorded. Then the Chief of Egypt told another story.

"There was a merchant in Egypt who had asked his niece's hand in marriage for his son. After the merchant's death, the son squandered his fortune over an unchaste woman and, having lost all he had, he mounted his horse and left the city. On his way he came upon a veiled horseman who called him by his name and offered to restore all his property to him if he would agree to give him his cousin who was betrothed to him. The merchant's son promised to do so. He brought his cousin to his own house, and although he grew fond of her, he decided to surrender her to the horseman. He therefore left her in the house, went to the place where he was to meet the horseman, and returned with him. But the house was empty and she was nowhere to be found. Unveiled, the horseman proved to be none other than the cousin. She had purchased all the property that the merchant's son had sold when he was infatuated with the unchaste woman. He rejoiced to know that he had such a wise wife."

Alexander married the remaining daughter of the King of Egypt, for she was chaste. When the army reached Andalusia, which was ruled by Qidafah [Candace], Alexander said to Aristotle, "I must go to this woman as a messenger and see her."

## How Alexander, Disguised as a Messenger, Visited Candace, the Queen of Andalusia, and What Happened between Them

The story goes that Alexander entrusted his army to the Sage, and he told his wife, the second daughter of the King of Egypt, that he intended to go to Candace as a messenger. His wife said, "May it please God that you succeed and obtain the object of your desire, so that we may rejoice at your success. I hope this slave will bring you good luck. But a sister of mine is wife to Candace's son. I beg that if they are disobedient the King will spare my sister's life." "Be it so," the King replied.

Then King Alexander dressed like a messenger and went to the city of Andalusia. Candace bedecked the court with a splendor that Alexander had never seen before. She veiled her face and sat on her throne. They placed golden chairs in the hall which was made of turquoise and decorated with an abundance of gold.

When Alexander was led within, he did courtesy after the manner of messengers, and sat on the golden chair. Candace said to him, "You have stayed in Egypt a long time, suffered much hardship, and seen many wonders. I know of all those circumstances. Your King, Alexander, has never enough gold and silver. But what is your message?" Alexander said, "The King of the World, Dhul-Qarnain, says thus, 'Prepare provisions for our army, come to visit us, and give us supplies for the journey to the Land of Darkness, that we may cross your land without doing you any harm.'" "Be it so," said Candace. "I will send provisions for the army, and go to visit the King. But stay here tonight; tomorrow I will make good my word and send you back."

Alexander bowed and said, "Be it as you command." They lodged him in the same palace, treated him kindly, and greatly honored him. Now Candace had a painter, a skillful master, whom she had commanded to visit every land where there was a king and paint his portrait. She kept these portraits in the treasure house. Among them there was a portrait of Alexander, done when he was in Egypt. Now, when Candace saw the messenger, she suspected him to be Alexander. She said nothing that day and she treated him kindly that night, until she had seen the portrait again and was assured that he was Alexander. But she did not reveal her knowledge to him and said nothing to those in her army, for her son Tinush, son-in-law to the King of Egypt whom Alexander had slain, was planning revenge. And if he heard from his mother who the messenger was, Alexander's life would not be worth two grains of barley.

And when Alexander went to Candace in the morning, he knew nothing of these circumstances. Candace conversed with him and asked him what wonders he had seen. "O Queen, I have seen many," replied Alexander. "Why did your King slay the daughter of the King of Egypt?" she asked. "She was unchaste," he replied. "How many wives does the King have with him now?" she asked. "One," he replied, "the daughter of the King of Egypt, Barqatisah." "She is virtuous and beautiful," she said. "I have seen her."

Then she ordered 100,000 dinars and great quantities of silk and other rare gifts to be made ready. When she told Alexander that all was ready, he said, "Did you not promise that you would give tribute, and you would go to see the King?" "I have paid the tribute as I promised, and," she said softly, "I saw Alexander, too." "Where did you see Alexander?" he asked. "Say no more," she replied, "for the wise know that you are King Alexander. I do not want to mar your grandeur; I intended to conceal my knowledge, for otherwise you would be humiliated. Be not so daring, for things do not always end well." Alexander was perplexed with fear of that woman. He said, "May a King never be without his sword." "What would you do with a sword?" she asked. "I would slay both you and myself," he replied. Candace watched him in his indignation and his rage. They were alone. "Temper your anger and go inside," she said. "Do not fear me, and be assured that I will not betray you. All my army seek revenge upon you. God forbid that something go wrong, and I be blamed for it."

But Alexander was in no way to be appeased. He retired from the Queen and went to his lodgings, saying to himself, "Whatever I have achieved in this world through manliness, this woman outdid in her womanhood. I wish she had slain me rather than do me kindness and thus make me indebted to her. I must be grateful to her. I have gone round the world and I have seen many kings, but I saw none as wise as she. She is a woman who is better than 1,000 men." He dared not stay there, but he could not leave then. Therefore he sat with a candle before him.

And when it was time for rest and sleep, Candace took Alexander's portrait and went to him, disguised as a slave girl. Alexander recognized her, rose, and did courtesy to her. Candace placed the portrait before him. Alexander looked at it and said to himself, "May this painter's hand be cut off! This is a miracle!" Then Candace bowed to him and said, reassuringly, "We are not given to duplicity. You will see tomorrow how I will handle this matter before the army."

And it is said that Alexander married Candace that night and stayed there for three nights, and that he lay with her. This is not true, but God knows best. She asked the King to promise to send for her after he had returned to Rum and had resumed his rule in peace. She would then leave kingship to her son, and go to Alexander. Alexander promised to do so, and he gave his word never to demand tribute from Andalusia, and from Candace's descendants. Then Candace returned to her chamber and Alexander was relieved.[33]

The next day, she called Alexander to her presence. She was ill at ease, for she was sitting on the throne while the King stood before her. After calling her men to her, she sent the King away. And in the presence of her army she sent someone to inform Alexander's messenger that she would prepare what the King had demanded within three days, wishing that Alexander might have his fill of gold. They said this to Alexander, and he felt secure.

And Candace addressed the army, saying, "We have no power against Alexander, but we have riches beyond measure. I will send him more than he has demanded. Let Alexander know that we think nothing of riches and be chastised." When they heard these words they bowed, saying, "Only our Queen and no one else could think of such a wise policy."

When night came, Candace adorned herself and went to the King. She bowed to him and showed him reverence, and she made many apologies, saying, "I did with the army as was your wish. But my son, who is son-in-law to the King of Egypt, has no intention to make peace, and is gnashing his teeth in anger at you." The King said, "Call him before you tomorrow and I will impart to him what will induce him to peace." And that night the King stayed with Candace until dawn. At dawn Candace returned to her chamber. In the morning she admitted Alexander and Tinush to her presence. When the son saw Alexander, he insulted him and was rude to him. Candace admonished her son, saying, "Stop backing the King of Egypt your father-in-law, that cruel tyrant. How dare you mistreat a messenger, and that in my presence?" The son was silent. Then Alexander said to Candace, "To make compensation for the way you have respected and honored me, I give you my word that if your son and 200 horsemen go with me to the camping-ground, I will deliver Alexander to him to do with him as he pleases." When Tinush heard this, he fell on his knees before Alexander, saying, "If you do so, I will count myself your slave."

They agreed that Candace should prepare the tribute within two days and send it to Alexander, so that Alexander might feel secure. And Tinush was to go with the messenger. They agreed to do so and thus Tinush was pacified.

When night came, Candace went to Alexander, paid him reverence and apologized many times, saying, "O King, what will you do to my son?" The King replied, "Be at ease. For the respect I owe you, I shall do nothing but good to your children." They spent the night together, and in the morning made covenant, and bade each other farewell. Candace returned, instructing her men to load the camels and the mules with gold and silver. She sent so many rare gifts to Alexander that the King was amazed.

Then Alexander came before her throne, and she put her son's hand in Alexander's hand and she entrusted her son to him. Alexander said to her, "I have given you my word that I will put Alexander's hand in that of your son in this manner." Candace knew that he said the truth, for Alexander's hand was in Tinush's hand. They bade each other farewell and Tinush departed in the company of 200 heavily armed horsemen.

But Candace was worried. She said to herself, "King Alexander has only twenty men with him. I am afraid that he will receive some harm. But the danger will be over as soon as they reach the city gates." And when he had left, she returned.

Nearing the camp, King Alexander said to Tinush, "Stay behind this wall until I bring King Alexander to you." No sooner had he said this than Aristotle and some soldiers arrived with the canopy. When Tinush saw that, he trembled with fear, realizing that the messenger was Alexander himself. He dismounted and he threw himself before Alexander, saying, "Have mercy, O King!" The King assured him and placed his own hand in his, saying, "Thus have I made good my pledge." Then the King honored Tinush and took him to his camp. He presented him with the robe of honor, a crown, and a belt. Then he sent Tinush back to the city.

Later, Tinush's wife came to the camp, visited her sister, and returned. On that same day the King departed with his army and moved onward, accompanied by the Chief of Egypt. The King was depressed. He told Aristotle that he wanted to hear a happy story. Aristotle called the Chief of Egypt, who related the story of Bakhtiyar, who, born and abandoned near a spring, was found and adopted by the chief of a gang of highwaymen that came to the spring, and was given the name of Khudadad. Afterward, he was arrested for robbery and taken to the King, who was moved with pity for him and admitted him to his service. Some time later, the ministers accused Khudadad of having dishonorable intentions toward the King's wife. The King decided to punish him. But each day Khudadad told the King a tale, until the tenth day when he was saved, and the King came to know that Khudadad was his own son. He gave the ministers who had plotted against his son's life to him to do with them what he wished. But Khudadad pardoned them all.

And this story exists as a book by itself, both in verse and in prose, and is known to many. We have referred to it briefly.[34] Indeed, this tale belongs to a later date than the time of Alexander, but God knows best.

When the Chief of Egypt finished this tale he said, "Khudadad pardoned the ministers and presented them with the robes of honor. Know then, O King Alexander, that this has been the policy of kings, and they should be so and act thus. Bloodshed is unbecoming to a king." And he meant this as a hint to Alexander. Alexander was beside himself with rage, and Aristotle knew that the Chief of Egypt had forfeited his blood. Alexander put his hand to his sword. Aristotle saw that, and, throwing himself before the King, intervened. "O King, he said this out of ignorance, for he is old and foolish." Alexander, out of respect for the

# ISHKANDARNAMAH 53

Sage, put his sword down. Then Aristotle motioned for the Chief of Egypt to leave. The latter did so, and that night passed.

Then the King said to the Sage, "We must prepare for the journey to the Land of Darkness." Therefore he called the inhabitants of that land and asked them the way to the Land of Darkness. They said, "There are ten prominent cities yet in the way. From here to the Land of Darkness there is a month's journey." "What people live in these ten cities?" asked the King. "They are Moors, O King," they replied. "Their men veil their faces like women, and their women go with their faces exposed. They are devout people." When Alexander heard this, he exclaimed, "O pure, great, Creator! I thought Andalusia was the end of the world, but there is more left."

Then he moved from there and came to a small town inhabited by devout but poor people. When they heard about Alexander, they prepared a modest offering, and 500 of the nobles, headed by a weak old man, came to the King and offered provisions. The King treated them kindly, accepted their offering, and left that land without doing them any harm.

As this town was by the sea, the King assumed that they had to continue the journey by sea. But he was told that the sea led to Syria, which could be reached by land also. Then he departed from there and he reached a city called Sagha. When he reached the gates, he saw a city wonderfully vast and pleasant, with a large population. The King of Sagha, who had a vast army, sent a messenger to Alexander with many gifts. Alexander accepted the gifts and he intended to depart, when, seeing a caravanserai built of hooves, he inquired who had constructed it. The Chief of Egypt, who happened to be present, said, "O King, this inn was built by Kaykhusraw the son of Siyavush, and the King of Kings. And this is how kings act." Alexander became angry again. He ordered his attendants to put the Chief of Egypt in chains and demanded 50,000 dinars before he would free him. The chief of that land, who knew the Chief of Egypt, lent him the sum, expecting to be paid back when the Chief returned to Egypt. The gold was submitted to Alexander, who then dismissed the Chief from his service. Then Alexander asked the inhabitants of that land who had built the inn. They replied, "It was King Kaykhusraw, the son of Siyavush, who came ashore with a great army and built this inn." Alexander visited that inn. He saw inscribed in that place: "Kaykhusraw, the son of Kaykavus, the son of Kayqubad, the son of Tahmuris, the son of Afridun." Alexander read that and he marveled at the inn.

Then he dismissed the Chief of Egypt and sent him back. And that night he asked Aristotle to tell him about Siyavush and Kaykhusraw and their story with Afrasiyab. He said to Aristotle, "I have heard about this story and in Turkistan I meant to ask you to relate it. Tell me the story tonight, for only God knows whether we will get to Turkistan again." Then the Sage related the story as it is told in the *Shahnamah* [of Firdawsi]. And the story is too long to be rendered here. Besides, most people know these stories from the *Shahnamah*. When Aristotle the Sage, had finished the story, Alexander's gown was wet with tears. "Be joyful, O wise Sage," he said to Aristotle, "for it did my heart good to listen to you."

Then he departed from there and he reached a land where he found strange and exquisite fruits the like of which he had never seen. And when the citizens came to Alexander, he asked them about the wonders of their land. They said, "O King, in our land there are many wonders. This region is the end of the earth and close to the Land of Darkness. It has twenty-four gates and a large population. We had a king, but he is no more. There is no king or judge in this land. The poor and the rich are the same. We have no locks to our gates, storehouses, and lodgings." Alexander marveled at what he heard, and inquired how this could be. They replied, "The rich and the poor are the same, for we have divided what we have equally. If I have something my neighbor lacks, I give him half of it that we may be equal. We have no king or judge, for kings and judges are needed to prevent people from taking one another's property, or doing one another injustice. Now, we are all equal; what need is there for a king or a judge? And doors to houses and storehouses are built to prevent stealing. What use are they to us? We have dug graves at our doors to remind us daily of our death."

Alexander marveled at them and he asked them what their religion was. "We worship the God of heaven and earth. We call upon him, and we do nothing but worship him by day and night." "Who taught you this religion and this truth?" asked the King. "A man called Khidr," they replied.³⁵ And as they were speaking thus, Khidr appeared. He came to the King and embraced and greeted him. Alexander rose, and, embracing Khidr, said, "Praised be God who granted me to see you." "Do you intend to go to the Land of Darkness?" asked Khidr. "Yes," said Alexander. "What do you seek there?" asked Khidr. "I hope to find the Water of Life," replied the King. "Such a great army as yours, will need large supplies," said Khidr. "Yes, but we cannot leave the army here," said Alexander. And nobody knew about the Water of Life except King Alexander, Aristotle the Sage, and Khidr. Then Khidr said, "I must go before the army." Alexander put all his army under Khidr's rule, and they departed from that region and reached another land. And Khidr obtained food and drink in the wilderness. Alexander knew that he could not reach the Land of Darkness except through him, and put his entire army under Khidr's rule. On their way they reached a land where the fields and pastures were full of cows and sheep. And the prophet Khidr would go before the army during the day, but when the army stopped for rest, he would disappear.

And the people of that land came to Alexander, saying, "We are poor and have nothing worthy of the King except our blessings." "What are the wonders of this land?" Alexander inquired. They went and brought an apricot, saying, "This is the wonder of our land, and the reason why we are Muslims. For formerly in our land there was a king, a descendant of Zahhak and an idol worshipper. And a prophet of God, called Ilyas, who is still alive but is concealed from man's eyes, had a disciple by the name of Yisaʿ,³⁶ who would go around, inviting people to the religion of God. When he came to our land and saw that we worshipped idols, he invited our king to renounce idolatry. The King demanded that he perform a miracle. 'I am no prophet to perform miracles,' he said. 'But you may demand a miracle and if God wishes that you become Muslims, it will come to pass.' Our King said, 'I want a tree to appear in this field and that same hour bear fruit, the color of my gown.' And the King was wearing a red and yellow gown. 'Let us go,' said Yisaʿ.' And we all left the city. Yisaʿ said his prayers and that same instant an apricot tree grew out in the wilderness, with the fruit half-red and half-yellow. And before this, there had been no fruit in our land. We reached with our hands and ate of the fruit. Our King accepted the faith, and some of us pretended to have done the same. Then Yisa' said to us, 'Keep the stones of the apricots, for they will be of some use, and God will yearly send you the fruit.' And we ate the fruits and kept the stones in our pockets.

"When we reached the city gate, Yisa' said to the King, 'Among your army and your people some have accepted the faith in truth, and some only pretend to have done so.' 'How do you know this?' asked the King. 'God reveals such matters to me. If you want to know for sure, send your horsemen to the gates to collect the stones. The ones with the sweet kernels belong to those who truly accepted the faith, and the ones with the bitter kernels belong to those who pretend to have accepted the faith.'

"The horsemen went to the gates and collected the stones, and it was as Yisa' had said. Those who had the sweet kernels were allowed to enter the city; those with bitter kernels were taken before the King. And Yisa' said to the King, 'These have confessed faith in falsehood.' With the second miracle all accepted the faith, and ever since we believe in the true faith."

Then the King demanded the legend of the prophet Ilyas, which is a good story. They said, "Khidr, peace be upon him, knows this story." Therefore when Khidr came, Alexander asked him to relate the story and Khidr did so. This story is related in *Qisas al-anbiya'*[37] in great detail, and in this book we intend to tell the story of Alexander, not the *Qisas al-anbiya'* or other tales.

## Alexander's Journey to the Land of Darkness and What Occurred There

It is said that after Khidr related the story of Ilyas the King said, "We will depart from this land without doing any harm, and without demanding provisions." "This is a wise policy," said Khidr.

They moved from there and reached another land situated within five days' distance from the Land of Darkness. Then King Alexander said to Khidr, "We have a long journey before us, and we need provisions for the army." But Alexander did not tell his men that the goal of his journey was to find the Water of Life. He said to them that he was going to Jabalqa,[38] on the mountain of Qaf.[39] He stayed there for a month. And Khidr would disappear during the night and reappear in the morning.

But Alexander was depressed at night, wondering whether he would find the Water of Life. For from the fourteen years which, he was told, were left in his life, nine had already passed. He was busy, supplying the army with provisions. For nearly a month, rice, peas, pomegranate seeds, barley, wheat, and honey were carried to them from the country.

One day, on one of the mountains of the West, Alexander saw an old hermit, his hair snow-white and his back bent double with age. The King was astonished to see him. He went to the hermit and asked his name. "My name is Hum," said the hermit, "and I am 750 years old. There is no mountain in the world that I have not reached." Alexander said, "Come to me and I will take you to the mountain of Qaf." The hermit replied. "In my 750-year life I could not reach the mountain of Qaf. Do you expect to reach it in the four or five years that remain in your life?" Alexander trembled to hear this. He said, "How do you know how much time remains in my life?" "I know," replied the old man. "I am going in search of the Water of Life. If I find it and drink of it, your foreknowledge will come to naught," said Alexander. "God willing," said the old man sarcastically.

*The King asked Aristotle about Kaykhusraw and Luhrasb. Aristotle told him their stories in detail, as they are recorded in the* Shahnamah.[40]
*They departed from there and reached a region near the Land of Darkness.*

Alexander prepared for the journey and the next day entered the Land of Darkness. His men were reluctant to enter that region. For four consecutive months they could not tell the day from the night. Alexander followed Khidr, who went before his army. The columns were so long that when the vanguard came to rest, the end of the column was still moving.

One day Khidr, peace be upon him, dropped something from his hand. As he picked it up, his hand came against water. He discovered a spring, the water of which tasted like honey. He knew that it was the

Water of Life and drank from it. Khidr had never tasted anything like that before. He said his prayers, and without telling the soldiers that he had drunk of the Water of Life he ordered them to stay where they were until he returned, warning them that if they moved one step further, they would perish. And he himself hurried to King Alexander, taking the rein of his steed, which happened to be a young mule. "Oh Alexander," he said. "I have drunk from the Water of Life and I have found the spring. I ordered the army to stay there, so that we would not lose the spring." And Khidr went before the King, holding his steed by the rein.

But when they returned to the spring it had disappeared. He asked the men whether they had moved away from that spot. They replied, "God forbid! We did not take one step further." They stayed there for seven days and seven nights, and the army rested. The provisions and the water supply, carried by the beasts of burden, were consumed, but the spring was not found. The King was sick at heart and full of regret; all his efforts and hopes had been defeated. After seven days, they departed and continued on their way until they left the dark and came upon daylight.

For four months, they had not seen the sunlight or the moonlight, or their own faces, and had not been able to tell the night from the day. They marched on gravel, not knowing what was under their feet. They tasted and smelled the stones, but because of darkness they could not tell what they were. Therefore all who had gone to the Land of Darkness were filled with remorse because of those stones. For when they left the darkness they discovered that the stones were all precious gems, rubies, and chrysolite. Therefore they were all filled with remorse, as the Prophet has said. The Prophet was asked, "Why, O Prophet of God?" He replied, "For they had done one of three things: some had taken a large number of the stones, some had taken only a few, and some had not taken any. Those who had taken many, wished that they had taken more. Those who had taken only a few, regretted that they had not taken more. Those who had not taken any, grieved the most. Know then that they were all full of remorse."

When they left the Land of Darkness and saw one another, they embraced and rejoiced, because they had not seen one another's face for months. But King Alexander was downcast. He had not found the Water of Life and had no hope for life. And when they left the darkness, he came upon the Qaf mountain and he saw Israfil with his trumpet to his mouth, one foot on the Qaf and one foot on the fourth sphere.[41] Alexander did not see the fourth sphere, but he saw the Qaf mountain and the leg of Israfil, who, holding the trumpet to his mouth, watches the sky, until He bids him blow. Alexander was puzzled and frightened, for he found no trace of the earth and its inhabitants there. An awesome voice addressed him: "You insolent man! Have you no shame? Now that you have reached the end of the earth, do you aspire to ascend to the sky? Return, for little is left of your life."

Alexander returned and started for the region where the sun sets. They said to him, "Your way lies to the west of the Qaf mountain, on the border of the Land of Darkness. It takes four days to reach that region. When you get there, tell your men not to be afraid. For when the sun sinks into the spring, a loud cry and uproar like the clamor of bells and cymbals is heard from the spring and this frightens people. There the sun is as big as four times the distance between the East and the West."

In spite of this warning, when Alexander saw the sun disk sink into the spring he fell unconscious. When he recovered his senses, he saw a tribe unlike any he had ever seen before. And then he reached the region that God mentions in the glorious Koran: "Until he reached the limit whither the sun set, he found it going down into a sea of black mud and found by it a people. We said: O Dhul-Qarnain! Thou mayest chastise or do them a good."[42] Alexander saw there a people both heathen and believing, and wanted to depart from the land. But God inspired Alexander to say to them, "I shall treat he who believes in God kindly, and God will grant him heaven as a reward. And he who is an unbeliever shall be slain and win hell as his reward. For the unbeliever death in this world and punishment in the next; for the believer, mercy and kindness in this world, and the joys of heaven in the next."

Then Alexander left that tribe. And scholars differ in regard to the warm spring. Some believe that the spring in which the sun sets is hot and boiling, and opinions differ concerning this.

After this adventure, Alexander prepared to depart from the land that had borders with Syria and was the region where the sun sets. Some believe the land to be the site of resurrection. Alexander stayed there for ten days, because the region was pleasant and temperate, though it was devoid of trees and plants.

One night the King was sleeping. When the night was partly over, he went out for some need, and he saw many serpents in the camping-ground. He feared that they might harm his soldiers. He awakened his men and advised them to stay up and protect themselves from the serpents. Many of the serpents were killed and some of them fled.

When day came Alexander ordered his men to begin building ships because they had to cross the sea that since the day of Kaykhusraw none had crossed. But he could not get all the provisions he needed from that land alone. Although there was much food to be found, it was very warm, and the food would spoil easily. He supplied his army with what was available, prepared for the journey as best he could, and built the vessels while seeking someone who was familiar with that sea and its wonders, but he found no such man.

## The Story of the Scorpion, the Snake, the Youth Who Was Sleeping in the Garden, and the Wonder That the King Saw

The story goes that at midday, when the sun was high and it was very hot, Alexander left his tent, his mind harassed by the black snakes he had seen. All alone, he left his tent, an Indian sword in his hand. He walked a while, and behold, he saw a scorpion as big as a duck, holding its tail straight to the ground, hastening on its way looking straight ahead. He marveled at what he saw. When he made an attempt to kill the scorpion, he heard a mysterious voice. "Spare the creature," the voice commanded, "for God has sent it for a purpose. Look where it goes." "I must see this wonder," thought the King.

All alone Alexander followed the scorpion, which hurried on its way as before until it had covered a good distance. The King grew weary. It was noon and very hot, and he was on foot. When the scorpion had gone a bit farther, it came upon a stretch of water. It waited, until at God's command, a turtle appeared on the water. The scorpion climbed to its back and the turtle returned to the water.

The King marveled at what he saw. He decided to follow the scorpion although he was tired, because the mysterious voice had said, "Look where it goes." He followed the scorpion until it came upon a wall. The scorpion climbed the wall and went to the other side. The King too climbed the wall, and, looking over, saw a pleasant garden. A dark youth, half-naked, wearing a loincloth, was sleeping peacefully while a dark serpent, curling on his chest, was about to bite him. The scorpion charged toward the youth, climbed upon his chest, and before the snake could bite him the scorpion stung it on the head and killed it. Having done so, the scorpion turned and after climbing the wall went to the stream. The same turtle appeared and carried it to the other bank, and the scorpion returned the way it had come.

King Alexander watched all this, wondering who the youth was to enjoy such grace from God. He awakened the youth, who asked him who he was. "It does not matter who I am," said Alexander. "Rather, consider God's grace unto you. Behold this snake." Then Alexander told him what he had witnessed. "Praised be God, the Lord of the Worlds, and to Him many thanks," said the youth. He went with the King, but did not know who he was. When they had walked for a while Alexander saw the Sage, who, accompanied by the troops, was looking for him. When they saw the King, they dismounted. The youth realized that Alexander was the King who had returned from the Land of Darkness. He did courtesy to the King and apologized. The King gave him gold and a rich gown. Alexander kept the youth in his service, for he knew the sea course and was familiar with that region.

Alexander ordered the Sage to record that adventure, so that the event might not be forgotten. Then he returned to his camp. When night came and he went to sleep, he dreamed of an angel who said to him, "Oh servant of God, Alexander, if you think that what you have done was accomplished through your own courage and wisdom, and that you saw all those wonders and reached the limits of the earth on your own, you are deceived. For all was done by God, the Creator of the seven spheres and seven earths. If you think that you can protect yourself from the snake and the scorpion, you are deceived. You rose in the night and killed the snake and the scorpion, thinking that if you were asleep, they would overcome you. What would you have done if they had overcome you in your sleep? Know then, O Alexander, that it is the Lord of the Worlds who guards you from all evil, as you saw by the example of the scorpion that He sent to slay that big snake and to save his servant. He who is in God's protection cannot be harmed by ferocious beasts, reptiles, demons, fairies, or man."

When Alexander heard this, he woke up. And going down on his knees, he bowed with his forehead to the ground and thanked God. Through his sagacity Alexander realized that God had thus shown him that his trust in Him was weak, for he had been afraid of the snakes. Again, through that adventure, God granted him to find the youth, who was familiar with the sea course—all this through the grace of God, the Lord of the Worlds. After these adventures were recorded in *Iskandarnamah* the King set out for the sea. He built vessels, but he was worried about the journey.

Then the youth said to Alexander, "O King, in this city there is an old man who has lived since the days of Moses. We can find him and ask him about this Green Sea."[43] The King was pleased. He said, "This old man is a wonder." The youth requested to have some companions on his mission. The King sent some of his attendants with him. They wrapped the old man in a blanket and carried him to the King. The King marveled to see him, and treated him kindly and asked how old he was. "I am 640 years old," answered the old man. "In the lifetime of which prophet did you live?" asked the King. "I have seen many prophets," replied the old man. "Which ones?" asked the King. "I have seen David, Solomon, Aaron, and Moses, peace be upon them, and I know their lives," said the old man. "Did any of them cross this sea?" asked the King. "Solomon crossed this sea without a ship; he was carried on the back of the wind," said the old man. "How many days does it take to cross the sea?" asked Alexander. "O King, this is a vast sea," replied the old man, "and there is none bigger than this in the world. When the blessed and the exalted Lord created the world, he made three-fourths of it from water, and one-fourth from land. The limits of this sea are nowhere within sight. If you choose to go by land you must return by the road that led you here. The road is difficult, and the Land of Darkness is in the way. If you go by sea you can reach the whole world. If the north wind is favorable, in eight months you will reach China and the China Sea; in a year, India; and, in two years the Mediterranean Sea. This sea is boundless." Then the King said, "In your long life have you discovered how long it takes to cover by land the distance covered by sea in a day?" "Yes," answered the old man. "The distance covered by a ship in one day when the north wind is favorable, is equal to 500 farsangs covered by horse on land." "Praised be God!" exclaimed the King.

And the sages of Rum had made many different medicines for the King, which he took daily; including electuaries containing snakes to give him courage so that he might not fear mighty deeds.

Alexander asked the old man to remember him in his prayers. The old man said, "I will give you a gift, O King, a prayer by virtue of which you shall cross the sea unharmed. For whatever conquest the prophets made was by virtue of this prayer. By it, Moses drowned the Pharaoh. God saves the possessor of this prayer from all evil." The King rejoiced to hear that. The old man said, "God sent this prayer from heaven to Daniel, who recited it when he was captive in the lions' thicket. By virtue of this prayer the lions bowed to him with their foreheads to the ground. Solomon brought the wind under his power through this prayer. It contains thirty names from the names of God. Those names are in heaven. You must hold this prayer dear." Then he copied the thirty names and gave them to the King.

And Sultan Mahmud, the son of Sabuktakin, may God have mercy upon him, found these names and asked Shaykh Abu Sa'id Khargushi[44] to copy them, giving him 1,000 maghribi dinars.[45] And all the conquests and wars of Sultan Mahmud were achieved by virtue of this prayer.

And Alexander gave 2,000 *Khusravani durusts*[46] to the old man to copy the names for him. The King received those great names and the next day he set upon the voyage. He gave those names to none but a prince who was accompanied by 24,000 men. The entire army crossed the sea by virtue of those names. Alexander had learned the thirty names by heart, and he recited them while steering the ship.

One night, when the ship was in anchor, the King sat with a candle before him, reciting the names. Suddenly a fish thrust its head out of the water. It was so big that it could make a morsel of the ship, the elephants, and the entire army. Alexander marveled at what he saw. He recited the thirty names and prayed to God, saying, "O Lord, by virtue of your exalted name, which is written in heaven, make this fish speak to me, so that it might answer my questions." After he made this plea, the fish thrust its head out of the water. King Alexander said, "What do you seek, O fish?" "God commanded me to speak to you," answered the fish. "Speak then," said Alexander. "You requested that I answer your questions. Now ask," said the fish. "Tell me what fish you are and whether there is any fish bigger than you in the sea," said Alexander. "When Solomon invited all his army," the fish replied, "and decided to feed all animals, he ordered giants, fairies, and men to carry food to the seashore for many days. (And God provides my needs mornings and evenings.) And the story goes that Solomon slaughtered 70,000 camels and 700,000 cows and 1,000,000 sheep for the feast, in addition to preparing other bounties beyond measure. And this is the number of the camels, cows, and sheep as Wahb ibn Munabbih has recorded. But God ordered me to thrust my head out of the sea and swallow all in one morsel, and that did not suffice my breakfast." "Is there any creature bigger than you?" asked the King. "Yes," the fish replied. The King prayed and recited the names. Soon, there was a tremendous convulsion and a fish surfaced, so big that the first fish could not be seen behind it. In a clear voice it said, "Praised be God, who created creatures in the land and in the sea. Before His greatness, they are as a mote in the air." Then the fish disappeared and Alexander crossed the sea in eight months and twenty days.[47] Many men and beasts perished on the way until they came ashore in the land of Machin, a region like paradise. Alexander saw many wonders at sea, but we will not mention them in detail; otherwise this story will become too long. While at sea, he saw strange creatures that he had never seen before and marveled at their voice and speech. When they came ashore, they were at the eastern coast. News was brought to the Emperor that Alexander had arrived after his journey to the Land of Darkness. No one believed that he had failed to drink of the Water of Life. And when Alexander finished his voyage in the Western Sea, he thanked God and they rejoiced. He inquired where the land led to. The inhabitants answered, "This is the

# ISHKANDARNAMAH 65

China Sea. From now on you will go by land. There are 360 cities in the way which, together, are called Turkistan. When you cross that region, you will be facing east, and the rising-place of the sun."

Then the King departed and led his army away on his journey to the East. He said to the Sage, "We have done with the West, and we have recorded its wonders. Now begin a second book for the wonders of the East, that it may be read after us, and we may be remembered by it, and our name may never die."

## Alexander's Arrival in Turkistan by Way of the Akhzar Sea, and What Happened between Him and the King of That Region

*Alexander came upon a city ruled by a deputy of the Emperor of China. Seeing that the ruler was an idolater, Alexander plundered the city and conquered a fort, inside of which he found barrels containing wheat, each grain as large as an almond. The ruler told Alexander that the barrels were handed down to them by their forefathers, and that they did not know what their story was.*

## The Story of the Barrel of Wheat Found in the King's Treasure House and the Life Story of Bahram, His Father, and Their Wives

*Alexander asked the elders of the city about the wheat. A man who was 600 years old told him that the wheat had been sown in the time of Kaykhusraw, during whose rule wheat throughout the world grew that large as a result of his justice.*[48]

*Afterward he came upon a tribe who told him of a palm tree, the fruit of which cured all ailments. The palm tree had grown out of the bones of a dead king. The King's daughter, eating of the fruit, had become pregnant and had given birth to a girl. When the King's daughter died, he built a cloister for his granddaughter, where she spent her life in prayer.*

## The Story of the Hermits and the King's Daughter, and What Occurred[49]

*Two hermits, who lived in the mountains, went to the cloister of the King's daughter and wanted to lie with her. She locked herself where they could not reach her. Fearing that the maiden would reveal this matter, they took the upper hand, telling the citizens that the King's daughter was unchaste. The King believed the hermits and decided to punish his daughter. But Alexander summoned the hermits to his presence separately and asked each to describe what they had seen at the cloister. They told contradictory stories, and thus it was proven that they had lied. The two hermits were burned on a pyre. Some time later, Alexander married the maiden.*

*The King of that land told Alexander stories about justice.*

## Alexander's Arrival at Siyavushgard and What Occurred between Him and the King of That Land

*Alexander visited Siyavushgard and the tomb of Siyavush, a place like paradise.[50] The earth on the tomb was red, and fresh blood flowed over the grave. In the midst of the warm blood there was a green plant.*

*People considered Alexander the son of Philip, but he knew that he was a descendant of Luhrasb. He therefore challenged Turanshah, the King of Darabgard, to war in order to avenge the blood of Luhrasb and Siyavush. Turanshah was defeated and later beheaded.*

*From there Alexander came to the paradise of Ganges,[51] where. he stayed for a month before he left for China.*

## Alexander's Arrival at China, the Wonders He Saw There, and What Occurred between Him and the King of That Land

*Alexander came upon a city where the houses and the walls were all made of stone. He was told that the city was built by giants in the time of Solomon. The inhabitants of the city were believers, the followers of*

*David the prophet, and knew the Torah and the Psalms. An old man who knew the Psalms of David and who was a psalm singer, told Alexander about David and Solomon.*

*Later, Alexander reached the city of Yaris the inhabitants of which were afflicted with blindness because they had refused to believe in God.*

## How Alexander Went to the Emperor of China as a Messenger and What Occurred between Them

*Alexander went to the Emperor as a messenger and demanded that he come to see Alexander and send him provisions. The Emperor agreed. However, he planned to poison Alexander while he was in his camp. The plot was discovered, and Alexander received no harm. He ordered his men to plunder the city, and he arrested the Emperor and his son.*

One day, Alexander said to Aristotle, "O Sage, we have traveled around the world, visited various lands, and reached the limits of the earth. In all this time, did you ever meet a man wiser and more learned than yourself?" "I did not," replied Aristotle. The King was displeased with that answer, for it is not proper for a man to praise himself. He asked again, "Is there anything in the world that is a mystery to you?" "O King, there is nothing that is hidden from me," Aristotle replied. "What if I ask you a question and you fail to answer it?" said the King. "In that case, my blood shall be forfeited," replied the Sage. "I will ask you two questions," said the King. "The first shall be about the doctrines of religion. I want you to answer promptly." "Ask," said Aristotle. "He who is king in this world," said Alexander, "owns the throne, the crown, the land, the treasury, and the army. What is it that God does not possess even though He is the King of Kings? And tell me also what the God of the World is doing this minute." "That which all kings have and God does not have, is wife and child and eating and sleeping, which God needs not." "You answered well," said the King. "Now tell me what God is doing this minute."[52] "O King, give me seven days to think about this question," Aristotle said. "If you do not find the answer within seven days, will you consider your life forfeited unto me?" asked the King. "I will," replied the Sage.

The King gave him seven days, but the Sage failed to find an answer. He looked into books, he summoned the nobility and the wise men of China, but none of them could answer the question. They said to him, "The King is looking for an excuse to spill your blood and appropriate your possessions, for who would ever know what God is doing?" "They are right," thought the Sage. "He who serves a King and wins himself a name, should be wary against his deceit."

It so happened that there was a Zangi[53] in the house of the Sage, in charge of the stove of the bath. He was some twenty years old and had never in his life possessed a new garment, and had never washed his face. He covered his nakedness with a rag and slept in the warm ashes of the bath's furnace.

On the sixth day, Aristotle's attendants found the Zangi singing and joyful. They beat him, saying, "What a time for such gaiety!" Weeping, he went to the Sage. The Sage was downhearted, sitting with his head on his knee; he had given up hope for life. The Zangi complained to the Sage that he had been beaten. "What was your fault?" asked the Sage. "I was singing," he replied. "Go today, for my heart is troubled. Tomorrow, I will put the offender in your hand," said the Sage. "I want him today," the Zangi insisted. The scholars present shouted at him, "Do you not know what has happened?" "Tell me what it is," he said. "I will not leave unless you tell me what has happened." The Sage called him to himself and said, "The King has asked me what God does in heaven." The Zangi said, "O Master! Do you not know what God does in heaven? Is this a mystery to such a learned man as you?" "I do not know the answer," confessed the Sage. "I know the answer," said the Zangi. "Tell us!" said the Sage. "I will give the answer before the King," said the Zangi. Then Aristotle went to the King, saying, "O King of the Earth! I have been in your service since the time your mother bore you. Through ignorance I claimed that I knew all things. The omniscient is God. I claimed that I never met anyone more learned than myself. Now, I say, I have a black slave, wiser than myself, and he will answer the question posed by the King."

"Bring him to me," said the King, "for I thought this was an unanswerable question." The Zangi was brought in, covering his nakedness with a rag, his feet smeared in dried dung a month old. The King looked at him and ordered him to give his answer. The Zangi said, "O King, tell your men to wash me clean and to dress me in your special gown." They did as he had asked. They took him to the bath, washed him clean, and dressed him in the King's royal gown. Then he said, "O King, tell them to bring me aloeswood and rosewater that I may smell good." They did as he had said. Then he said, "Give me a house and a horse with its trappings." That done, he said, "I want a beautiful Turkish maiden to be my wife, and ten handsome slaves to serve me." Alexander gave him one of the four Chinese maidens presented to him by the Emperor of China, and ten slave boys as beautiful as the moon. Then the Zangi said, "Now, O King, what was the question you asked?" The King said "Tell me what God is doing this moment." "O King," the Zangi said, "what God is doing is this: in this hour, he brought me from the bath furnace and raised me from that mean state to such honorable position that I may sit in the minister's seat in the presence of the King of the Earth. God in this hour is making this take place."

When the King heard that from the Zangi he realized that this was a warning from God, so that it might be known that in the seven spheres and earths the omniscient God is the sole possessor of perfect knowledge.

Then the Sage said to himself, "The King will stay here for two or three months. He will find excuses to criticize me every day." Therefore he went home, took 50,000 dinars, and sent the money to Alexander. Later he went to Alexander himself and kissed the ground before him. The King did not accept the sum. "I do not keep you for gold or silver," he said. "You should be wiser than to think so, for all my treasure house is yours." Aristotle bowed before the King.

The King stayed in that land for three months. He called the nobles and the learned men of that land to himself and asked them each a question. They told many stories and Alexander ordered that the stories that were most pleasant and wonderful be recorded. One day it was snowing hard. The wise men of China gathered in the King's presence, and told anecdotes and stories about women and their foolishness.

Among them, one said, "O King, whoever obeys women has even less wit than they do, and he who humbles himself to them is even less than a cock. I know a pleasant story on this theme. I will relate it, if the King so pleases." The King gave him leave. And since the story is pleasant and short, we will narrate it. This much will cause no boredom and will not be without benefit.

### THE STORY[54]

Once upon a time, in the days of Solomon, there was a man, a friend of Solomon, who later became Solomon's attendant. He had lived long and grown to be old, without having ever told a lie. One day Solomon said to him, "Make a request from me, so that I may compensate you for your services." The old man had no need for riches; he was rich himself and owned many beasts of burden and an abundance of land. He had a stable with a balcony high up, where he slept at night. And from there he could hear the animals making noise and talking until morning. The old man had often said to himself, "I wish I knew what the animals are saying, and could understand their speech." Therefore, when Solomon asked him to make a request, he said, "O Prophet of God, I have a petition to make to you." "Say it," said Solomon. "I want to comprehend the speech of animals, so that I may know what they say. If you fulfill this request, I will be indebted to you." Solomon replied, "Wait until Gabriel comes. Then I shall ask your petition from God. For only God can bring it to pass."

And when Gabriel came, Solomon asked God to reveal these mysteries to the old man. Gabriel went to the presence of the Lord of the Worlds, and returned, saying, "O prophet of God, the request you made on behalf of the old man has been granted." Then Solomon thought to himself, "There are strange and mighty mysteries in the words of animals; and this man, being truthful, will repeat them as they are. I must find a way to stop him from revealing what he hears to others." Therefore he said to the old man, "Your petition has been granted, but on the condition that you do not tell anyone what you hear the animals say; for the minute you do so, the Death Angel will take your life. Be warned, and tell no one what you hear them say." The old man said, "O prophet of God, your will shall be obeyed." That night he returned home very happy. He went to the balcony and lay down, and God enabled him to understand everything the animals said. From that time on, he would sit there all the time, observing the animals. And when God granted this man's petition, he brought all kinds of animals and fowls, adding them to those he already kept in the stable, and he listened to their speech from morning to the time for the evening prayer. One day, a quarrel broke out between a donkey and an ox. Everyday the two did together what there was to do, such as carrying wood, grain, stones, and the like—chores that belong on a farm. Then in the night there was a fight between the donkey and the ox. The donkey said, "I will take revenge on you tomorrow." "How?" asked the ox. "I will drop to the ground and will not get on my feet. This way you will have to do what we did together everyday, and that will serve you right," said the donkey. "They will beat you until you get to your feet," said the ox. "I will put up with the beating until they leave me alone," said the donkey. The old man heard their debate. He marveled at them, and wondered how their quarrel would end.

In the morning, the servant came and put the packsaddle on the ox, and the donkey's master came to fetch him. The donkey was on the ground. The master tried to make it rise, but in no way could he get the donkey to its feet. The man beat it with a stick a few times. The donkey rolled on the ground, braying, but did not rise. It cried to the ox, saying, "I made my escape, and I hope they will work you to death." "You have not yet," replied the ox. "For this minute they will make you get up by the stick." Then the donkey's master returned and began to beat the poor creature. The old man, who was looking from the balcony said, "What do you want from this donkey? Let him be today; he may be ill." The master left the stable, and the donkey remained behind. And that day, the donkey rested and grazed leisurely. When it was time for evening prayer, the ox arrived, exhausted. He said to the donkey, "You did this to me today, but some day I will take revenge on you." The donkey answered, "I did this today, and what is to come tomorrow is unknown."

The old man, who was sitting on the balcony, heard this and laughed aloud. His wife, who was with him, asked, "What did you laugh at? What have I done to make you mock me?" And she swore that she would leave his house unless he told her what she had done that made him laugh at her.

The man was perplexed and could not decide what to do. He had never told a lie and did not want to do so now. But he was afraid that if he revealed what the animals had said he would die. And his wife was of noble birth and beautiful. She threatened that she would leave him. "Do what you will," said the man. This convinced her that he had laughed at her, for otherwise, she thought, he would not let her go. She grew more quarrelsome, saying, "Tell me truly why you laughed at me, and what it was I did that deserved to be laughed at. If you do not tell the truth, I will go to Solomon and complain about you." And she was a relative of Solomon.

The man did not know what to do. He said to himself, "I am old, and my life is nearing its end. I would rather die than tell a lie." So he said to his wife, "Give me three days, and I will tell you why I laughed." The woman agreed and gave him three days. The man prepared for death. He had grown offspring from another wife. He called them to himself, made his will, and told his wife that he was about to die. On the third day, he sat on the balcony full of sorrow, and listened to hear what the animals and fowls would say. But they were all silent and sad, for they knew that their master was troubled. After an hour or so, a cock entered the stable merrily, beating his wings and chasing the hens. He wanted to mate with them, but they would not let him. Finally the cock said, "What is the matter with you? Why do you avoid me?" And the hens kept running away from the cock, as the man watched.

Then the hens got together and said to the cock, "You should be ashamed to think of your pleasure while our master is preparing for his death." When the man heard this from the hens, he wept. It so happened that his wife was present. She asked him why he wept. As before, he could not tell her why, so he asked her to leave him and return to him at the end of the day. Then he would tell her both why he laughed and why he wept. The woman left him, and the man went on watching the fowls to see what they would do. After a while, the cock said, "Our master has no sense of honor. It is his own fault to have become subject to a woman's will. If he had any manliness, the minute his wife asked him what he had laughed at, he would take the whip and give that meddlesome woman some ten strokes and say, 'What is it to you why I laughed?' He did not do this then. But he could have done it even now, when she asked why he wept. Had he done so, the woman would have behaved herself and asked no more questions, and he could have saved himself from this predicament without telling a lie. Why should one die for a woman? And you hens! Are you not all my wives? If you do not obey me I will dig out your brains with my beak and pull out your eyes. What is a woman worth, anyway, that a man should die for her?" As the cock said these words, he mated with the hens one by one, and beat them all.

When the man heard the cock, he thought to himself, "Praised be God! I should not be less than a cock. Why should I be resigned to die?" He braced himself, and sat there happy. He ordered his men to give a generous ration of sesame seeds to the fowls.

When the evening prayer was said, and the day had come to an end, his wife came to him and asked him why he had laughed and wept. The man pretended to get angry. He rose, rolled up his sleeves, took a whip, and struck her, saying, "You nosy woman! What is it to a woman why a man laughs or weeps? What is it to you to want to know?" And he called for a rope, pretending that he was going to tie her to a pillar to chastise and punish her. The woman was trembling with fear. "Laugh and weep all you want," she said. "I will ask no more questions." And thus the cock's advice freed the man from trouble.

*Alexander asked the Chinese astrologers to cast his horoscope. They found his sign to be Leo and his planet the sun. They prophesied that great deeds would be accomplished at his hand and that he would conquer the East.*

*Alexander asked how many years remained of his life. But they were unable to answer that, for death is a mystery to man.*

## How Alexander's Aunt Contrived a Plan to Murder Him and What Occurred

*Alexander's aunt dug a hole in the hallway in the women's quarters for Alexander to fall into. She told Alexander that she had discovered a treasure there. The King and Aristotle went to see the treasure at her request. But when they reached the hallway, Aristotle refused to follow her any farther; and a cat, clinging to the King, would not let him enter the hallway. Seeing that the King had not followed her, the woman returned. But as she carefully passed by the edge of the pit the cat jumped at her and caused her to fall into the pit.*

Later the King asked Aristotle why he had refused to enter the hallway. By way of an explanation, Aristotle told him the story of a young man who squandered all that he had inherited from his father, except for 3,000 dinars with which he bought three wise sayings. The sayings were: "Do not speak before you are asked to do so"; "Do not give away a good day for a bad day"; and "Do not do what is of no use to you." By following these sayings, the youth saved his life on many occasions.[55]

## How the Son of the Emperor of China Contrived a Plan to Poison Alexander through His Concubine, and How the King Discovered That by Sagacity

The son of the Emperor of China sent some poison to a concubine of Alexander and asked her to poison the King. But Alexander found the poison in her bosom and made her confess her intention. He beheaded the Emperor's son.

Two angels asked God to give them leave to go to Alexander, to be his companions, and to pray with him. God granted their request and they came to Alexander assuming human appearance. Alexander asked them how much longer the world would last. The angels told him of the signs that would occur when the world would end and advised him to follow God's wishes in all he did.

From there Alexander came to Taghmaj.

## How Alexander Arrived in Taghmaj and Visited the King of That Land as a Messenger

Shahmalik, the King of Taghmaj, believed in the religion of Abraham. One night he heard a mysterious voice in his dream telling him that Alexander would go to him as a messenger.

When Alexander came to Shahmalik, the latter recognized him and told him of the dream. He told Alexander of the Land of the Giants and the Fairies, promising to give the King an amulet to protect him against them.

Then Shahmalik said to the King, "I will come to your presence at noon when the King is alone, for I am afraid my men will recognize the King." King Alexander laughed, and, exposing his two horns which he always kept concealed, said, "Come openly, for your soliders will not recognize me."[56]

## Alexander's Arrival in the Land of the Giants and the Cannibal Zangis, and His Battle against Them

*The size of Alexander's army terrified the giants, forcing them to take refuge in a fort. When night came, the giants tried to attack Alexander's camp, but they could not break through the magic circle.*[57] *Their King, seeking to make peace, sent a messenger and offered to go to Alexander's presence. But Alexander knew that if he spared their lives, they would always be a nuisance to man. Therefore he killed them all.*

*From there, Alexander set out for the Land of the Fairies.*

## Alexander's Arrival at the Well, the Story of the Maiden, and What Occurred between Alexander and the Zangis

*Coming upon a well, Alexander's men tried to draw some water, but the rope broke every time they pulled the bucket. A man volunteered to enter the well and see what was wrong. Inside the well, he found a gigantic Zangi, the Zangi's servant, and a maiden. There were houses and buildings under the ground, and the Zangi lived there as a king.*

*Alexander slew the Zangi and his servant. The maiden, who was a king's daughter and had been kidnapped by the Zangi, was rescued. An old man had given her an amulet that protected her against the Zangi's advances.*

## Alexander's Arrival at the Hermit's Cloister on the Mountaintop and What Occurred

*Alexander met an old man, a follower of the religion of Abraham, who told him about Solomon and gave him an amulet containing the great name of God. That night, until morning, lions and wild beasts came to pay homage to the name of God and brought offerings of food.*

*Alexander married the maiden whom he had saved from the Zangi. The old man brought Alexander many varieties of fruit as a gift for his wedding and told the King stories about Solomon.*

*Alexander departed from that region and reached the Land of the Fairies.*[58]

## Alexander's Arrival in the Fairyland, His Meeting with Araqit, the Fairy Queen, and What Occurred

The story goes that when King Alexander was some four parasangs from the fairyland, he came upon a region full of sweet-smelling herbs and plants, and springs and streams like those in the paradise of Eden. He ordered his men to camp there and fear not. The men pitched their tents in that heavenly meadow. When night came, they went to sleep, and the King took the great name of God and other talismans. They drew the magic circle around the camp for safety, and they rested peacefully. When some time had passed, the camping-ground was surrounded from all sides by creatures, some like animals, some like wild beasts, and some like human beings with legs like those of beasts. The men saw them approaching the camping-ground and running back, for they could not get inside. And the fairies said to one another, "He has drawn the magic circle. Perhaps Solomon has come to life again, for it was he who drew the magic circle." They surrounded the camping-ground until morning, but in no way could they enter it. When day came, they departed.

In the morning the King ordered his men to blow the bugles and beat the drums, the kettledrums, and the like, as is the custom. The clamor frightened the fairies and they escaped, hiding under the ground. Their Queen, Araqit,[59] sent some of the fairies to find out what the clamor was. They returned to Araqit, saying, "From the time of Solomon no king has had power over fairies. We do not know what they are, and who this king is." Then Araqit said, "We will send someone and call him to our presence and thus learn who he is."

In the morning Alexander's men went to him and informed him of what they had seen the night before. King Alexander said that he had seen the same, and wondered what would happen next. The next day 200 fairies arrived on horseback. The King saw them as he and his men were riding in the meadow. He returned to his camping-ground and went to his tent. But the fairies could not enter the camp because of the magic circle. They wondered if the King was the prophet Solomon. They called out, "Let one of you come to us, so that we may deliver our message." The Sage went to them to hear their message. They said, "O King, Araqit says, 'Bid Alexander to come to our throne, so that we may see him.'" Aristotle returned and made their message known to the King. "I am not accustomed to go to people, especially to women," said Alexander. "Let her come to our presence, visit us, and give us provisions if she wants us to depart without doing her any harm."

The fairies returned and gave Araqit the answer to her message. Araqit was perplexed. "What is to be done?" she said. "We must find out what religion he has. If he is an infidel, we will fight him; but if he is a Muslim, he will cross our land and do us no harm."

Meanwhile, Alexander called the Rumi sorcerers to himself. He asked, "What kind of fairies are these?" They said, "O King, these fairies look like human beings, except for their legs. They do not harm people and they are believers. Their females are more beautiful than the moon and the sun. They are numerous. It is no lie to say that there are a hundred thousand times a thousand of them and more in this land. No one is equal to them in battle." When the King heard this, he was at a loss. He turned to God for protection.

Now, Araqit had decided to attack Alexander's camp that night if he failed to come before her. And the King knew nothing of this until night came and he did not renew the magic circle; for the King did not know that the circle had to be renewed every night. Such untoward things happen sometimes. The King knew nothing about the fairies' intention, and he was occupied with his prayers to God.

That night thousands and thousands of fairies came to attack the camp. When they drew near the camp, they discovered that there was no magic circle, and that the men were asleep. The fairies gathered their strength and attacked the King's army, killing many and taking captive many more, among them the Sage and the King's wife whom he had rescued from the Zangi. But they did not take any property or any beasts with them.

When the King saw what they had done, he mounted his horse and cried to the elephant drivers to beat the drums. Alexander's men started fighting and they killed some of the fairies and took some captive. But the fairies had killed more and taken more captives than the King. The King was downhearted. He summoned the sorcerers, but they could not be found. He thought that they had fled, but he discovered that they had been taken captive by the fairies. The Sage and the King's wife were also missing. But the King was secure. "They will not kill them," he said to himself, "as long as we do no harm to the fairies we have taken captive."

Then Araqit sent a messenger to the King, saying, "If you come that I may see you, I will return all the captives to you and I will forgive you the blood you have shed. Otherwise, mind you, tonight hosts of fairies will arrive from all parts of the world to set fire to your camp, and you will have no power against them." Alexander replied, "I will not let this affair last until night. Before the evening prayer, my elephants will trample your camp and your land. But, if you prefer, come forth from your army, and let us do combat and see who will win." Araqit replied, "It is late now. I will come tomorrow. We will fight and see who will triumph." "Let it be so," said the King. "I will trust your word." And fairies keep their word; however, the King did not feel secure that night and guarded the camping-ground. But none of the fairies approached that night.

When day came and it grew light, the fairies began to arrive one host after the other and stood in line, until there were so many of them that for every man in King Alexander's army there were ten fairies. When the King saw that, he was afraid. "I made a mistake," he thought. "I should have crossed their land and made no claims. Indeed I brought this down upon myself. I cannot tell how this affair will end." As he was thinking thus, Araqit mounted a horse like those used by human beings, and, properly armed, she entered the battlefield, her hair and face unveiled. You would think that the moon had come to the earth. When they told Alexander of this, he too entered the battlefield. His men were downhearted. Wearing the great name of God on his arm, the King entered the battlefield, circled around, and raised his voice, crying, "*Allah Akbar!*" And as the King uttered the name of God, the infidel fairies, 100,000 in number, flew away. Only the Muslim fairies remained.

But when Alexander looked at Araqit closely, strength left his limbs. He stood motionless, like a picture. Araqit wanted to attack the King, to take him by the belt and unhorse him, but she could not get near him. Therefore Alexander took the opportunity, caught her by the belt, and was about to tear her from her horse when she gathered her strength and tore her belt. Before the King could make another move, the fairies flew to him from the air, and threw something into his eyes that darkened his vision. The King was afraid. He released Araqit's belt and she escaped. And when she was gone, the King returned to his men. But his eyes and his heart were infatuated with that woman, so much so that the army and his sovereignty were degraded in his eyes. All day he tried to find a solution.

And on that day Araqit began to fear the King and his strength. She decided that Alexander could be subdued only by cunning. Now, when the King surveyed his army, he discovered that the commanders of the army had all been taken captive. Moreover, his own heart was in bondage. He was perplexed and did not know what to do. Therefore he did ablution and prayed to God. The next day, he ordered his men to beat the drums and blow the war bugles. They all mounted, and 400,000 men armed themselves. When the news came to Araqit she became afraid, but she armed herself and led the fairy host to war. The men could not distinguish the fairies well, for they could assume any appearance they wanted: lions, dragons, and all kinds of animals.

The battle was fierce that day, and many were killed on both sides. Araqit did not have the courage to go to the battlefield, and remained behind. When the battle was done, the King sent one of the fairies, who was taken captive, as messenger to Araqit, saying, "Let it be known that I have no desire for your kingdom, your grandeur, or your power. If you send my captives back to me, I will depart. I do respect you, but do not be obstinate, for you are not more numerous or stronger than the giants, whom I defeated."

When the fairy came and gave this message to Araqit, she sent word to Alexander by the same fairy, saying, "I know better what it is to show respect, for I did not slay any man I took captive from you and I treated the captives well, while you killed many of those you took prisoner. Now, if you seek peace, come to me and fear not, for you shall not be harmed. Come, so that I may see you and know you, and let us find a way, so that you may cross the land unharmed. If you do not come willingly, I have the power to bring you here in chains and put you in prison like other captives. I do not wish to do you harm, but the fairies bear a grudge against you and if it were not for me, they would have destroyed your entire army. Come to our presence and free yourself from this trouble. Otherwise, wait and you will see."

The message displeased Alexander. In his anger he thought, "I would rather bear with her; but if I put up with this, she will grow bold and say, 'He is afraid of me.' Moreover, it is a great shame that I who have seen the East and the West, and subdued all kings and conquered all lands, should be ruled by a woman and go to her presence." Therefore he sent her a message, saying, "I have been to the farthest limits of the world, and I have accomplished great conquests. The wonders that I have discovered in the world make *Iskandarnamah* a camel load. I never went to any king; all kings came to me, and he who disobeyed me was brought to my presence by force. Come to me, you and your horsemen and the chiefs of your army. If you have anything to say, say it then and hear my answer. Otherwise, prepare for war tomorrow, for we have stayed here too long, and we have a journey before us."

When Araqit received the message, she said, "He means no truth. I must kidnap him." Therefore she sent word, asking Alexander to pitch his tent outside the city the next day, and promising that she would go there at noon and do as he desired. "Let it be so," said the King. Then Araqit sent two fairies to the King's tent and told them to find out what he did. The fairies found Alexander at his prayers. They brought the news to Araqit. She sent them back a second time. An hour later they returned and said that he had finished his prayers and was asleep in his bed with a concubine. When Araqit heard this, she rose and with those two fairies flew to the King's tent in the camp. The King was making love to the concubine, and had removed the amulet containing the name of God from his body. When he had finished, he fell asleep. The fairies came and lifted him in his sleep and with the help of Araqit they carried him away.

When the King woke up, he found himself in a hall as beautiful as paradise, bedecked with silk and golden verandas. Alexander thought that he was dreaming. When he turned in order to sleep on his other side, he saw Araqit sitting near his bed, all by herself. There was no one beside her. And when the King saw her there and found himself a captive in her hand, he said to himself, "Had I a knife, I would strike myself." Araqit and the fairies, who knew that the King was strong, had his toes tied together.[60] For that reason and because he did not have the name of God with him, Alexander was unable to free himself no matter how hard he tried. Besides, he had to perform ablution. He stopped struggling. Araqit said to him, "O Alexander, do you know who you are and what this place is?" "Sleep is the brother of death," replied the King. "There is no honor in stealing away a sleeping man by magic. And there is no shame in being kidnapped by a fairy while asleep. If you wish to see the manliness of men, untie my feet." Araqit knew that the King was right in what he said. She remained silent. She untied his feet, and she kept him in a place as beautiful as an idol's temple. And her army knew nothing of this. She sent the fairies to bring food for the King, for the food of the fairies is different from that of human beings. When day came, Alexander's men looked for him, but could not find him. The army fell into a state of confusion.

Alexander said to Araqit, "Do not act thus. If you set me free and return my chiefs to me, I will depart tomorrow and leave your kingdom." "I will never let you go," said Araqit. "It would be a strange thing to set free the bird one has caught. I will not set you at liberty, nor will I slay you, nor let my army know about you. The fairies have gone to bring you food to eat." Then Alexander said, "Leave me a while to do ablution." And beneath the place where the King was, there were streams of running water. The King asked Araqit to untie his hands, so that he might do ablution. Being half-witted and injudicious like all women, she told her attendants to untie the King's hands. Then the King said to her, "I am ashamed to go into the water naked before you." Araqit left, and the King entered the water and performed ablution. Around the stream he saw wide pastures and many orchards. He said to himself, "If I follow this stream, I will eventually reach inhabited land and free myself from these witless women."

Araqit had set a slave girl to watch the King's clothes. She asked the King why he did not come out of the water. The King said, "I will be grateful to you if you do me a good turn and free me from this woman by letting me follow the stream and escape." "You must not follow the stream," she said. "I will show you a shorter way." "Where?" asked the King. "When you come out of the water," she replied, "leave through that small door which is shut, for that is the shortest way to your camping-ground. But tie my hands and my feet and leave me here, and give me your word that when you gain victory over this fairy, you will deliver me from her hand. I am a human being and the daughter of the King of the East. My father, Arsalankhan, is King of that region, and Shahmalik is my brother. Araqit fell in love with my husband, who was a descendant of Qarakhan, the King of Transoxania. Every night she would come and trouble my husbnad. But because of the love he bore me, he would pay no attention to her. One night, as I was sleeping beside my husband, she came and carried me away, hoping that he would comply with her and desire her; but he would have none of her, of course. It has been seven years since Araqit brought me here, and two years since my husband passed away. For five years he wandered around the world, searching for me." The slave girl wept as she spoke these words. "Come with me," said the King. "I cannot," she replied. "You will find it difficult enough to get to your army by yourself. Think of a way to rescue me after you reach the camp."

Then the King put on his clothes. He tied the maiden's hands and feet, and left through the small door. Meanwhile, Araqit was preparing food for the King. When the King failed to return from the water, she became worried and went to see what had happened. She found the maiden with her hands and feet tied fast, and realized that the King had made his escape. "How did the King go?" She asked the maiden. "He came out of the water, tied my hands and feet, and left through the small door," she replied. The world darkened before Araqit's eyes, and she almost lost her wits. She untied the slave girl and said to her, "Beware! Say nothing of this." But Araqit's army knew that she was very fond of human males, for her mother was human and her father a fairy, as in the case of Bilqays, the Queen of Sheba. But no man had had his will with her. And fairies live long.

When the King left through the small door, he found himself in a wilderness with green pastures and streams. But there was no sign of life and it was noon. He bowed to the ground and he said, "O omniscient Lord, show your sinful servant the way." No sooner had he spoken than God made a deer appear before him. King Alexander tried to catch the deer, but the deer ran away. Through his sagacity Alexander realized that he was to follow the deer. He did so for about half a parasang, until he was unable to go any further, for he was barefoot. But when he stopped, the deer stopped also, until the King started again. Alexander realized that this was God's doing. When he had gone a little farther, the camping-place came into view. It was noon; the army was in commotion and the chiefs were searching everywhere for the King. But the King did not want the army to know that he had been kidnapped by a fairy, for kingship depends on reverence from the subjects. He said to himself, "Let me not be weaker than a woman, who kidnapped me and revealed it to no one. I too shall conceal it, else, my subjects will lose respect for me."

Then the King looked from the border of the camping-ground, saw the elephants, and approached them. The elephant keepers had been overcome by fear. Some were preparing to escape, and some were asleep. Alexander took hold of an elephant, mounted it, and suddenly entered the camp. When the men saw him, they blew the longhorn, beat the drums, and raised their voices so high that the land trembled with convulsion. The fairies hid under the ground, alarmed by the uproar. Araqit said to the slave girl, "The King has entered his camp."

Alexander said to his men, "I had gone to attend to some affair. Go to the city as you are, crying aloud, with the bugles and the drums, and trample the fairies under the elephants' feet." The army moved toward the city gate in that fearful uproar with 1,500 elephants, each like a mountain of iron. They destroyed the rampart and the gate. Still on the elephant's back, the King led the attack.

They captured some 2,000 fairies and did much destruction. Then the King said, "It is enough for today," and they returned. Later, Alexander went back to the stream with fifty horsemen, hoping to rescue the slave girl. They found the door firmly shut, and there was no one in sight. When King Alexander returned to his camp he asked that the captive fairy be brought to the field, and he sent a message to Araqit, saying, "You have captured 1,000 men and one woman belonging to me, and 2,700 of your fairies are in my hand, imprisoned inside the magic circle from which, you may assure yourself, they cannot escape. Send me your captives and receive mine in return. Then I will tell you what is to be done."

Araqit agreed, but she sent a messenger to Alexander, saying, "Send me a man in whom you can confide, so that I may speak to him without the knowledge of the two armies." The fairy came and delivered the message. Alexander replied, "I have no one who can keep a secret, whereas you have many slave girls. Send one to me." And the King was hoping that she would send the daughter of Arsalankhan. When Araqit heard the message, she said to herself, "The secret that I had caught Alexander and he escaped is known to this maiden. It is better to send her." Therefore she called the daughter of Arsalankhan to herself and said to her, "Today you are like a sister to me, and I have chosen you above all the fairies to confide this secret to you. Rise and with two or three fairies go to the King's camp and say to him, 'You escaped from me. That was not worthy of a king. I brought you here out of love and not enmity, and I would have set you free in the right manner myself, for I know that you will not forgo your kingship. But this is useless talk, for you are gone. I have become attached to you and this woman is my confidante. Beware not to break your word, and keep your covenant well.'"

Then the maiden and the two fairies whom Araqit trusted came to the King and bowed before him. The King asked, "What are you here for, O woman?" "I carry a message," she replied. "What is it?" asked the King. "Only inside can I speak it," she replied. Inside, she told him about

Araqit and gave him the message. The King said, "I will not trust this woman until she returns my army commanders. Then I will send back her captives, and hostility will end between us."

Alexander asked the maiden what he could do to help her. "O King, you know best," she replied. The King's heart was moved with compassion, for she was very beautiful and the daughter of a king. But he said to himself, "It is not to my advantage to give her shelter now, for if I do so, Araqit will detain my captives." He said to the maiden, "Take heart, for I will not leave this land before I rescue you from Araqit. I will go to your father's kingdom and take you to your father; and, if you wish, you can be my wife."

The maiden bowed before the King and praised him. The fairies were waiting for her in the air. The King said to her, "Bring the answer to my message soon." She said, "O King, her army are all hostile to you; but she is your friend, and the two fairies accompanying me are those who that night carried you away in your sleep." "I will do nothing to them now," said the King. "But you will see for yourself what I plan to do to them later." Then the woman said, "O King, you see Araqit, all fair and beautiful; but only her upper half is so, for her feet and her legs are hairy like a beast's." That made the King lose interest a little. Besides, Alexander was a wise man and would not set his heart on such things.

When the woman returned to Araqit and gave her the King's answer, Araqit sent for the chiefs of her army. She said to them, "Alexander has sent a message, saying, 'Yield your captives and receive mine in return.' What is to be done?" "The Queen knows best," they replied. "Since they have three captives for every captive we have, we will do well to return their captives and get ours." Then Araqit ordered that the Sage and all the captives be sent to the King. But she detained Alexander's wife.

When the King saw the Sage, he embraced him and he wept, saying, "All the sorrow in my heart was for you. Praised be God for restoring you to me." Then the King had the fairies brought to his presence. When they were taken to him, he said, "Is any of you a relative of Araqit?" Fifteen of the nobles among them were relatives of Araqit. The King had those fifteen fairies detained so that Araqit would return his wife. He set the rest at liberty, and they went to Araqit, saying, "King Alexander says that he will not release your relatives until you return his wife." Araqit sent the King's wife to him, for fear of her subjects; otherwise she would have kept her.

When Alexander's wife returned, Alexander rejoiced and told his men to place the drums on the elephants' backs. The men cried out aloud and marched towards the city gates. They caused great damage and killed many of the fairies, but following the King's command they refrained from taking any captives. When Araqit heard about the event, she became disconsolate. She said to the daughter of Arsalankhan, "This King is treacherous. I have driven his love out of my heart. I will have him here by tomorrow, dead or in chains." She ordered the fairies to be ready and planned to attack the camp at midnight. The King knew nothing of this. But when Araqit left the city to array the army, the daughter of Arsalankhan set out for his camp through the opening in the wall. It was night. She reached the King's camping-ground in no time, for she knew the way, and went straight to King Alexander's tent. The servants and watchmen informed Alexander, who was at his prayers. When he had finished, the maiden told him all the circumstances. The King mounted his horse and armed himself. He sent the woman to his tent, where she stayed secure. Then he ordered the elephant riders and the soldiers to mount and be ready. He instructed them to raise a louder uproar from the drums, the bugles, and the cymbals than they had done on other nights and to move toward the fairies. The men did as they were told.

Meanwhile, Araqit was biding her time to surprise the King's army with the fairy host at midnight. But when the fairies heard that uproar and clamor, they were frightened and all fled to the city. The men chased them with the elephants. Bearing the great name of God, the King himself started for Araqit's palace, entered it, and won an abundance of riches, as well as many slave girls. He carried away the slave girls, so that Araqit might think that Arsalankhan's daughter had been taken together with them. Araqit and all the fairies disappeared in the air. Then the King ordered his men to withdraw. Many fairies were killed and those who survived fled. The King returned to his camping-ground and offered thanks to God. "O wise and pure Lord! You are the Creator of all beings. The good and the evil are subject to your will. You give victory to whom you like, and you humble whom you will." Then he went to Arsalankhan's daughter. He showed her much kindness and courtesy, for he was very grateful to her. He gave her rich gowns and gold and jewelry, and he promised to marry her when they reached her father's kingdom, and then to take her to Rum.

Now, when Araqit came to her palace, she found everything in ruins. The palace had been plundered, her jewelry was all gone, the slave girls were missing, and Arsalankhan's daughter was nowhere to be seen. "Alas!" she said, "he has taken that maiden captive. He will marry her, for she is his own kind and the daughter of a king. But what is to be done? I will think of a strategy tomorrow, and see how it works." And Araqit came to bear a grudge against King Alexander. When daylight came, she called the fairies to herself, telling them that she needed several thousand fairies to go with her that night. When the fairies were gathered, Araqit said, "I want you to dig a tunnel between my palace and the King's camping-ground and his tent, so that from here one can go to where he sleeps. This you must do tonight." They promised to finish the task by midnight. At midnight they finished digging and reached the place where the King was sleeping, so that with one more blow of the pick the King would fall through.

Meanwhile, the King inquired of Arsalankhan's daughter what Araqit intended to do. She said to him, "O King, she has taken many men and kept them in chains in secret. She plays with them for a time, without ever giving herself to any of them. Her captives either make their escape, or die in her prison. Sometimes she lets them go on her own. She intends to do the same to the King, but she says, 'I will not do this to the King, for he will not forgo his sovereignty and his rule for the world.' Yet, day and night she contrives plans. I do not know what the outcome will be." "It will be nothing but what God has decreed," said Alexander, and resumed his prayer. Then suddenly he saw the earth sink, while Queen Araqit and several thousand fairies set upon his army. The King marveled at their craftiness. He uttered the great name of God aloud, drew his sword, and attacked the fairies. In this incident, the King's camp received more damage than it had ever before. The ground between the King's camp and the city had all sunk, but none of the men was injured. The King ordered his men to kill whomever they found. His eyes hunted Araqit, whom he meant to capture. But she had made her escape through the tunnel to her palace, and gone into hiding. The King and his men captured and killed as many fairies as they could, but the camping-ground was in ruin.

Then the King instructed his men to withdraw four parasangs and camp on the mountain. "If I depart from this land without defeating them, I am not Alexander," said the King. The men pitched their tents on the mountain happy and content, and secure from all sides. And when they were settled there, Araqit sent a messenger to the King. "If you want us to give you leave to cross our land unharmed," she said, "return the maiden in whom we confide, along with the other slave girls you have taken prisoner."

When the King heard this message, he replied, "Go and tell this shameless woman that Alexander says, 'I will not leave this land before I take your life. You know yourself the trouble you have caused. I have sent everywhere for fighting men and elephants. It will not be long before they trample your palace and your kingdom under their feet. As for yourself, I will try to capture you alive and hang you. The maiden in whom you have confided is the daughter of the King of the East, Arsalankhan. I have informed him that I have rescued his daughter from you, so that he may join us, and, by divine favor, we will take vengeance upon you and give this land to mankind.'"

The messenger returned and took his answer to Araqit. The message increased her enmity. She summoned the flying fairies and told them to go around the world, make what had occurred known to fairies everywhere, and call them to her court. Then the sorcerers she had taken captive sent word to her. "If you unchain us, we will assist you with magic and deliver you from this trouble," they said. Araqit was pleased. She set the sorcerers free, and they came before her throne. "Send us to Alexander as messengers," they said, "and we will frighten him and force him to leave this land." "You lie," said Araqit. "You said the same thing to the giants. Do you think that I have not heard about you?" "You are right," they answered, "but the giants' case was one thing, and the Queen's is another." "Will you be my allies?" asked Araqit. "I have one wish; I want to capture him." "This is easy to do," the sorcerers replied. "Send us to him, and some night we will put him to sleep through magic. He will not awake until the next day. And while he is asleep, you can send your fairies to take him to you." Then Araqit said, "You must give me your word and five of you must remain here as hostages, that I may know you speak the truth." The sorcerers, who were seventy-five in number, left five men behind. The rest went to the King and bowed before him. The King inquired how they had managed to go to him. "O King, we escaped from her hand," they said. "How did you escape?" the King asked, knowing that sorcerers with all their magic are no match for fairies, and suspecting them of treachery. He urged them to tell the truth. They said, "O King, we were able to make our escape because she did not know that we are sorcerers. But five of us have remained there." "You lie," said the King. "You have come to do some mischief. You must have agreed to do her a service, and you have left those five as hostages." Then the King had them put in chains and imprisoned them.

Now, it so happened that Alexander had captured a fairy called Ghilan, whom he had put in chains. (And when a fairy is in iron fetters, he can in no way free himself.) Soon after the sorcerers were put in chains, the brother of that fairy came to Alexander, bowed before him, and said, "If the King sets my brother free, I will tell him a secret." "Who is your brother?" asked the King. "Ghilan," replied the fairy. The King's attendants took him to the fairies who were in chains, so that he might set his brother free and take him to the King. When they all returned with the fairy's brother, the fairy said, "O King, these sorcerers have come to bind you through magic, so that our Queen might steal you away. I have said this to you out of despair, hoping that you will release my brother. If Araqit finds out about this, she will slay my brother and myself." "Where do you intend to go now?" asked the King. "We will return to the sea, and see how your quarrel will end," said the fairy. "I will set your brother free if you promise to keep me informed of all that happens in your land," said the King. The fairy agreed and promised to do so. And fairies keep their word and do not break their vows. Then the King freed Ghilan's brother. The two went to Araqit and told her that they had escaped. Araqit was glad, for the fairy was of noble birth.

Alexander did nothing for three days, but on the fourth day, he ordered his attendants to take the sorcerers to him and said to them, "You evil, foul creatures. You have come in treachery and deceit to put a spell on me. Do you not know that I have the great name of God and can put sorcerers to destruction? Tell me the truth." But of course they would not tell the truth. And the King knew that the fairy had not lied. Therefore he punished the sorcerers by cutting off the right hand of each. He called for witnesses and made the sorcerers promise that they would return to Rum that night. But when they left the King's camping-ground they said, "Thus injured, with no provisions and with our hands cut off, how can we go to the sea? It is wiser to go to Araqit, and show her our predicament. And we will ask that the five who are with her join and serve us. Perhaps we will succeed in destroying this man."

After they had reasoned thus, they rose and went to Araqit, with their hands cut off. They said, weeping, "We lost our hands in your service, and we have come here that we may find a way to deal with this man." Araqit replied, "I have tried every trick known to fairies, but to no avail." "If you summon the sorcerers of Rum to aid us," they said, "together, through witchcraft, we will set fire to Alexander's camp and burn it to the ground." Therefore Araqit sent someone to Rum. Soon after, the fairies returned with those they sought. And those sorcerers who had been dismembered wept before the sorcerers who had come from Rum and said to them, "Unless you help us, we will destroy ourselves. We lost our hands serving your King. What is to be done now?" They replied, "We will blind Alexander and all his men within an hour." The dismembered sorcerers knew that they would succeed and were content. Then the day reached its end and night came. The King bore the name of God and of course would not divide it from himself. By divine providence, that night the old man who had given Alexander an amulet containing the name of God left the cloister, bearing the great name of God, and all animals and wild beasts went to pay homage to that great name. Meanwhile the sorcerers went to the camping-ground to blind Alexander and the soldiers, who were asleep, by throwing some substance into their eyes. When they arrived at the camp, a lion, by virtue of the great name of God, took the news to the old man, saying, "The sorcerers have gone to destroy Alexander's men." The old man asked where they were, for he was blind. Then he rubbed the great name of God against his eyes. That instant he gained his sight and was able to see the sorcerers. Then he said to the lions, "By virtue of God's great name, destroy these sorcerers." The lions, which were many, attacked and caught the sorcerers, and killed all but one of them, who made his escape. The rest were torn to pieces.

The next day, the old man went to the King and told him all that had occurred. The King knelt with his forehead to the ground and thanked God. And when he went to the camping-ground, he found the sorcerers dead. Then he said, "Even after their hands were cut off these evil men persevered in doing evil until God destroyed them."

They left the bodies as they were. The soldiers saw the mangled bodies and marveled at God's doings. That day Alexander did not admit anyone to his presence and spent the day in prayer. And when Araqit heard what had happened to the sorcerers, she was frightened. "Is this man Solomon come to life again?" she wondered. Meanwhile, the King stayed in that land, waiting to know God's will. He said to himself, "I wish the angel who is my friend would appear and inform me of the outcome of my war against the fairies."

Meanwhile Araqit thought of a new scheme. She said to herself, "This time I will go myself. I will find him and either satisfy my will by him, or kill him and free myself. Indeed, if my uncle had arrived, this affair would have been settled by now." Therefore when night came and it was time for rest and sleep, she set out for the King's camp and went to his tent. The tent was empty, except for two watchmen. She said to herself, "The King is not in his tent in the night. Where could he be? Perhaps he has cunningly entered my palace." But when she returned to her palace, she did not see anyone. She waited that night and went to the camp again the next night, but could not find the King.

The next day, 100,000 giants and fairies came from the sea and went to Araqit's presence. They said to her, "What is your will? What do you want us to do to this man? We will drown him with his entire army if you want." Araqit replied, "It is not as simple as you think. The giant Sindah is a captive of his and my uncle is his prisoner.[61] And from the day he took my uncle captive more than 5,000 fairies and sea giants have been slain." Alexander had captured these chiefs without knowing who they were.

The gaints inquired whether Alexander was protected by the magic circle. She said that he was. The chief of the giants said, "I am glad we came here to see this man, for he is like Solomon. He has been to the

Land of Darkness, whereas Solomon with all his glory did not go to the Land of Darkness. We must go to see him and find out what gives him power to capture giants and fairies. We will go to see him today." "I will not give you leave," said Araqit. "Beware! This man does not keep his word. He is contentious, discourteous, dishonest, and untrustworthy, and he has conquered the whole world. Do what you will. Go, if you are certain that you can return unharmed." "O Lady," they replied, "we will go and return unharmed."

Then the chief of the giants said to his troops, "Go and keep watch near Alexander's camping-ground. If we need you, we will signal with smoke. Come to us if you see smoke. Otherwise, wait until we return." Then Ghilan's brother, the fairy who had become ally to the King, came to Alexander and said, "The giants and the fairies have come from the sea, but they all regret what they have done. The King of the giants is approaching your camp with his troops. He is going to move his army near your camping-place in secret. Be on your guard." Then the King had the elephants covered with steel, for giants are afraid of steel. And he ordered his men to blow the longhorn, beat the drums, and cry aloud. The King's army raised such a clamor that the whole world trembled. The uproar frightened Araqit. She said, "He has heard of the arrival of the giants. I wonder who informed him of it."

Now, when the giants saw the elephants, they were frightened and they withdrew. News was brought to Alexander that 100,000 giants who were approaching his camping-place withdrew when they saw the elephants. They said to the King, "We saw them near the camping-ground, some twenty giants, each the size of a mountain. They are led by the fairies. They were planning to attack you, but they are afraid of the elephants." When the King heard that, he sent the name of God and the amulet with which they drew the magic circle to the elephant riders and said, "Fear not and set the elephants upon them." The elephant riders attacked and three or four giants were thus trampled to death. The chief of the giants withdrew, leading away his troops. He said, "My sons and my brother were slain. What business did I have here? It was a mistake to come." He went to Queen Araqit and said, "This man is above Solomon, who was a prophet of God. Fear and pity have no place in his heart. They set the elephants upon us and they killed my two sons and my brother." The giants and the fairies mourned for three days. Then the sea giants said, "We will not leave until we have avenged the blood of those four youths on these people." "We will assist you, for our Queen is helpless before him. We will resort to every means to take Alexander's life," the fairies promised.

Then King Alexander called the old man to himself and told him how he had defeated the giants. The old man consoled the King and said, "All this happened through God's grace, for no man is equal to the giants and none has ever subdued them. All this is by virtue of the great name of God. As long as this name is with you, none can do you harm. Neither man, nor fairy or giant can harm the man who has God on his side." Then he said, "Know, O King, that all deliverance is from God. If you conquer the giants, fine; if not, turn for help to God, so that He may aid you to destroy them completely, for this is a mighty task." Then the King said, "Each day they obtain new aid." The old man replied, "Know, O King, that you set too much value on this world. Consider the kings of the past. First, Jamshid, who ruled for 1,000 years, and Zahhak, who ruled for 1,000 years. Then Afridun, who ruled for 500 years. Then there is the rule of Manuchihr, Kayqubad, and Kaykhusraw. They are gone and turned to dust. And King Solomon, as you must have heard, was a prophet of God. Consider the prophets. Where are Adam, Noah, Hud, and Salih?[62] And in the time of Hud, among the tribe of 'Ad there was a man called Shattad of 'Ad, who lived for 1,000 years and never had any trouble. He built the Iram Garden, like a paradise, and when he had finished building it, he made streams of milk and honey in it. But when he went to see his creation, the Angel of Death claimed his life even before he had taken his foot out of the stirrup, and made away with it as Shattad had one foot in the stirrup and one just taken out. He remained motionless in that posture, and that paradise disappeared from man's sight." (And this story is well known. We wrote it here briefly, and now we return to the story of Alexander.) Then the old man said to the King, "I say this to you, for it is not wise to bear so much trouble for this world." King Alexander said, "O peerless old man, the affairs of this world have their own charm. But it is as you say, especially in regard to kingship. However, it is a shame that after me men should read the *Iskandarnamah* and the wonders that I have seen and of which I have written, and then say that Alexander was defeated by the fairies, or, still worse, by a woman."

At Araqit's request, from all over the world giants and fairies came to fight Alexander. When most of them were killed by the King, Araqit sent for the sea giants and the great giants. The latter were like thunderclouds and fought from above.

## How Alexander Invaded Araqit's Territory and Araqit's Uncle Came to Her Aid

Aided by a witch, Araqit kidnapped Alexander, took him to a palace, and proposed to make peace with him. Alexander rejected her offer and with the help of some fairies made his escape.

## The Arrival of Araqit's Uncle and His Fairies at the Camping-Ground and What Occurred between Him and King Alexander

Araqit's uncle, who was a Muslim, had come to visit Alexander rather than to fight him. Araqit warned him against Alexander's treachery; nevertheless, Ruvid went to see Alexander and advised him to leave that land in peace. Alexander told Ruvid that he would not leave before he had won the land from the fairies and returned it to mankind. Ruvid said that the land was given to them by Afrasiyab, whom they had aided in his battle against Kaykhusraw. Alexander replied:

"I shall not surrender to you what was once owned by man, but which a tyrant seized and gave to you. Leave this land to man, to inhabit and to cultivate, that when strangers and wayfarers arrive at this region, they may not be at a loss for bread and victuals. You have seized these four cities whose inhabitants were put to flight and had to seek shelter elsewhere. I will not allow this. If you want to save your lives and go unharmed, withdraw from this land and return to the sea. Give me your word and a written pledge that you will never claim this land again, and leave. Only then will I depart. Otherwise I shall not leave any of you alive. I will do with you as I did with the giants, all of whom I slew and threw into the sea."

*Ruvid was imprisoned, and Araqit, trying to kidnap Alexander, was seriously wounded. Then the fairies who were taken captive told Alexander that if the object of his sojourn there was to marry Araqit, they would ask her to consent to that. Alexander replied that his object was to give the land to mankind.*[63] *The nobles of the giants and the fairies went to Araqit and asked her to go to Alexander and tell him that they would do as he wished. Araqit went to visit Alexander.*

The King was informed that Araqit had arrived. She was led to his presence. "O King! I seek quarter here," she said. "I shall obey you in all things. I will do whatever you command with all my heart." Then she rose and bowed before the King. The Rumi and Persian nobility who were in the King's presence marveled at the beauty of her face. They said, "Let us remain silent, until the King gives his answer." Then the King spoke. "Your life and your property will be in our protection," he said. "But you must leave 100 of your relatives with me as hostages and depart from this land." Araqit said, "O King! I have come to you on my own and abandoned my kingdom. Take me for a slave that you have bought. I have no fortitude for war." "That would be easy," replied the King. "But if I capture you now you will be disgraced. Return to your camp and dispatch the troops that have come from the sea and other lands to their own place. Then tell your army that you have sought shelter with Alexander and intend to go to the East with him. Let them depart from the land and return to the sea. After you have done as I have said, come to me and I will see about your affairs."

Araqit gave her word and asked the King to promise that he would not shed her blood or put her in chains. The King said, "I will not shed your blood, and, if you keep your word, I will not put you in chains." Araqit returned to her camp and informed the chiefs of the circumstances. They said, "It is best that you go to him. We will all leave. Your own army can wait at sea for a month, and some can accompany you. After he returns from the East, you can come back to your own land and the entire army will return to you from where they are."

But the fairies were reluctant to leave their home and accused her of being in love with Alexander. When Araqit heard this, she addressed herself to the fairies who had come from other lands, saying, "Let it be known that my army is speaking evil of me. What am I to do when you fail to defeat him? I went to him, as you had said, and sought quarter. Now, if you are dissatisfied, prepare for war. We will attack tomorrow."

And Araqit secretly sent someone to the King and told him what had happened. The King knew that her subjects had blamed her. He sent her word, saying, "Either carry out your promise, or prepare for war."

Araqit told her troops to go outside the city and mount their horses. When her army went to the field, Alexander's men arrived from the other direction with the elephants. There was a great battle. Many giants and fairies were slain, and 70,000 of the chiefs of Araqit's army were captured. Araqit and her host learned the news and the world darkened before their eyes. They said, "Tomorrow we will fight so hard that the whole world will tremble."

The next day, Araqit told her army to go to the field. They prepared for a great battle and took the lead. When the King heard of this, he came to the field. All the men armed themselves and the elephants were prepared for battle. The King called a fairy to take a message to Araqit. "Tell her," he said, "I was not the one who broke his word. If I leave any one of you alive, I am not Alexander." Then they engaged in a battle, which is called "the great battle." On that day the Persians and the elephants fought as they had never done before. The giants and the fairies who had been summoned from other lands saw that their lives were at stake. Saying to themselves, "Why should we suffer all this?" they turned back and fled. And the King's men set upon Araqit's host. They crushed several thousand of them under the elephants' feet and captured Araqit. The King said to his attendants, "Do not bring Araqit to me, but put her in iron chains." They put Araqit in chains, and delivered her to Aristotle. As for the other fairies, some begged that their lives be spared, and promised to take their wives and children and leave that same day. The rest were beheaded.

Alexander and his men entered the city. They found a place like paradise, with all kinds of fruits and green trees. The jewelry and ornaments the King found there were beyond measure. The fairies' domain covered four parasangs of land. And after a day's journey, the King would reach a different city each day. In all these cities the inhabitants knew that Araqit, her uncle Ruvid, and the giant Sindah had been taken prisoner. The news made them vacate the cities and return to the sea, from whence they had originally come. The King cleared that land of giants and fairies, and the original inhabitants, who had scattered around the world, returned. They praised the King of the Earth. The houses of their fathers and ancestors were given back to them. They would give witness to one another's ownership, and regain possession of their homes. The King stayed there for four months, until the land was settled by man and completely freed from giants and fairies. The war was over; Alexander stayed in that land secure, with Araqit his prisoner.

One day the Sage asked him, "What is your will concerning this woman and the captives?" The King replied, "I will summon them to the court tomorrow and consider their case." The next day the King sat on his throne, and the Sage brought Araqit to his presence. Some 700 fairies and giants were in the King's prison. Alexander had those who showed impertinence beheaded, and spared the rest. And when Ruvid was brought to him, he took pity on him, for he had not captured Ruvid in war; rather, Ruvid himself had come to him. He ordered his men to unbind Ruvid and sent for Araqit. Ruvid bowed before the King and looked at Araqit in chains. She had grown pale and her body was bent under the weight of her fetters. The King was in love with her, but he showed manly self-restraint. Then Ruvid said to Alexander, "O King of the Earth! This woman is the Queen of all fairies and her father was the King of all fairies. The King should regard her more highly." "I will have her slain this moment," the King said angrily. "You do not know what I have suffered at her hand. I will show her no mercy. Be grateful that I spared your life and do not ask for more." Then the King called for the torturer and when he came said to him, "Behead this shameless woman." Aristotle, the Sage, and all the nobles bowed before him. "O King," they pleaded, "she is a woman and of the seed of kings. Please spare her life." The King forgave her, and ordered his men to unbind her and take her to Aristotle's quarters.

He then ordered Ruvid to take Araqit to Istakhr in Pars, where she could stay with him. But Ruvid refused, saying, "The fairies will seize her from me and demand that she become sovereign." "You are right," Alexander said. That day passed. The next day, he summoned the giant Sindah to his presence. The giant was an infidel; therefore the King had him beheaded. He presented Ruvid with the gown of honor. Ruvid prayed for him, saying, "Oh King of the Earth, accept this advice from your servant and marry Araqit, for she is worthy of a king. It is wise that she herself does not rule but spend her life in ease." The Sage and the chiefs of the army all said, "O King, this is wise to do. For Araqit was born of a human mother, and it is fitting that she be ruled by the King." Therefore they called the religious authorities, and Ruvid gave Araqit to Alexander in marriage after the custom of the Muslims. Alexander gave gifts to Ruvid again, and sent him to the region of Pars.

Thus the King married Araqit and stayed in that land for four months. He spent his time with Araqit in private, and his men rested. When summer was over and autumn came, the King decided to move. He said to Araqit, "How far is this region from the East where the sun rises, and what regions are in the way?" Araqit replied, "The next inhabited land is forty parasangs away, and there are four kings on the way. The first is the King of Russians. The Russians are heathens and do not believe in God. They have a vast territory, which we will have to cross. Having crossed their land, you will come upon a vast country inhabited by fair-faced, proud Turks and ruled by a great monarch. We will have to cross a great river that runs by the city gate. The bridge is in the city. They have built bridges out of leather. The passage is narrow and difficult, and the water massive. They open the passage when they want. After you pass that land, you will reach a country like paradise, forty parasangs by forty parasangs. The king of that land is Arsalankhan, whose daughter I had taken captive." "Have you seen all these regions?" asked the King. "Yes," replied Araqit. "Every time I flew over these parts 70,000 fairies flew with me. Those people obey me; all except the Zangis, against whom I have no power." Then the King said, "Were the fairies with you the night you kidnapped Arsalankhan's daughter?" Araqit was embarrassed. She bent down her head, burning with shame. She made no reply, and the King said no more on that theme. "With God's help we will cross those forty parasangs of land and victory shall be ours," he said.

The next day Araqit said, "O King, I desire that you sleep with no other woman." "Say no more of this," said the King, "for it cannot be done. Do not set your heart on this, for nothing will come of it but torment. I am a king and have many wives and concubines both here and in Rum. Kings cannot help but be thus. You had better show yourself worthy of respect." "How many wives do you have in Rum?" she asked. "Ten who are daughters of kings," he said, "and here I have ten wives and forty concubines. The slave girl I seized from you is now my wife. And God has given me such prowess that in one night I have entered ninety chambers.[64] What you ask will bring you nothing but ill feeling. I will hold you above all other women, but I do not know whether I will take any more wives before we reach the East." Araqit was a wise woman, even though she was a fairy. She said no more, for she knew that she would get nowhere. And Alexander was hers three nights a week, and four nights he would go to other women.

After Araqit's territory was settled by man, Alexander prepared to leave. Araqit said to him, "I have 1,000 fairies who attend on me. They can go nowhere. Let us take them with us." The King consented. And those 1,400 [sic] fairies entered the King's service and joined his army. There were fair maidens among them who married the King's soldiers, and their males asked human females in marriage.

Then Araqit decided to honor Alexander. She dug out hidden treasures and brought them to the King. She offered him such an abundance of gold and jewels that what he had brought from India and Rum looked meager beside it. The King marveled at the bounty and said, "God has willed nothing but good for me. It is profitable to stay long in this land!" The King gave of those riches to his soldiers, rewarded the Sage generously, and favored Araqit more than before. Since the region was secure, the inhabitants began to cultivate the land. Brave men came forth in that country and freed themselves from the giants and fairies. And that land will remain in man's hand until the Day of Resurrection, and its inhabitants will continue to pray for the King of the Earth, Alexander.

Four months later, the King departed from that region, reaching a country with many cities the inhabitants of which were heathen Turks who did not believe in God. Their King, Julbab, had over a thousand times a thousand soldiers, all heathens and idolaters. They had learned that Alexander was bound for the East and had prepared for battle. They had decided to allow Alexander to cross their land peacefully, but to fight him if he showed hostility. The news of what Alexander had done to the fairies and the giants had reached them, and they were in great fear of him.

## Alexander's Arrival in Russia, What Happened between Him and the Russians, and the Dream He Had in That Land

The story goes that when Alexander reached the land of the Russians, Araqit said to him, "Send someone to the Russians with 100 fairies." "I will do so," replied the King. But Alexander neither sent a messenger nor asked for provisions, and none dared question him. For two days he admitted no one to his presence, and spoke to no one. The soldiers grew worried. They said to themselves, "God forbid that this fairy woman should conspire against the King while we are at the city gates and for every one of us, there are ten Russians in the city. What has happened to the King?" Rumors spread among the soldiers. Everywhere they whispered together quietly until the camp was in a commotion. The chiefs met, trying to find out the cause of Alexander's strange behavior. At last the rumors got out of hand, so the chiefs sought the Sage to inquire what had happened to the King. "Do not speak of this," said the Sage. He went to Alexander's tent, but he was not admitted. When it was time for evening prayer, Araqit went to the King and found him sitting on the prayer-rug with his head on his knees. "What troubles you?" she asked. At the end of the day, the Sage sent someone to Araqit and said, "Tell us how the King fares, for the day has ended and we fear disorder in the army." Araqit answered, "Our King is in good health. Tonight [sic] he was by my side. Suddenly he woke up, and he has been praying since dawn. I went to him a while ago and found him at his prayers. With a gesture he ordered me to leave him alone for the day." The Sage was saddened by the news. But when night came they opened the tent and the King admitted the Persians to his presence. Before them all was the Sage. He saw the King had grown pale, and bowed before him and said, weeping, "O King, may the evil eye be far from you! You did not admit us yesterday. Nothing is wrong, I hope." The whole army was waiting, downhearted, and 400,000 men had gathered before Alexander's tent to hear what was said. The King, who could hear the commotion in the camp, said to himself, "Before all else, the army must be appeased and the soldiers sent back to their place. Then I will reveal the secret to the Sage and the chiefs of the army." Therefore, mounting his horse, he left his quarters gracefully, pale but smiling, bearing a sword in his hand. When the soldiers saw the King, they blew the longhorn, beat the drums, and cried aloud. They threw themselves to the ground, as if the sky had thundered and the earth were trembling.

Alexander reassured them that all was well, saying, "I spent this day in the presence of God." When the soldiers saw the King, they departed content. The King returned to his tent and summoned the nobles and the Sage. "Tell us, O King, what has happened to you," they said. "I have had a strange dream, and I am terrified by it," said Alexander. "What dream?" they asked. "I dreamed about a statue. The statue's head was made of gold, its chest of silver, its thighs of brass, its legs of iron, and its feet of baked clay. Then a rock fell on the statue, breaking it to pieces, and I heard a voice from the statue, saying, 'O son of Nahid, thus is your temporal career and your kingship.'[65] I was frightened. Then an angel appeared to me and said, 'Fear not and take heart, for the faith still remains.' When I woke up, I was very depressed and wished to rule no more. Today, I pondered this decision for a long time and I was sad. I said to myself, 'I will divide my treasures and my riches among my men, return to the cloister of the old hermit, and worship God until the Lord of the Worlds calls me to him.' But then I thought, 'I am responsible for the lives of thousands of men. How can I abandon them?'"

Then the Sage said to the King, "Be joyful, for Bukht al-Nasr had this dream and Daniel interpreted it. I have the book of interpretation of dreams. There it is written that Bukht al-Nasr, the son of Ruham Gudarz, became the king of Syria and had this dream after his slaughter of the Jews. None could interpret it, except the prophet Daniel. He said to Bukht al-Nasr, 'The head of the statue, made of gold, is your rule which shall excel the rule of all kings of the earth. The statue itself represents the world. Its chest, made of silver, represents the rule of those who will come after you. Its thighs, made of brass, represent those kings who are inferior to you. Its legs, made of iron, represent the Messiah, whose creed is above all creeds in strength, just as iron is above all things in solidity. And the feet, made of baked clay, represent the world, which shall at last end in destruction.' Here is the interpretation of the dream. And, know O King, that God sends dreams to his fortunate servants. For they can give to charity if the dreams are ominous and thus divert the disaster; or, if they are propitious and favorable, rejoice at them. And the angel who addressed you by the name of your mother at the end is the angel who tomorrow, on the Day of Resurrection, will call every man by his mother's name." "What is the significance of this?" asked the King. The Sage replied. . . .* The King was pleased. He prayed, and begged God to grant him to see the angel who was his friend. The next day God made the angel manifest to Alexander. The King rejoiced and asked the angel many questions. "Was it right or wrong to drive the giants and the fairies from their home?" he asked. "It was right," said the angel, "for they were evildoers." Then Alexander said, "Was it right to take a fairy to be my wife?" The angel replied, "It was right and God. . . ."† For this reason the King stayed there and waged war against the Russians day and night. They killed many Russians and awaited the mysterious thing promised by the angel. A few days later King Alexander won the victory and entered the land of the Russians, discovering that the inhabitants had dispersed. His men drew their swords and slew many of the Russians. The battle continued until it was time for the evening prayer.

Then the King came to a house the doors of which were locked. Inside the house, they found a great number of deer. The King marveled at that and said, "Deer should be in the field; why are they in this house?" The deer were striving to escape, but the King told his men not to let them go until he had found out why they were in that house. Then they caught a Russian and forced him to reveal why the deer were kept there. He said, "O King, these are the deer that produce musk. Ever since you camped here, we have been sending horsemen to the field every day, to catch the deer and bring them here. We were afraid you would catch a deer, find the musk and say, 'This land is very pleasant, for it yields musk,' and seize it from us." And King Alexander had come to this region for the deer. He took the musk from the deer's navel. The next morning he sat on his throne in his camp. The chief of the Russians was taken prisoner, a great many were killed, and the rest fled, homeless.

*Blank space in the manuscript.
†One leaf is missing from the manuscript here. The mysterious thing later said to have been promised by the angel must have been recorded on this leaf. Perhaps it is the zebra that leads Alexander to the chest guarded by a serpent. See pp. 103–5.

The next day a zebra as beautiful as 1,000 idols entered the King's tent. The King marveled at its beauty, and told his men to catch it alive, being careful not to harm it. The zebra playfully dodged them, trotting away, but coming back to the tent. Then the King himself set out to catch the zebra. It began to run from him and the King followed. Then he thought, "One cannot follow a zebra on foot." Therefore he mounted his horse and said to his men, "Do not follow me. I want to catch the zebra by myself." He chased the zebra on horseback for some distance. He was all alone. Fearing that the zebra could be a demon, he decided to go no farther. But he remembered the angel who had said, "A great wonder will be revealed to you." With that in mind, he set forth again. Looking around, he found himself at the seashore. He saw a chest, a Zangi who had fallen dead, and a black snake that had curled around the chest. The King marveled at what he saw. "What is this chest?" he wondered. When Alexander approached the chest, the snake unwound itself and sat apart. The King dismounted, and the snake and the zebra both stood before him. The King looked at the Zangi fallen dead, and marveled at his height and his stoutness. He was eighteen *gaz*[66] tall. A mule loaded with household utensils was standing nearby. Then the King turned his face to the sky and said, "O glorious Maker and perfect Creator, such things are your doings and no creature can fathom your mystery." When he went to the chest, he found a solid lock at its lid. He could not open the lock, hard as he tried. Then he uttered the great name of God and the lock turned open. The King lifted the lid and inside found a maiden like the moon and the sun, like 1,000 idols, like the nymph of paradise, adorned with jewelry and gold beyond measure. And the moonfaced girl had her face on her knees, weeping bitterly.

When the King saw her face and her beauty, his heart grew faint and he marveled at her, a maiden not yet attained puberty, tall and graceful as a cypress. Her hands were tied behind her back. Then the King looked back, discovering that both the snake and the zebra had disappeared. He unfastened the maiden's hands and helped her out of the chest. He marveled at the beauty of her face and wondered at the creative power of God.

An hour after Alexander had left in pursuit of the zebra, his men set out to find him, following the footprints of the horse. The King saw the dust from the distance of an arrow shot, and realized that it was the army. Then he asked the maiden who she was. "My story is long," she replied. "I am of the seed of Afrasiyab and the daughter of the King of Turkistan. My father is the King of the paradise of Ganges. One day I went to a festival with slaves and slave girls. When night came, the servants and the guards all rested, and I was fast asleep. Suddenly I woke up and left my bed for a need. I saw this frightful Zangi who jumped at me, caught me, and carried me away. There was a fort nearby with Zangis more frightful than this one. They kept me in the fort for ten days but did not do me any harm. They said that they intended to take me to their king. 'Be joyful,' they said, 'for our King is obeyed by all the Zangis. We will take you to him to be his bride.' They tied my hands, fearing that I would kill myself, and they placed me in this iron chest with the jewelry and gold they were sending to the King by way of kindness. They entrusted me to this Zangi to take me to their king. We were at sea for twenty days. Every day he would give me two loaves of bread and some food, and take me out of the chest for easing nature. Once he said to me, 'Be joyful, for we have only one day's journey to cover.' And he gave me food, which I ate, and I resigned myself to whatever God had decreed. I called God to my aid day and night. Then the Zangi put me back into the chest and said, 'I will sleep for an hour, for I did not sleep last night. Home is near, and tonight shall be your wedding night.' I was frightened; I said to myself, 'The bridegroom is black and frightful, a cannibal like the other Zangis.' In this chest I prayed to God to save me from this Zangi. That same minute I heard the Zangi cry out, 'I am slain by the snake.' He cried a few times, then he was silent. And I knew that he was dead. This is my story as I told you. Now, O courteous man, tell me who you are." The King replied, "I am the grandson of Shahmalik, who is the King of Turkistan." "Show me the sign of royalty," she said. The King did so. Then she said, "Know, O good man, that for two years our land had been subject to disturbance. But lately it has grown better." "What was the cause?" asked the King. She replied, "After King Alexander left the Land of Darkness, he started for our land. Many kings in this region were slain. Then Alexander brought justice to the land and departed."

 The King and the maiden were thus conversing when the elephants arrived with the royal canopy. And when the men saw the King, they bowed to the ground before him. The maiden realized by this that he was a king. And King Alexander was very handsome and still young. The maiden said, "Praised be God who saved me from those cannibal, infidel Zangis, and put me in the hand of such a king. But what king is he?" The King informed the Sage of all that had occurred. The men kept arriving and bowing before the King, and the King told them of his adventure. When night came he said to his men, "Behead the Zangi, bury the body, but keep the head and stuff it with straw, for it will prove useful." They did as they were told. And the spot where the Zangi had died was about two parasangs from the fort.

Then King Alexander mounted his horse and they placed the maiden in a *howdah* and took her to the camping-ground. But they did not send her to Araqit, for fear of her envy. The king bowed to the ground and said, "O omniscient Lord and powerful, able Creator! You have been more benevolent to this servant of yours than to anyone else. How can I ever thank you enough." And that same night Alexander married the maiden, who was more beautiful and more delicate than all the women that he had seen in his expedition around the world.

The news reached Araqit, and when the King went to her she inquired what had happened. The King told her all about the Zangi, the snake, the maiden, and the Zebra who had led him to that spot. Araqit asked the King how many wives he meant to have. It passed his tongue that this was his last one. The divination proved true, and Alexander took no other wife except for maidens who fell into his hands and whom he made his concubines.[67] But on that day he had four wives, including Araqit. Then the King said to Araqit, "Be merry, for I will come to you as often as before." Thus he humored her, for the battle with the Zangis was ahead of him and he did not fully trust the fairies.

When the King was through with the wedding, and the Russians were mostly killed and the rest driven away, those among the Russians who were believers were brought back, the land was given to them, and they were content. The King said to them, "Rejoice and be not afraid. If the Russians trouble you or attack your territory, turn for help to Araqit's kingdom, for that land is now in the possession of man and ruled by my deputies. I am in this region at present, and on my way back I will cross your land."

The King departed from there, and having covered two parasangs, he and his men reached the fort of the Zangis. They said, "It is not advisable to camp here; we should go a little farther." They camped at a short distance from the fort. The camp stretched for four parasangs, and it faced the road. Yet Alexander did not camp along the road. And it was time for the evening prayer.

The King told his men to blow the bugles and beat the drums and the cymbals all at once. The whole world trembled with the clamor, and the Zangis were frightened. They knew nothing about King Alexander. They took the news to the King of the Zangis, saying, "Such and such a Zangi is coming and bringing the daughter of such and such a king, with abundance of gold and jewelry." Their king ordered them to leave the fort, find out what that great noise was, and bring him the news. They looked down from the top of the fort, found a vast army with numerous elephants, and heard voices saying that it was Alexander, the King of the Earth.

## Alexander's Arrival at the Fortress of Qatil, the Zangi, the Seizure of the Fort, and What Happened between the King and the Zangis

The story goes that when Alexander camped there, the King of the Zangis said, "We must inquire why he has come here. Has he come to fight, or will he only cross the land?" "We do not know this," his men replied. And in that fort there were 7,000 cannibal Zangis; each ate a whole ox every day. And in chronicles and early writings it is stated that the Zangis were remnants of the tribes of 'Ad and 'Uj. They had huge bodies; their heads were as big as a *lahd*;[68] their mouths were like the opening of a cave, and their teeth like the tusks of a boar. They sent one of the Zangis who was bigger and more fierce-looking than the rest as a messenger to Alexander.

The attendants brought the news to Alexander, saying, "Someone has come fierce as a dragon, more awesome than the fairies we saw. Even the elephants and the horses stampeded to see him." The King took the great name of God in his hand and sat on his throne. The men and the elephants surrounded the King's tent. When the Zangi came near the tent, they did not grant him entrance, but first asked the King for permission. The King gave him leave. The Zangi entered and bowed down. His appearance frightened the King. "What do you want?" asked the King. "Qatil the Zangi, the King of the cannibal Zangis, wishes to know what you want here," replied the messenger. The King said, "Tell him I have come to seize your fort and fortifications, to trample your army under the feet of my elephants, and to kill every single one of you." The Zangi raised his hand to seize the King, paying no heed to the 10,000 Turkish slaves belonging to the King's household, who were guarding the King, bearing unsheathed swords in their hands. When the Zangi raised his hand to seize the King, the latter, holding the great name of God in his hand, jumped to his feet and drew his sword. The Zangi stretched his arm to unfasten a stone club which was tied to his belt. He stamped on the ground, and roared so loud that of the women and children in Alexander's army a number died. Meanwhile the King was on his feet and the slaves stood there with their swords drawn, but the Zangi took no heed of them. Only the Sage knew how to handle the Zangi. So he ordered the men to bring the stuffed head of the Zangi and throw it at the foot of the throne. By divine providence, it so happened that the two Zangis were brothers. And as the Zangi looked at the head, the Sage ordered the men to attack him. The slaves took him by the sword and cut him to pieces, so that, except for his head, not a single part of his body remained whole. The King told them to bury the body, but to save both of the heads. They did as he had said.

 The Zangis waited a day or two for the return of the messenger, but he failed to arrive. On the third day they sent another Zangi to the King, more fierce-looking than the first. They told him to ask the King why he had gone to that land, and what he intended to do. They demanded that the King pay the road-toll if he wanted to cross the land, and declare his intention.

 News was brought to the King that a Zangi had left the fort and was coming toward the camp. He told his men to carry his throne to the field, and cover all the elephants with iron. "Watch for my signal," he told the elephant drivers, "and if the messenger of the Zangis swears or acts discourteously, do as I say. He had better do no more than deliver his message and leave."

 On his way, the Zangi asked Alexander's men what had become of the first messenger. They said that no one had gone to them. The Zangi was perplexed. When he came before Alexander's throne he bowed and said, "The sovereign of the Zangis, King Qatil, says thus, 'I sent a messenger to make inquiries about you. You did not send him back. Why? What do you seek in this region? If you want to cross the land, pay the road-toll and depart in peace. And if you have another intention, say what it is.'" The King replied, "First, none of his men has come to us except you. As to your second question concerning my purpose, I am going to the rising-place of the sun, and I come from the West. In my journey around the world, I have confronted more dreadful enemies than you. I passed many great kings, and the East and the West came under my rule. The kings of the earth all obeyed my commands. Those who defied me forfeited their lives. I have stopped in this land to relieve mankind from your nuisance, to seize this fort with the help of God, and to destroy every one of you with the help of God."

The Zangi was wise and held his life dear. "I will deliver this message," he said, "and will see what he has to say." On his way back, the Zangi saw the awe-inspiring sight of the elephants, the soldiers, and the camp. When he returned to the Zangis he repeated Alexander's answer as he had heard it.

The King of the Zangis was displeased. He jumped to his feet and seized the messenger, pulled and cut off one of his ears, and said, "How dare you repeat these words in my presence? Why did you not pull him down from his throne when he spoke thus? You should have wreaked havoc upon them, even if their army were a thousand times thousand in number." He removed the messenger from office, sent another messenger, more fearful than the former, and he said, "Go and tell the King that unless he leaves this land, I will descend from the fort and trample him and his men like so many ants. And if he gives a harsh answer, tear him limb from limb and fear not."

The Zangi, who was very rude, came to the King's tent and was admitted. The King asked what he wanted. "I am here to order you to leave this land," said the Zangi. "Otherwise, King Qatil says, he will come and cut you and your men to pieces." The King replied, "Tell him that I will not leave this land before every one of you is dead. I will seize the fort from you and you will pay for what you have done to mankind."

"It cannot be otherwise," began Aristotle, when suddenly the Zangi jumped and pulled the Sage down from the golden chair. The army fell into commotion. The King rose, drew his anvil-cutting sword, and hit the Zangi on the neck. The men fell upon him and cut him to pieces. They kept his head and buried his body.

The next day the King moved his army nearer the fort, within one parasang distance from it. He told his men to beat the drums and blow the bugles. They made a great noise.

When day came and the messenger did not return, the King of the Zangis called the one-eared messenger and said, "Our first messenger did not return, and the one I dispatched yesterday has not come back. Go, make inquiries, and bring us the news, for the army has come near the fort."

The Zangi went before Alexander's throne, bowed, and did as rules of conduct require. He said, "O King, the first messenger who came to your presence has not returned. The day before yesterday another was sent; he too has not returned." "No one has come here but you," the King said. "But we have heard that a bride is being brought to you. Perhaps they have gone to welcome her." When the one-eared Zangi heard this, he rose, bowed to the King, and returned. He said to King Qatil, "The messenger did not go to Alexander. It seems that Alexander has sent his men to capture the bride, and both of our men were informed of this and went to rescue her." King Qatil gave arms to 100 men and sent them to look for the messengers and the bride. They descended from the fort in the night. The fairies saw them, and informed King Alexander. The King sent 100 elephants with 1,000 brave horsemen to the seashore and said to them, "The Zangis are bound to come. Kill whomever you find and throw them under the feet of the elephants."

They went to the seashore, and, finding no one there, waited. When an hour had passed, the Zangis arrived and asked them who they were. "We are Alexander's men," they replied. "What do you want here?" the Zangis asked. "We have come to capture Qatil's bride and take her to Alexander," they said. "We will not permit you," the Zangis replied and started to fight. It was a great war, and the Zangis proved to be very strong. They struggled aginst the elephants and beat down two or three of them, and slew some of the men. Alexander's men grew afraid of the Zangis. They continued fighting, but could not defeat their adversaries. They brought the elephants into action but still could not subdue them. Then God inspired King Alexander to send them aid. The King dispatched 1,000 horsemen and 500 elephants. Meanwhile, the war had grown fierce. The Zangis had destroyed ten elephants and slain many of the men. Alexander's troops were about to flee, when the aid arrived. The men cried, "*Allah Akbar*," and said, "Here comes King Alexander." They rushed at the Zangis and set the elephants upon them. They slew every one of them, cut off their heads and took the heads to the King. The King told them to stick the heads on lances, cry aloud, beat the drums, and blow the bugles. The King's army shed tears of joy. The Zangis looked from the fort, watched the rejoicing, and heard the uproar. When they saw the heads of their own people stuck on lances, they wailed and cried.

From a hundred Zangis only one had made his escape. He returned to the fort and said, "O King, the Zangis were all slain. The army is still near the sea and the bride has not yet arrived. We must be on our guard, for an abundance of jewelry was sent with the bride. It must not fall into their hands."

Then King Qatil prepared 1,000 men and sent them to the seashore to guard the bride. The fairies informed Alexander of this. Alexander was pleased. He said, "Let them stay there. We will do nothing today." When night came the King himself mounted his horse and said to the fairies, "Go and make inquiries about them." The fairies returned soon after and said, "O King, they all are fast asleep and dead to this world." The King with 5,000 excellent horsemen and 200 elephants surprised them at night. Of those one thousand Zangis, only ten made their escape. The King had the heads of the dead stuck upon spears and carried before the host. His men rejoiced at the victory.

But the Zangis were angry. They said, "Tomorrow we shall fight from the fort." The next day the chiefs of the Zangis and their men bombarded the King's army from the ramparts with arrows and stones. The King and his men were all armed, but many were hit and injured by the arrows and the stones, for the enemy was above them and they could not fight back. Alexander did not know what to do. When night came, the armies retired. The King was very sad. He said, "What is to be done? It is difficult to fight them while they are high above. We have no power against them. We will waste our time and many of us will be slain." The fairies said, "O King, two parasangs from here, there is a gay and pleasant garden called the Haft Anbur. We had better camp there. The Zangis will think we have fled. They will follow us and in the plain we will be able to fight them." The King replied, "If we leave this spot they will never come after us. But perhaps some of them will go to the seashore in search of the bride."

When it grew dark, the King went to the Haft Anbur Garden. He saw a garden like an earthly paradise. "Whose garden is this?" he asked. "In this country there was a king called Mahjasb," they replied, "and this garden belonged to his daughter, 'Ayn al-Hayat. The King camped in the garden.

In the morning the Zangis discovered that Alexander's army was missing. They thought that Alexander had escaped. One of them descended the fort to see where the footprints of the horses led. He found the footprints leading to the Haft Anbur Garden and took the news to Qatil, saying, "Alexander has gone to the Haft Anbur Garden. I wonder what scheme this is." When night came, the King of the Zangis dispatched 1,000 men from the fort in secret and ordered them to remain at the seashore. They went to the seashore, called a ship, and boarded it, hoping to find the bride.

After they had sailed for a day, they saw a ship approaching from the opposite direction with an abundance of riches and property, many slave girls, and a great amount of musk and ambergris. They had piled all this in a second fort and were sending it to the King of the Zangis. When the Zangis reached the ship, they inquired where the bride was. They were told that she had been sent to them ten days before, with such and such a Zangi and an abundance of gold and jewelry. The Zangis said that she had not arrived. The fairies went to Alexander and informed him of the circumstances. The King realized that the Zangis would soon return. Therefore he sent a large number of his men with some elephants to the seashore, and ordered the fairies to go to the sea and keep watch for their arrival. The men stopped at the seashore.

It so happened that the King had a premonition that his army would come to harm. One day, they saw more ships sailing toward the shore. The fairies informed the King that the Zangis had returned with riches and treasures beyond measure.

*Alexander and his men put the enemy to the sword when they disembarked. The ship's cargo was carried to the Haft Anbur Garden.*

*Qatil sent a messenger, promising Alexander more gold and riches and requesting him to return the bride to him and leave in peace. Alexander rejected the offer and denied that the bride was in his hands. Qatil came to think that the bride had been driven to an island, having been caught in a storm.*

## How Qatil the Zangi Sent 2,000 Men to Seek the Bride, and Alexander Made a Surprise Attack on Them

*The Zangis went to the seashore, and waited for ships that would take them to the sea in search of the bride. They were all killed by Alexander's men. A second group sent by Qatil were all captured. Qatil sent to his brother, Rafi', and asked him to come to his aid.*

## How Rafi' the Zangi Came to the Aid of His Brother and They Fought Alexander

*Rafi' joined forces with Qatil but they were defeated. Alexander took Rafi' prisoner and after many more wars and adventures, finally hanged him Qatil sent for Rafi' 's son, 'Anbar, to come to his aid.*

*Qatil, angered against Land, the one-eared Zangi, cut off his other ear. Land secretly joined Alexander's service as a spy.*

## How 'Anbar Received Qatil's Letter, Gathered an Army, and Went to the Aid of His Uncle, and What Happened between Them and King Alexander

The story goes that when 'Anbar, the son of Rafi', received Qatil's letter and was informed of his father's death, he wept and lamented. 'Anbar's fort was on the border of the Zangis' territory, and it was manned by a great number of Zangis. 'Anbar mourned for his father. Then he sent someone to gather the Zangis who lived in and around that region. So many of them committed themselves to take revenge that they could not be numbered.

Then 'Anbar left the fort in charge of one he trusted. He prepared the ship, and remained on board for a month until he had gathered all the Zangis. When some 20,000 black Zangis had come together, 'Anbar prepared for the voyage and set out on his course.

King Alexander and Land knew nothing of this. The King was occupied with the building of the Haft Anbur Garden. He meant to ask Araqit to finish the tale of 'Ayn al-Hayat, but Araqit was still weak. One night King Alexander continued praying until it was morning. Then he sat on his throne, troubled. He ordered the Sage and the entire army to come to his presence. King Alexander delivered an address and praised God and the prophets. Then he said, "Let it be known, O chiefs, that last night I prayed to the God of gods until morning, hoping that he would forgive my sins, and my sins are many. I pondered upon my sins. When the night ended, I slept a while. The angel who is a friend to me came to me in a dream and said, 'O Alexander, since you left Rum, you did nothing of value in the other world, except the war with the Zangis. The slaying of one Zangi is enough retribution for a year's sins, which would deserve to be punished by hell. You will slay so many of the Zangis that only God will know their number. You must stay in this land, for a friend of God is in a trial from which he will be relieved at your hand. The term of his trial is not yet ended. Remember that God's doings are inscrutable and unlike man's habits and customs. You must be patient.' Since that is what God has commanded, and by His command we shall win heaven, we must be patient and wait to see what God's will is. It is fourteen months since we came to the land of the fairies, the giants, and the Zangis, and the time of departure is yet unknown. According to accurate calculations today I am thirty-five years old, no more and no less. I wish to God I would live to old age, for then all things would be well."

The Sage said, "O King, life and death are mysteries known to no one but God. You must not surrender to sorrow. Did you ask the angel at all?" "Yes," replied the King, "I have asked the angel many times. The angel says, 'The unknown is known to the Omniscient, not to us.' I am full of sorrow, and merriment and joy are empoisoned for me." Then the King asked the Sage, "How many months are there in thirty-six years?" years?" "Four hundred and thirty-two months," replied the Sage. The King said, "From what I have heard, some seventy months still remain of my life." Then he bowed with his forehead to the ground and said, "O God! Bless what remains and grant me success in obeying your will."

Meanwhile Araqit was pregnant, and the King was full of anxiety on that account.

*'Anbar arrived with 2,000 men, and 10,000 more were to join him later. With him was a hermit whom he had kept prisoner for thirty years. He brought the hermit to the fort inside a chest. It was God's decree that the hermit should be freed by Alexander after he had defeated 'Anbar.*

## How 'Anbar Descended from the Fort with 2,000 Men, and the Battle between the Zangis and the King

*Alexander's men defeated the Zangis in battle. Then 'Anbar himself came to the field and challenged Alexander to combat. But Alexander's men did not want their King to fight in person. Seven men from Alexander's army confronted 'Anbar, but they were defeated and taken captive one by one. Eventually 'Anbar was defeated and taken captive by Araqit. He was tortured and finally put to death.*

*Qatil sent messengers to Zangbar and asked Shahmalik to come to his aid.*

## [Scribe's Commentary][69]

When the scribe of the present copy reached this point, he found a few contradictions in the story, which are annoying to the wise. The contradiction lies in this: When Alexander reached the East and came ashore, in this copy it is written that he arrived at the town of Divas [?], in the country of Tamghaj, and that the King of Tamghaj was Shahmalik, a Muslim and a just man, a follower of the faith of the friend of God, Abraham. And the angel said to Shahmalik in a dream, "Tomorrow Alexander will come to you as a messenger. Treat him kindly, so that he may depart without doing you any harm." And when day came and Alexander went to him as a messenger, Shahmalik fell upon his knees before him. In short, he showed so much respect to the King that Alexander was embarrassed and made peace with him. He entered into a treaty with Shahmalik and departed without doing any harm. Then he went to the country of the giants, and from there to the land of the fairy Araqit.

At this point in the story we are told that Shahmalik sent an army before Alexander and between them there were great wars, for no reason. This is an erroneous contradiction, and is occasioned by careless and ignorant copyists. In short, 'Abd al-Kafi ibn Abi al-Barakat, the scribe of the book from which this copy was made, studied many copies. In all of them the story was written in this manner. And so it is in the original copy which is in the Jami' Library at the end of the bazaar. Nobody had noticed the contradiction before, and carelessly they had written and read the story.

The truth is that when the King went ashore he arrived at the town of Divas, whose king, Tamghaj, was a relative of Shahmalik and owed his kingship to him. Alexander made peace with him and left. The region where he fought to capture the fort of the Zangis was close to Shahmalik's kingdom. Shahmalik was the King of the entire East, and all the kings of the East obeyed him. Shahmalik's brother was Arsalankhan, and he was under Shahmalik's rule.

Another contradiction is that early in the story, where Alexander fights with Queen Araqit, it is said that the maiden whom the King seized from Lady Araqit was the daughter of Arsalankhan; and here it is stated that she was Shahmalik's daughter. This is a strange contradiction and God is the best judge of its truth.

And this chapter was written so that the scribe of this story might be excused, for the original copy reads thus, and such things are not unusual among ignorant scribes. But there is no doubt that the contradiction existed from the beginning, for Tamghaj, who was a relative of Shahmalik, was taken for Shahmalik himself, and for this reason the story sounds contradictory. And let us be done with that and return to the story of Alexander.

*Alexander's men pitched camp in the garden and prepared to face Shamalik and the Zangis.*

## How Buqraquz, Shahmalik's Son, Made a Surprise Attack on Alexander's Army, and What Occurred between Him and the King

*Shahmalik's son, Buqraquz, was defeated and captured by Alexander, who put him in chains. Alexander reproached Shahmalik and his son for having initiated the hostilities. Buqraquz told the King that his father had gone mad out of grief for the loss of his daughter who was kidnapped by the fairies, and that he himself had warned his father against uniting with the Zangis.*

The next day, the King ordered his attendants to bring Shahmalik's son to his special quarters in private. The King, the Sage, and a few servants were present. The son of Shahmalik prostrated himself. He had grown ill and his face had turned pale in Alexander's prison. The King said to him, "I have learned all the circumstances. Now, answer truly to what I ask. Tell me first what your religion is." He replied, "O King, the religion of the Arab Zahhak, Jamshid, and the kings of the Turks." "Why is it that you are not idolaters?" asked the King. Then he said, "You answered this truthfully. But tell me, how far is your land from the rising-place of the sun?" The son of Shahmalik replied, "We can reach the rising-place of the sun in five days." "Have you ever gone to the rising-place of the sun?" asked the King. "We dare not go there," he replied. "Why?" asked the King. "For it is five days' journey from where we are. There, in the morning at sunrise, they hide the women and children underground, for fear that they should perish from the terror of that great uproar and tumult," he replied. "What is the uproar and the tumult like?" asked the King. "Like the sound of cymbals, bells, and terrible cries," he replied. "Are there any inhabitants in the land?" asked the King. "Yes, there are," he replied. "But they are naked and of different kinds. Among them are Gog and Magog who have remained there from the other side.[70] Their original dwelling is on the left of the rising-place of the sun. There is another tribe yet unvisited by man, whose members know nothing except themselves and their nakedness." "Are they not harmed by the rising of the sun?" asked the King. "They have become accustomed to it," he replied. "Did your father ever attack these tribes?" asked the King. "With all his power, my father is resolved to bear with them," he replied. "How far does your father's kingdom extend from the rising-place of the sun?" asked the King. "Our kingdom extends from the rising-place to where we have dug the ditches," he replied. "It contains four cities, and having crossed the kingdom, you reach Jabalsa." "How many soldiers has your father?" asked the King. "He has more soldiers than can be counted," he replied. "A thousand times thousand?" asked the King. "Twice as many, and more," he replied. "Has there been any war between your father and any other king?" asked Alexander. "Yes, with Queen Araqit and the cannibals," he replied. "Who excelled?" asked the King. "It would depend, O King. Sometimes we excelled, and sometimes they did," he replied. "I know that you have answered all this truthfully," said the King. "Will you recognize your sister if you see her?" "Yes," he replied. Then the King said, "She was in the hands of the fairies. When I conquered that land, I rescued her from the fairies, and now she is my wife." Shahmalik's son fell to the ground for joy. The King ordered his men to remove the chains from his feet and treat him well. "I will spare your life. Stay here," said the King. And he entrusted him to the servants to take him to his sister. When she saw her brother, she jumped to her feet and they embraced each other and both swooned for joy.

Buqraquz was a wise youth. He knew it was not right to stay there longer. He took his leave from his sister, and, with the servants, returned to the King. The King delivered him to the Sage and said, "Treat him kindly, and let him remain unbound. But do not feel secure about him until I see how this affair develops."

Meanwhile, the King was awaiting the arrival of Land, Qatil's messenger. A number of slaves were assigned to serve Shahmalik's son, and the King would send him a banquet twice a day. One day Shahmalik's son said to the Sage, "May I send one of these slaves to my father and give him the news about my sister so that this enmity may come to an end?" "It can be done if the King gives leave," the Sage replied. "I will ask permission from the King." But when Alexander heard Buqraquz's suggestion he replied, "I will not grant this, for Shahmalik will think that I am afraid of him." Then the King summoned Shahmalik's son. "What is your name?" he asked. "Your slave Buqraquz khan," he replied, and he dared not use the title of *shah*. Then the King said, "You have asked to send a slave to your father and tell him of these circumstances.

Indeed your father shall not know of these affairs neither now nor later. May it please God, I will capture him and send him to his daughter in chains, so that he may realize what he has done. It was because of your truthfulness that I forgave you, and it was pity for your youth that made me pardon you. I did not do so because of your sister or your father." Then Shahmalik's son bowed before the King, and returned to his quarters. He stayed with the Sage and the days went by.

Meanwhile news was brought to Shahmalik that his troops had not succeeded, that Alexander had excelled, and Buqraquz and thirty princes were taken captive. This drove Shahmalik to madness. He wept, tears rolling down his white beard. He beat himself, saying, "I could not bear being separated from my daughter. How can I endure the absence of that moonfaced beauty who used to stand before my throne? Cursed be the Zangis."

Then he called the ministers and said to them, "We contrived a scheme, but it did not work. Now both my daughter and my son are lost; and so will my home, my kingdom, and my rule be lost. What is to be done?" The ministers said, "We warned you that the scheme was unwise, but you did not listen." "You were right," he replied. Then his minister said, "O King, Alexander is no small ruler. Today he is the King of the East and the West. The kings of the earth pay him tribute out of fear. He has subdued all kings wherever he has gone. He slew those who rebelled against him and disobeyed him. It is advisable that you write a letter to him and send him messengers with presents worthy of such a king and say, 'It was the Zangis who incited me to this strife. If you show magnanimity as is worthy of you and return my son to me, we will be indebted to you.'" "Be it so," said Shahmalik. He sent a letter to Alexander together with 10,000 Khusravani durusts (each durust worth five dinars), 1,000 musk buds, three or four pairs of deer, bisons, and two ostriches with gem-studded leashes. He prepared all this and sent it to King Alexander with an eloquent messenger.

A few days after this, news was brought to the King that Shahmalik's messenger had arrived. The King told his men to decorate the Haft Anbur Garden with great splendor. They adorned the elephants and placed the lions at the entrance. When the messenger entered, the King was sitting on the throne and the fairies were standing in line, above the King's head in the air. The messenger bowed to the King and placed the presents before him. The King looked at the presents. The messenger handed the letter, but said nothing. The Sage opened the letter. Alexander remained silent for an hour after he had seen the presents. Then he raised his head and said, "How dare Shahmalik block my way when God has opened the whole world to me from the East to the West?" The messenger bowed and said, "O King of the Earth, who would dare oppose your will? Heed that which is in the letter." After the letter was read, the messenger added his message. The King said to the Sage, "Give the messenger lodging for the night. I will give my answer tomorrow." They provided the lodging for the messenger and sent him food. The King had told the Sage to make sure that the messenger did not see Shahmalik's son or hear anything about him.

Thus that night the messenger stayed with the Sage. The King prayed all night long to God. At dawn, having said his morning prayer, he went to sleep and rested. When he awoke, Land, the Zangi who served him as a spy, came to the camp. He said to Alexander, "O King, tomorrow is the day of strife: 400,000 Zangis will descend from the fort." The King ordered that Shahmalik's messenger be detained until the battle had ended. Then he commanded his men to prepare for war. The next day, the drums and bugles sounded from the fort. Soon after, the Zangi troops descended from the fort and stood in line. Qatil too descended from the fort, huge as a mountain covered with steel.

When Alexander's soldiers saw Qatil, they trembled with fear and they said, "Who will dare to meet him in combat? Alas! We are ruined. What is to be done?" The King realized that the army was afraid of Qatil. He ordered his men to prepare for battle and to station the elephants.

## Alexander's Battle against Qatil the Zangi and What Occurred between Them

*The angel came to Alexander with good tidings of victory over the Zangis but warned him against the infidel Turks. After a number of battles Alexander won the victory and Qatil fled to his fort.*

*Alexander refused Shahmalik's presents and sent him a harsh answer. Meanwhile, Buqraquz accepted Islam.*

*Some time later, Alexander and Qatil faced each other in combat once more. Their battle lasted until the end of the day, with neither side winning. Meanwhile, Araqit and the fairies conquered the fort and put the Zangis to flight. The old hermit was rescued from Qatil's prison.*

*Araqit gave birth to a son whom they called Iskandarus. They celebrated the event seven days and seven nights.*

*Qatil was tortured and finally slain.*

## How the King of Zangis, Mankus, Came to Shahmalik with the Zangis, the Battle between Shahmalik and Alexander, and What Occurred

*In addition to the Zangis, Shahmalik had sent for the Elephant-ears, a tribe who lived near the rising-place of the sun. Alexander allowed Mankus and 600 of his men to enter the fort, only to trap and kill them. In the battle with Shahmalik, Alexander won the victory as well. The Zangis sent for Mankus's son who arrived with 50,000 Zangis to avenge his father's death.*

*That night Alexander prayed to God until midnight.*

At dawn, God most high made the angel who was Alexander's friend appear to him. The angel said to him, "Take heart, for you have won complete victory upon the Zangis. The engagement against the Zangis is over; now you have to deal with the infidel Turks. It is unwise to advance any farther. Your place is here, for here you have two solid shelters: the fort and the garden. These infidel Turks will not let you cross as long as they can resist you. You have great tasks before you. Protect yourself from these unbeliever Turks and trust in God, for victory will be yours in the end."

When the King heard these words from the angel, he bowed to the ground and offered his thanks. Then the angel disappeared. The King guarded the Haft Anbur Garden and the fort carefully. In the morning he went to the hermit's cloister, where the hermit prayed for him and gave him encouragement. The night before the angel had said to him, "There are great wonders in store for you, and you shall see them." "Are they to my advantage or disadvantage?" the King had inquired. "They are for your good and nothing else," the angel had replied.

One day King Alexander was sitting before the hermit, watching the road. He saw two horsemen galloping, one following the other. When they came near, the King said to the army, "See who these horsemen are who are dressed in green and are galloping." "We see no one," they replied. "Now they are near us," said the King. The horsemen greeted Alexander, but Alexander did not know who they were. When he answered their greetings one of the horsemen said, "Do you not recognize me?" "No," said Alexander. "I am Khidr, the prophet, and this is Ilyas, my brother.[71] We have covered seven months' journey in an hour. God has sent us to you with the good tidings of victory. Be on your guard, for 100,000 infidel Turks lie in ambush. Soon they will reach your camping-ground. You knew nothing of this. The Zangis have contrived a scheme to capture the fort. There is an underground passage from the fort into the sea, and all the remaining Zangis have gone to the sea, planning to return to the fort through the passage at night to seize your wives, your concubines, and your treasury. Be watchful, now that we have warned you, and God will aid you."

Then Khidr assumed the appearance he had in the Land of Darkness. He gave the King the glad tidings of great conquests and good deeds that were to be accomplished at his hand in the rising-place of the sun—all this, through the grace of God. "Do not grieve over death," he said to Alexander. "When death comes, one must perforce depart, for death is just. When the time comes, it is happier there, for you will be close to God. Be merry, for one must not grieve over death before it comes. Send your men in two directions." Khidr showed Alexander both directions and said, "Keep the fort from the Zangis tonight. Victory shall be yours in the end. And if you ever face weakness or failure, do not be sorrowful, for it is not good to succeed always." Then Khidr bade them farewell.

*Alexander prepared for war as Khidr had instructed him. Meanwhile, Araqit defeated an army of 100,000 Turks who had planned to attack Alexander at night. She returned to the fort, searching for the underground passage mentioned by Khidr. The secret passage was discovered, and the Zangis were allowed to enter the fort through it only to be put to the sword.*

## How Shahmalik Seduced Araqit for His Son, Tafqaj, and What Occurred

The story goes that Shahmalik found himself completely helpless in fighting Alexander and was at a loss. He thought to himself, "First we should do away with this fairy woman, then it will be easy to deal with Alexander." Therefore he contemplated the case of Araqit. His son Tafqaj, the elder brother of Buqraquz, was very handsome and Araqit had sought after him for many years. He had asked the daughter of the King of Sind in marriage, but she had passed away, and he had not yet remarried. Shahmalik decided that Araqit could be deceived through gentleness. He ordered two noblewomen to prepare themselves and he inquired whether Araqit was in the garden or in the fort. They informed him that she was in the fort. Shahmalik sent a spy to keep watch near the fort and bring him news as soon as Araqit went to the garden. The spy remained there.

When King Alexander defeated the Zangis, he ordered the passage between the fort and the sea to be sealed off, so that no one could enter it. He said to his men, "Let this fort remain; this shelter must not be destroyed. It may prove useful some day, and we may come to need it. Ours is a hard task, and time is passing. But we are nearing our goal. Be it as God wills."

Afterward, the corpses in the fort started to decompose. The King ordered Araqit to go to the garden for two or three days, until the corpses were thrown into the sea. Then Araqit returned to the garden. Having made sure that she was in the garden, Shahmalik's spy took the news to Shahmalik. The two armies were twenty parasangs apart. The spy covered the distance in two days and gave the news to Shahmalik. Meanwhile, Alexander, who had sent out scouts and set up watchmen, was resting and waiting to know God's will, free from care.

When Shahmalik was informed that Araqit had come to the garden, he sent two women and a servant to her as messengers, and he wrote a letter in which he said, "O Queen of the Earth, we are surprised at you, for you have united with the enemy, given up your home and a seventy-year-old kingship, and turned your back on your own people. All these wondrous deeds are yours, not Alexander's. What has Alexander done that did not start and end with you? Now, heed these words with wisdom and prudence, so that you may understand. Know that Alexander will stay in this region until he has visited the rising-place of the sun. He will take you with him to Rum; but at Rum [he will not treat you as he does here], for he has many wives, all daughters of great kings. Here too, he has two or three with him. Soon he will have no regard for you.

"You know that Buqraquz, my son, is in Alexander's prison. My elder son, whose name is Tafqaj, has no wife. His wife passed away a year ago. Leave Alexander and unite with us. And when he leaves, I will restore you to your kingdom and your rule. My son will be your husband; he will be under your command and your rule. I myself will be as your slave. If you believe these words to be true, and consider it wise to do as I say, think of a strategy. Once you abandon him, he will not be able to resist us for one day, for we have dispatched swift messengers to the Zangis and they will arrive soon. We have also called the Birahnigan [the Naked Tribe] from the border of the rising-place of the sun. When they come, they will attack the camp and tear them all, limb from limb. But you are the cause of our undoing. It would be better for you if you do as I have said. I will make Tafqaj swear not to look at any other woman after marrying you."

Shahmalik sent both those women and the servant to the King's camping-ground. They arrived there in secret, and when night came they boldly entered and sought admittance. Araqit was sitting on the throne. The daughter of Shahmalik was standing before Araqit's throne, waiting. The two women recognized her and they wondered greatly, because for all that had occurred Shahmalik did not know that his daughter was in the hand of the King. The two women had thought that she was in Araqit's hand, for when she disappeared there were rumors that she had been kidnapped by the fairies.

They stood there silent, and, when the daughter of Shahmalik left, those women and the servant said to the fairies, "Tell the Queen that we are messengers, sent to her by Shahmalik. We will deliver our message if she so commands. We have come unknown to King Alexander." Meanwhile, Shahmalik's daughter was listening unobserved and she heard these words. Araqit knew that Shahmalik's daughter was still there. Therefore she ordered the fairies to hide the messengers. When Shahmalik's daughter was gone, Araqit called the messengers and treated them kindly, as is the custom. Then she ordered them to deliver their message. They gave the message and handed the letter to her.

Araqit read the letter, thought about Shahmalik's offer, and was perplexed. She said to herself, "Shahmalik is right. I will be dear to Alexander only as long as he is here. Once he leaves this land and returns to his kingdom, he will make me jealous of his wives every day. Tafqaj is better for me, for he is young and he will be ruled by me. I have done so much for the King, but he does not think anything of it." Having reasoned thus she thought again, "Alexander is the King of the East and the West. He has seen me naked, and I have borne him a son. What will people say afterward?" She was greatly perplexed and did not know what to do. She displayed signs of uneasiness and could not give them an answer.

Meanwhile, after leaving Araqit, Shahmalik's daughter went to Alexander immediately. "O King," she said, "Two women and a servant have come to Araqit from my father." "What did they say?" asked the King. "They did not let me hear," she said. "Alas! this cursed woman has done her evil deed," said the King. He rose and entered Araqit's quarters unexpectedly. Araqit saw the King. She left the messengers and ran up to him, bowing and flattering as was her way. The King ascended the throne and seated himself. When Araqit saw that she sat too. But she was pale and nervous.

"What news?" asked the King. But Araqit said nothing of the arrival of the messengers. The King became more suspicious, for he had expected her to reveal the circumstances to him. Then he lay on the throne and feigned sleep. Araqit ordered the fairies to hide the messengers until night. The King, who was awake, heard this. The fairies took the messengers away. The King stayed there for an hour. Then he rose and left. When he returned to his tent he summoned the Sage to his presence and told him all that had happened. The Sage said, "O King, true nature never errs. Her deeds have always been so. But we must let be, else there will be commotion in the army." "I will go this moment and put her in chains, and I will seize the messengers and learn the circumstances," said the King. "This is no time for such action," replied the Sage. "But send someone to seize the messengers on their way back, so that we may get Araqit's letter and see what answer she has made." The King replied, "She will send the messengers [ under the protection of] the fairies so that they may go undetected by man." "O King," said the Sage, "This is more difficult than the case of the Zangis." Then the King rose from his perplexity and went to Araqit's quarters, a naked sword in his hand.

Seeing the King in that manner, Araqit grew fearful and asked, "What troubles you, O King?" The King said, "Be honest with me and speak the truth." He repeated these words three times. Then he ordered the fairies to bring the two women and the servant before him. Araqit despaired of life, but she said nothing. The fairies brought them before the King. Alexander ordered that they behead the servant, and put the two women in chains and deliver them to the Sage. Araqit bitterly regretted what she had done. She trembled for fear of the King, staring at the ground for shame. The King was on his feet. He beheaded fifty fairies with his own hand, breeding great terror and fear. And Araqit was standing, shaking with fear. Then the King seized Araqit's hands, tied them with her hair, which reached down to her feet, and took her inside the tent. No one knew of these circumstances except the concubines.

"What have I done?" said Araqit. "You have revealed your evil nature," replied the King, leaving and ordering his men to guard the tent. The remainder of the fairies escaped and hid in the sea for fear of the King. They cursed Queen Araqit, saying, "You foul, evil, wanton woman! Do you want a husband superior to Alexander?" And of the King's army, except for Aristotle, no one knew of all this.

The King did no more until the next morning. When he entered the tent, he found Shahmalik's letter on the edge of the throne. He read it, and he stuffed it in the upper part of his boot. When night came, the King sent someone to the Sage and asked him to bring the two women before him. They were taken to the King. One of them was a beautiful free woman, the other a slave girl. Then the King ordered his attendants to unbind them and treat them kindly. He said to them, "What women are you?" One of them replied, "I am the wife of Shahmalik's cupbearer." The other said, "I am Shahmalik's concubine." "Never again will you see Shahmalik, or you the cupbearer," the King said to them. "But if you answer my questions truthfully, I will spare your life, honor you, and grant you high positions. And if you lie, I will spill your blood." "We will speak nothing but the truth," they replied.

*The two women told Alexander that Shahmalik intended to seduce Araqit; consequently, Araqit was put in chains. One of the two women, who had been nurse to Shahmalik's daughter, decided to stay with her. The other, a crafty woman who was the wife of Shahmalik's cupbearer, went to Shahmalik with the false news that Araqit would be waiting for his son near the garden that night. Shahmalik and his son rejoiced to hear the news.*

## How the Cupbearer's Wife Deceived Tafqaj and Surrendered Him to King Alexander

*Aided by the cupbearer's wife, Alexander seized Tafqaj and imprisoned him. Meanwhile Shahmalik and Mankus's son, Akhtaf, united and waged war against Alexander.*

And when the day was nearing its end, from the army of the infidel Turks a youth came forth, like the moon and the sun. He marched between the two armies, brandishing his spear above his head and calling for an adversary. One by one they went forth from the King's army and fell at his hand. In this manner seventy men belonging to Alexander's army lay on the battlefield. Alexander and his men were surprised and marveled at the Turk.

From the King's army no one dared go forward. The King's heart was full of dread as the horseman kept circling the field, calling for an adversary. Never before had anyone slain seventy men from Alexander's army in combat. Alexander saw that his men were afraid. He thought to himself, "The army will be defeated through fear, and if we are defeated on this account I will fall into ignominy. First, this is a difficult place and the limit of the earth. Second, they will say, 'whatever Alexander achieved was through the fairies and now that Araqit is in chains, he is defeated.' But I hope to conquer and be victorious, for God promised me victory."

Having thus considered the matter, he pulled the rein of the horse, intending to fight the Turk himself. But at that moment a horseman emerged from the King's army on a black horse. He charged into the battlefield, swift as wind, and attacked the Turk the instant he reached him. The horseman from the King's army was in reality Alexander's wife, Shahmalik's daughter. She held the Turk by his belt, and, putting forth her strength, snatched him from the saddle and in that manner brought him before King Alexander and threw him to the ground. Then she prostrated herself and went back among the troops. No one knew who she was. "This horseman did well!" said the King. "But it was a woman and not a man. Although I do not know who she was, I am certain she was a woman. But this is no time to make inquiries about her; it is time for battle and manliness."

Then another man from the Turks entered the battlefield. The Turk who was taken captive was a brother of Shahmalik called Turanmalik. He was equal to 1,000 men in battle, and he dearly loved Shahmalik. Turanmalik, from the start, had warned his brother, saying, "Do not ally yourself with the Zangis, for it will bring you harm; and do not strive against Alexander, for he is blessed with good fortune and you cannot withstand him. For he who is blessed with good fortune overcomes all who choose to wage war against him." But Shahmalik had paid his brother no heed.

The Turk who came to the field after Turanmalik was taken captive was Turanmalik's son. And when he entered the field he behaved rudely. (The maiden who was now King Alexander's wife had been once betrothed to this man, and Shahmalik had given her to him.) When he entered the field, he slandered and abused her; for he had asked this maiden's hand in marriage from his uncle, but the maiden had refused his hand and would not consent to marry him. And for her sake, Shahmalik had refused to give her to his nephew. It was then that

Turanmalik and his son slandered her and claimed that she was unchaste and in love with that prince [?]. And because of this quarrel there had been a blood feud between them. It was after this that Araqit carried away Shahmalik's daughter while she was sleeping beside her husband. Having been separated from her, her husband passed away some time later. (And this story has already been related in detail.) When the husband passed away, Turanmalik said to his son, "Arise and go to your uncle, ask his daughter in marriage, and say to him, 'If you give her to me, I will go round the world and search for her.'" But when Turanmalik's son went to his uncle and told him thus, his uncle replied, "Why ask for a harlot to be your wife?" And meanwhile she had disappeared.

When this youth, who was Shahmalik's nephew and Turanmalik's son, entered the field, he circled around and he cried out, "O Alexander! Do you know whom you have taken captive? It is my father and the brother of Shahmalik. His capture will bring you no profit but do you great harm, for he sought your good day and night. Let him go." The King replied, "Fight and do not worry about him, for he can shift for himself."

From the Iranian host a horseman confronted Turanmalik's son and was slain by him. Then others came forth, and one by one seven men were slain. Once more the King, moved by manly zeal, decided to enter the field. They blew the golden horn to announce that the king would fight, but they discovered that same horseman on the battlefield again, bedecked with fine ornaments. The horseman struggled against the Turk for a long time, until finally, getting hold of the Turk's belt, he snatched him from the saddle. But being unable to hold the Turk, the horseman threw him to the ground, placed a noose around his neck, and dragged him away. When the infidel Turks saw that, they charged in a body. King Alexander attacked also. The two armies were entangled. Dust rose to the sky over the battlefield, and in that commotion and tumult, the horseman disappeared from sight.

Having dragged the Turk to the Haft Anbur Garden, Shahmalik's daughter disarmed him, and delivered him to her attendants to bind his hands and feet securely. They said to him, "You villain! Will you accuse a chaste maiden of unchasteness again?"

Then they discovered the horseman to be Shahmalik's daughter, whom King Alexander had married. She had long implored God to surrender her uncle and his son to her. Since the time she had been separated from her father, she had meditated revenge day and night, for they had slandered her. And after the enmity and the war between her father and King Alexander, one night she saw in a dream that her uncle was torn limb from limb by a lion, and he and his son were slain. Then she said to herself, "I am a helpless woman. I do not know whether my father or Alexander follows the right faith." She lifted her face to the sky in prayer. "O omnipotent God!" she said. "Disclose this mystery to me. If Alexander's religion is the right faith that leads to heaven and saves from hell, give me a sign. Lend me the strength of forty men, so that I may capture my uncle and my cousin in combat and surrender them to the King. That will raise my state; for Araqit is no more than a woman, yet she has fought many battles." And she prayed to God to grant her request.

And on the night of the Turks' arrival, she dreamed that they said to her: "Arm yourself tomorrow and go to the field, for your request has been granted. Both your uncle and your cousin will fall into your hands, so that you may be convinced that this faith is rightful and not false." This maiden was very timid, so much so that she could not lift a stick. Yet God gave her great strength and fortitude. She went to Alexander's armory, and she called her brother Buqraquz and told him all that had happened. Since she could not arm herself, her brother helped her. None looked as handsome and vigorous as she after she was armed. The servants marveled at her courage. She mounted a black horse that belonged to her brother. Then her brother thought to himself, "If this frail woman overcomes those two great princes, I will be convinced that this is the right faith. I will leave my father altogether, and join Alexander's service wholeheartedly."

As he mused thus, his sister entered the field. She defeated Turanmalik and captured him. Some time later, she entered the field in a different array, and returned victorious and joyful, bringing her cousin with her in chains. But for fear of the King, she did not show him to her brother. She tied him securely in her quarters and delivered him to the guards. Then she and her brother accepted the faith with certainty, saying, "Now there can be no doubt that this is the true faith." And having won victory in two combats, Shahmalik's daughter unarmed herself, dressed in women's clothing, and went to her quarters. She knelt, bowing to the ground, and thanked God.

Now, this event lowered Queen Araqit's standing, for there was a reason behind the strength of Shahmalik's daughter. And because of her strength and her combat, all forgot Araqit and exalted Shahmalik's daughter; as is the nature of this world, that when the new appears the old is forgotten.

*When the day ended, Alexander returned to his camp. In his tent, he found the Turk in chains. His servants told him that the Turk was brought there by Shahmalik's daughter.*

The King attributed her victory to God's grace. He bowed to the ground, saying, "O God of all gods! All are ruled by you from the gnat to the elephant. You give strength and fortitude to whom you will, and victory to whom you choose. Your servant had a wife who would come to his aid in every battle. When she was beguiled, you gave your servant another, so that he might not be dismayed. O Lord! Give your slave grace that he may praise you as he should."

*When Araqit heard how Shahmalik's daughter had assisted Alexander in battle, she became so jealous that she fainted and remained unconscious for twenty-four hours. Later, she implored the King to pardon her, but Alexander refused to do so.*

*Turanmalik and his son were hanged after they refused to accept the faith.*

## How Tafqaj's Letter to Araqit Was Discovered by Alexander

*Tafqaj, who was imprisoned in the fort, sent a letter to Araqit, urging her to set him free and escape with him. Araqit wrote him a favorable answer. Her letter was intercepted, and she was imprisoned in a dungeon. There were rumors that she was caught with Tafqaj.*

*Later, the Zangis freed Tafqaj from prison and took him away with Qatil's bride and Alexander's concubines. When the King was informed of this he went to Araqit's dungeon, only to discover that she too was missing.*

## How Araqit Pursued Tafqaj and the Zangis and Fought Them

The story goes that when the fairies heard that Alexander had arrested Araqit with Tafqaj, they grew heavyhearted. But when they came to the King they realized that the rumor was untrue. They said to themselves, "This woman is ruined. The King will slay her sooner or later. Let us return to the sea with those of our kind. Let us be spared this infamy and the pain of having to witness the death of our lady." And they cried and wept. When night came, they went toward the sea and at midnight discovered the Zangis, who had returned through the tunnel that was near the fort and were leaving through the opening. They were about 400 and had brought Tafqaj and the King's wife with them, saying that she was Qatil's bride. They were carrying the bodies of Qatil, Turanmalik and his son, and the Zangi, Land, with them.

When the fairies saw them they said, "Let us contrive a plan and restore our lady to her position." They went to Araqit whom they found miserably tied in chains. They said to her, "If you are not in love with Tafqaj, and have been falsely accused, be apprised that the Zangis have gone to the fort through the sea tunnel. They have taken Tafqaj and the King's wife, together with an abundance of goods, and they are still at sea. They will return by morning. They do not exceed 400 in number, and they carry with them the bodies of Qatil, Land, and Turanmalik and his son. Let us unbind you. The horses are ready. Mount, and we shall take you there in an hour. Through this victory you can make amends for your deed. We had decided to leave, because the King intends to slay you; but we said to ourselves, 'Let us go and see.' If this victory is won, and the King is pleased, we will gain what we desire. Otherwise, we will take you and go back to the sea, where we will be free from this misery." "Let it be so," Araqit replied.

Then they untied her hands and she went to Alexander's bed, where he was sleeping next to Shahmalik's daughter, and took his sword from his bedside. She armed herself, and mounting the King's steed, rode away with the fairies. The Zangis had gone no more than one parasang when Lady Araqit caught up with them. She addressed them, saying, "I am King Alexander, Conqueror of Countries. You villains! Where are you taking these?" Then the fairies attacked the Zangis, and Lady Araqit set upon them and slew 200 of them. The rest escaped but the fairies pursued them and killed many of them. They won back the King's wife and untied her hands and feet. The fairies also captured Tafqaj, who recognized Araqit and said to her, "O Lady! Was this fair?" Araqit replied, "You foul villain! Because of you I endangered my life and displeased such a man as Alexander." With her sword she struck at his shoulder so hard that she severed his arm. Then she had the heads of the Zangis stuck on lances and she returned. When daylight came, they saw the dust from the troops and heard the drums. Araqit recognized Alexander's army. When she came near she saw King Alexander riding in full gallop, like a madman who has broken his chains. The men followed him. Araqit too was galloping fast. The King addressed his men, saying, "They are few in number and are coming toward us. Go and see who they are." He slackened the reins, riding slowly. Araqit saw the canopy of the King, but did not go to him because she was ashamed. And when she saw the King's face, she dismounted and fell to the ground. Then she sat and she kissed the King's stirrup. The King was astounded. The fairies brought his wife to him, and showed him the dead and the heads of Turanmalik and his son. The King examined all this. The chiefs of the army looked at one another in amazement. When they realized what had happened, they all dismounted, following Araqit's example. Four hundred gold-belted princes bowed with their foreheads to the ground and they said, "O King! There is nothing left." Then Araqit placed the halter around Tafqaj's neck with her own hand and brought him before the King. The King saw him and he said, "Who cut his arm?" They replied, "O King, it was Queen Araqit." And they repeated Araqit's words to Tafqaj. Then the King looked at Araqit's hand. He found her holding the sword that he had placed at his pillow the night before, and riding his special horse. Araqit threw Tafqaj to the ground and said to him, "You villain! You planned to deceive me, and you caused such a king to become displeased with me." Then she struck him with the sword, severed his head from his body, and stuck his head upon a lance.

The King rejoiced at this victory and he prostrated himself with his forehead to the ground, saying, "O pure God! You can do what you will. How can I thank you enough? At dawn I was so heavyhearted; by morning I am so joyful!"

*Araqit was placed in a howdah and taken to the camp. She told Alexander how, rescued by the fairies, she took the King's sword from his bedside, defeated the Zangis, and seized Tafqaj. The King was pleased with her.*

## How Shahmalik's Daughter Tried to Poison Alexander, How the King Discovered Her Intention, and What Occurred

The story goes that it was God's decree that Shahmalik's daughter should grow jealous of Araqit. She wanted to make the King lose interest in Araqit. For ten days the King went to Araqit every night and the wife who was Qatil's bride attended her day and night. Therefore Shahmalik's daughter became very jealous. And she also turned against the King and Araqit for the slaughter of her brother, Tafqaj. Although Tafqaj had been her enemy, he was still her brother. If the King himself had killed him, she would not have taken it to heart as much as when she knew that Araqit had slain him with her own hands. Therefore she set her heart on killing both the King and Araqit. One night she called her brother Buqraquz and said to him, "O brother, this fairy, as you have heard, has killed our brother. What are we to do to be secure from her? Our old father has lost his son, and I brought his brother and nephew to destruction, trying to prevent the King from making peace with Araqit. Now once more this fairy harlot is restored to kingship and all the chiefs are at her service."

Her brother replied, "If you were good, neither you nor I would be in prison." "I will never act this way again," she said. They wondered what to do, and at the end they decided to send a letter to their father by a slave girl, tell him all the circumstances, and ask for poison. "Whether we poison Araqit first or the King, this mighty deed will be accomplished at our hand," they said.

*The plot to poison Alexander was exposed. The King slew Buqraquz and surrendered Shahmalik's daughter to Araqit to do with her as she pleased.*

## How the Cupbearer's Wife Deceived Shahmalik and Surrendered Him to Alexander[72]

*Alexander poisoned Shahmalik's daughter and placed her in a chest with the dead body of Buqraquz. The cupbearer's wife told Shahmalik that she had brought his daughter and Alexander both unconscious in the chest. Shahmalik rejoiced at that.*

## How Shahmalik Was Taken Captive by Alexander, and How Arsalankhan Became King in His Place

The story goes that Shahmalik took his daughter out of the chest, embraced her, and, placing his face upon hers, said, "My heart is gladdened to see you again." Then he asked his attendants to bring a *howdah* and place her there to sleep. He instructed them to carry her to her own room the next day so that when she awoke, she would find herself in her own room. "Take out Alexander," Shahmalik's attendants suggested. "I will take him out tomorrow," he said. They called the musicians, drank wine, and celebrated the event. One of the nobles said to Shahmalik, "Be careful, for Alexander may wake up suddenly." They looked inside the chest, and, finding a sword inside, said to Shahmalik, "O King! If Alexander comes out of the chest with that sword, we and our entire army will be no match for him." "I know that better than you," Shahmalik replied. "That is why I have kept him in the chest." Then they closed the chest firmly and were secure. When an hour passed, the servant in charge of the *howdah* called Shahmalik in alarm. "Has my daughter awakened?" He asked. "No," answered the servant. Shahmalik went to his daughter's bed and found her dead. Terrified, he returned to the other chest. "Alas!" he said, "My daughter is dead. Open the other chest and take out Alexander."

When they lifted the lid and took out the body, he saw his own son, slain, his head sown to his neck. Shahmalik fainted. Overcome with fear, his men fled on horseback. The fairies went to Araqit and informed her of all that had happened. Thus Araqit learned that Shahmalik's men had deserted him. She mounted her steed, and accompanied by the fairies went to the road and blocked their way.

*Araqit and Alexander killed many of the Turks, Shahmalik's army were all dispersed, and he himself was seized by Araqit. Shahmalik's brother, Arsalankhan, ascended the throne. He made Mankus's son chief of the army and prepared to fight Alexander.*

The fairies came to Araqit and informed her that they had found Shahmalik's daughter in a most unseemly condition. Araqit was displeased. She ordered them to wrap a cover around her and bring her to the garden. After that, she surrendered Shahmalik to Alexander. They bound his hands and feet tightly, placed him on the back of an elephant, and brought him to the camping-ground, so that the entire army might see him. Later they carried him to the fort and imprisoned him in a dungeon.

And when Araqit came to Shahmalik's daughter, she found her dead. She examined her womb and found her pregnant with a girl from the King; the fetus was yet unripe. She wept bitterly at what she saw. She called the King and blamed him severely, saying, "None ever did what you have done! You have murdered a helpless pregnant woman. Beware! This shall not go unpunished." "God forbid!" said Alexander. "I did not murder her. It was the cupbearer's wife who said this was wise to do." "I swear to God I will kill this woman," said Araqit. Then she buried Shahmalik's daughter with her own hands. And she mourned for some days. And on the day the girl was buried the angel appeared to Alexander in a dream and said to him angrily, "You will be punished for slaying this woman." When the angel had disappeared in anger, the King awoke, pensive and fearful. He went to the tomb of his wife and wept a long time. He admitted no one to his presence for a week, and day and night he wept and prayed to God. After a week, the angel appeared and said, "O Alexander! You should not have slain this woman. God is displeased with you. The angels of the seven spheres trembled at this deed, for she had accepted the true faith and she was a believer. The destruction of an entire world does not weigh with God as much as the slaying of a believing Muslim. For the evil you have done you must suffer at the hand of the infidels, for God has thus decreed. But victory shall be yours in the end. Remember the saying, 'Whatever in this world to whoever in this world.' Since you aim to conquer the whole world, you must be willing to take the world's troubles upon yourself." Then the angel said, "Be wary of these infidel Turks; henceforth, if you capture anyone, first call him three times to accept the true faith and warn him. If he accepts the faith, spare his life even if he has slaughtered many. If he refuses the faith and will not turn to God, kill him even if he has done you much good. Belief in God and Islam redeems all evils. Give shelter to those who seek protection. Much good shall be done at your hand while you cross the rising-place of the sun and the Bayn al-Saddayn."[73] Then the angel bade the King farewell and disappeared. Penitent, the King bowed with his forehead to the ground, wept, and begged forgiveness, day and night praying to God until seven more days had passed. Then he resumed his royal duties as King.

*Alexander did not kill the cupbearer's wife, because she had done him much service. He rewarded her with gold and precious gowns. The woman said that to repay all the good he had done her, she could do no better than to keep away from his court.*

## How Arsalankhan Became King and What Occurred between Him and King Alexander

*Arsalankhan succeeded his brother, Shahmalik, and became king. The cupbearer's wife went to Alexander and offered to deliver Arsalankhan and Mankus's son to him. She instructed Alexander to wait near a certain hill with his princes. When he did as she had said, she went to Arsalan-*

khan and told him where he could capture Alexander and his princes. Arsalankhan set out with 50,000 horsemen. He captured Alexander and all his men except for two who made their escape.

Alexander instructed his companions to treat him as an equal and say that Alexander was not with them. Arsalankhan's messenger, Qaymun, who recognized Alexander, bribed the guard and took Alexander to his own house. Arsalankhan was led to believe that Alexander had not been taken prisoner.

## How Araqit and the Sage Were Informed of King Alexander's Captivity and Contrived a Plan to Rescue Him

The story goes that the next morning the news reached King Alexander's men, and his wife, Qatil's bride, went to Araqit and said to her, "It was that foul woman who played this trick. The King was in my chamber when she came and proposed this scheme." Araqit was angered against the woman. She ordered the entire army to arm themselves. Then the Sage came, his sleeves torn, a small turban on his head, and tears running down his face. When Araqit saw him, she fell in a swoon. The men came to her in a body and they said to her, "Beware, O Queen of Queens, beware! The lives of thousands of men and beasts depend on that single man." Araqit wailed and tore her hair, and sounds of lamentation from the camping-ground rose to the sky. The two princes who had made their escape were brought before Araqit to tell her of what they had seen. "They made the King run with a noose around his neck, together will all the princes," they said. When Araqit heard this, she bit into her arm and hand, tearing off the flesh. And the King's wives and concubines were all standing bareheaded before Araqit.

Then the Sage said to her, "Beware, O Queen! This is no time for mourning. The army will arrive any minute." "I have sent ten fairies to find out the circumstances," said Araqit. "If the King is yet unharmed, I will not sleep or eat until I bring him here; and if, God forbid, it turns to be otherwise, I will drown myself in the sea, for I do not want the world without King Alexander," she said, tears running down her face.

On the first day of the King's captivity in the hands of Arsalankhan, the fairies went after the King, finding him bareheaded and in chains, detained among the princes in the midst of a closure. They returned and told Araqit what they had seen. She flew into a rage, but she addressed the army, saying, "Fear not and be at ease, for he is safe. Arsalankhan has not the courage to look the King in the eye." She spoke thus to pacify them; in reality she was deeply vexed. Having been reassured that the King was alive, she called all the fairies and she asked the Sage to order that the treasury, the spare goods, and the women be carried to the fort and the passage between the fort and the sea be sealed. Then Araqit armed herself, and 400,000 horsemen armed themselves to accompany her. She stood before the troops, wearing a helmet and holding a lance in her hand. They removed the royal tent and carried it to the fort. About 1,000 men were at the fort; another 1,000 remained in the garden.

*Meanwhile, Alexander remained in Qaymun's house for four days, and Arsalankhan came to believe that Alexander either had not been among the princes when they were captured, or had since made his escape. The cupbearer's wife volunteered to go to Alexander's camp and find out the truth.*

Then the fairies visited the princes a second time. When they returned, they said to Araqit, "Take courage, for the King is not in the hand of the enemy. You and the Sage must find a strategy to rescue him." Araqit said to the Sage, "I deem it advisable to take the army and go to war. I will declare that you are Alexander, and you shall dress in the King's array. We will send messengers and liberate the princes, and in this way defeat the enemy all at once." "It is yours to command," the Sage replied.

Then he ordered the entire army to mount their horses, arm themselves, and set on the way. They requested Araqit to mount with them and they rode together. On their way, they saw a horseman galloping fast. Araqit ordered the men to seize the horseman and bring him to her. They seized the horseman and when they looked closely, they discovered that it was the cupbearer's wife, the evil woman who has caused them so much trouble. Araqit was glad, but she said nothing;

instead, she treated the woman kindly, asking her where she had been and how she had become involved in the capture of Alexander's men. The woman said, "O Lady, it was the King's fault, for he deserted his men and the rest were all caught." Araqit realized that she knew nothing about the King. She told the men to arrest her and put her in chains. And she said, "You foul, cursed woman! If I do not slay you in a manner that shall be a lesson to mankind, I am not Araqit." And the woman was young and fair.

Araqit told her men to put the woman in chains and place her on the back of the elephant, and they moved on. The woman did not know that the King was not among the army. She said to the elephant driver, "Is there anyone who could take a message from me to the King?" The elephant driver replied, "The King is in the rear of the troops; when he dismounts, I will take you to him myself." It was night and the army was moving ahead. And when the elephant driver, who was an Indian, saw the woman, he came to desire her. She said to him, "If you set me free, I will be your friend and I will give you gold, and costly robes and jewels beyond measure." She gave him her bracelet, her earrings, and whatever else she had. The Indian received them from her and he lay with her two or three times before it was day. In the morning he helped her get off the elephant, and she walked away.

The next morning, Araqit camped within two parasangs' distance from Arsalankhan's dominion. She chose an eloquent messenger, instructing him to go to Arsalankhan and say, "Alexander says thus: 'There was no quarrel or battle between us, but you captured 400 men from my army through treachery. It is better that you do not displease me, so that there may be no enmity between us. Return the princes, and let the army cross your land in peace. Otherwise, be prepared for war tomorrow.'"

The messenger departed with fifty horsemen. When news was brought to Arsalankhan that Alexander's messenger had come, he ordered his attendants to decorate the court, and he sent someone to summon Amir Qaymun. When the messenger entered, he bowed before Arsalankhan. They gave him a seat, and he delivered his message. Arsalankhan looked at Qaymun questioningly. "The King knows best," said Qaymun. Then Arsalankhan said, "Blood has been shed between us, for he has slain two nephews of mine, and my brother and his daughter are his captives.[74] How can I give him leave to pass? Only our swords shall speak for us. Moreover, he has slaughtered a great many Zangis and they have come to me to seek justice and to avenge the blood that he has shed. Fifty thousand Zangis are at sea. In two or three days, they will arrive and tear you, your army, and your elephants to pieces. I would be mad if I allowed you to cross my land. You are mistaken." Having said this, he sent the messenger away and returned to his quarters.

Qaymun came to Alexander and said, "Know, O King, that your army has arrived. Were it not for the toll collector at the gate of the city, I would send you to your own camping-ground this very day. Now we can do nothing but wait. But be at ease, for nothing outside these two possibilities can happen. If the Turks are defeated, all will be as you desire, and if they are victorious, we will think of a strategy." "Be it so," replied the King.

Meanwhile the messenger returned to Araqit and told her what Arsalankhan had said and what threats he had made. Araqit commanded the troops to array the center, form their lines, blow the longhorn, and beat the drums.

From the top of Qaymun's palace, Alexander looked at the camping-ground and saw all the tumult. He raised his head toward the sky and said, "Oh righteous God, I did wrong. Be merciful and generous, and forgive my transgression." Then he came down, for he dared not stay there. When the army reached within one parasang distance from Arsalankhan's camp, he sent forth his troops. The two armies stood face to face.

Araqit asked forty fairies to rescue four of the Iranian prisoners. The fairies said, "Lady, you know well that this is hard to do, and cannot be achieved except at night, for we cannot go to them in the daytime." Araqit said, "Alas! I should have done this [last] night, then would I have shown them the star in the light of the day."

The armies engaged in battle, and the fighting spread from there. The fairies shot arrows from the air, fighting as they had never done before, and killing a great number of the Turks. Arsalankhan marveled at their fighting. He entered the battlefield himself and shouted, "O Alexander, come forward!" The Sage was standing in Alexander's place, wearing a helmet. Then Araqit gracefully entered the battlefield and cleverly removed her helmet. (She was a resourceful woman and knew what to do.) Her dazzling beauty overshadowed the sun. She said to Arsalankhan, "I am Queen Araqit, a slave of Alexander, the King of the Earth. Come, you wicked, infidel villain, if you can withstand me in battle."

When Arsalankhan saw her face, he fell in love with her with a thousand hearts, and strength left his limbs. But he was wise, and he realized that if he fought with her he would be captured or killed. He said to himself, "This evil woman will spoil the joys of sovereignty for me." Then he said to her, "You wanton harlot! I am ashamed of fighting with you. Return, for I shall not fight except with King Alexander."

Araqit resented what he said. Attacking, she hit him with a spear, piercing his shoulder. Arsalankhan almost fell from his horse. He said to himself, "My beloved will take my life. Another blow will be the end of me." He turned to flee, but Araqit followed him and hit him with the spear a second time, wounding him again. Arsalankhan took refuge among his own men. Then the Sage attacked and Arsalankhan's army was defeated. Araqit's troops followed them to the gates and put many of them to death.

*Arsalankhan returned to the fort wounded; the cupbearer's wife, who had returned, told him that Alexander was not in his camp.*

*Meanwhile Qaymun, seeing Arsalankhan wounded, regretted that he had taken Alexander into his own house. But he said nothing that day.*

*Arsalankhan asked the cupbearer's wife to help him win Araqit's heart. The woman went to Araqit in disguise, and she did not reveal her identity or her mission until Araqit had sworn that she would spare her life.*

When she removed her veil, Araqit recognized her. The woman threw herself to the ground before Araqit and said, "Know, O Queen, that twice before I acted to the King's advantage: I surrendered Tafqaj and Shahmalik to him. This time, it was the King's fault, for kingship and love do not go together." "What is it you speak of?" asked Araqit. The woman replied, "O Queen, Alexander has fallen in love with a Turkish woman who lives in this land. She has built a cloister in which she lives a pious life. Her name is Zubaydah. I was messenger between them." "Where did she and the King meet?" asked Araqit. "They first saw each other in their dreams. Zubaydah saw the King in her dream first, and then I carried messages between them. That is why the King would not put me to death, and would not allow you to do me any harm." The evidence was convincing; and when Araqit heard what the woman had said, she believed her. Female jealousy affected her deeply.

The woman who lived in the cloister was a maiden, in beauty like the moon and the sun. She was the daughter of the King of Turkistan. Long ago, she had had a dream in which she was warned that heathens are punished by hell. She accepted Islam and fled from her mother and father, taking refuge in a cloister built of stone by fairies and giants in the days of Solomon. Her father and mother came to her and pleaded with her to return, but she did not consent. She had been in the cloister nearly ten years. Araqit had visited her as a pilgrim and she had seen her face. There was neither a woman nor a fairy like her; Araqit always said that she wished she had Zubaydah's face.

Then Araqit said to the cupbearer's wife, "Is the King there now?" "Yes," she replied, "And never again will he return to the camp. To save his honor, I concealed this from Arsalankhan, who thinks that the King is in the camp. Otherwise he would capture him this instant." When Araqit had heard these words, she treated the woman kindly and promised to hold her dear. She said to herself, "The army must know nothing of this. If the King has visited this maiden, seen her face, and lain with her, never again will he so much as look at me or any other woman. Meanwhile, the whole army have put their trust in me, and I know not what is to be done."

The maiden's cloister was on a mountain. Its gate was always open to pilgrims, and it was the refuge of all in need. Anyone who fled from a king would go there, and the maiden would grant him shelter. Araqit herself knew all this. Having heard and believed the woman, Araqit hid her. Then she sent two fairies to the maiden's cloister to inquire about the circumstances and bring her news in truth.

By God's decree, it so happened that Arsalankhan's army was defeated that night; three of his men who had survived sought refuge at the cloister, and the maiden had given them shelter. She had dispatched them the next morning, and they had gone to the city. Horse dung and footprints of horses could be seen at the gate of the cloister. Now, when the fairies reached the cloister, they found the gate firmly locked. They knocked, but no one opened the door for them. Returning, at the foot of the mountain, they met some villagers and inquired why the gate of the cloister was shut. "Perhaps some prince from the defeated army has taken refuge there," the villagers replied. All the evidence bore witness that what the cupbearer's wife had said was true.

The fairies returned and they told Araqit what they had heard and seen. She trembled at the news, but said nothing to the army and asked the woman what was to be done. The woman said, "O Queen, I know another secret, which I will disclose to you if you promise to spare my life." "I promise," said Araqit. "Know that yesterday in the battle when you uncovered your face, Arsalankhan saw you and fell in love with you, so much so that he cannot move a limb. That is why you beat him in battle; otherwise, you would have seen his manliness, his horsemanship, and his vigor. Now you have rendered him powerless. He called me and he told me all this. And I came here to tell you of both these matters." Araqit was perplexed. She said to herself, "If Alexander has abandoned me and given up his kingdom for a woman, I too should seek my comfort. But there can be no doubt that the King will return to his army. For the words of the angel cannot be false, and the angel said to him, 'Victory shall be yours in the end.'" Then she said to the woman, "Go to the cloister and bring us correct intelligence." "Your will is to be obeyed," said the woman.

The woman's story was completely false. King Alexander had never seen the cloister; nor did the maiden know anything about all this. The vile woman meant to beguile Araqit with these lies. After she left Araqit, she went to Arsalankhan and gave him the good tidings, saying, "Your desire is fulfilled. If Alexander does not return to his camping-ground today or tomorrow, you will achieve your goal. But if he does return within the next two days, our task will be hard." "I will find Alexander and seize him this day," said Arsalankhan. "Even though he is not in the camp, he cannot have gone out of this world." And the woman herself could not rest until she had carried out her evil scheme.

After the woman had left, Queen Araqit thought to herself, "She lies. For would a king like Alexander abandon all his subjects and leave his kingship to stay in a cloister at the gate of the enemy? This is beyond the bounds of possibility." After she had reasoned thus, she summoned the fairies. And the camping-ground of the King and Araqit was three parasangs from the cloister and two parasangs from the city. She said to the fairies, "Carry me to the cloister of the pious maiden in secret. Perhaps through her prayer the King will be restored to us." The fairies carried her and after an hour's flight reached the cloister. The gate was open, so they entered.

The devout maiden recognized Araqit, whom she had seen many times before, and said, "May it be for a happy cause that the Queen has honored this place at this time." "I have come for a visit," said Araqit. "I intended to come yesterday as well, but I was told that the gates were closed." "Yes," said the maiden, "last night two horsemen from the host of the infidel Turks had sought shelter here—and this is a place for refuge. They both left in the morning. I had to say my prayers and do ablution, and, as you know, on ablution days one must shut the gates. If there has been any mishap, tell me, that I may plead to God to change that discomfort into ease." When the maiden had spoken thus Araqit's heart was set at ease and she realized that the cupbearer's wife had lied about Alexander and the maiden. She told the maiden how the King had disappeared and the princes were taken captive. "Be at ease," said the maiden. "I will pray to God tonight and, may it please God, tomorrow you shall hear from the King."

Araqit bade her farewell and left. She returned to the camp immediately, so that no one noticed her absence. And when she returned she asked Alexander's wife, the maiden who had been sent for Qatil, whether the cupbearer's wife had yet returned. "Where did the Queen go?" she asked Araqit. "I had gone to search for the King. He was nowhere to be found. We must wait tonight. Tomorrow, may it please God, we will hear the news of his safety," Araqit replied. Then she lay down to rest for a while. When she went to sleep, she had a dream and saw the King in a castle. The King addressed her, saying, "Where are you?" Frightened, she woke up, wondering where the castle was and to whom it belonged. She put herself to sleep again, hoping to see the King a second time, but she did not. When she awoke, she said to herself, "I am glad that I did not bring myself to shame by trusting that evil, wicked woman. I know that the King is on a high place, and, may it please God, we will have good news from him today or tomorrow. For the prayers of the devout maiden will not go unheard. Had I listened to that woman, I would be now shamed before the King and all this effort would have been wasted."

When an hour had passed, the cunning woman entered boldly and sat before Queen Araqit and close to her. "What did you do?" Araqit inquired. "I went to the cloister," she replied. "The gate was shut, therefore I knocked. They opened, but I did not see that maiden. They led me upstairs where I saw the King sleeping by her side. But she had not yet given him leave to lie with her, for they needed someone to make them man and wife. But both were sleeping in one place. The King said to me, 'Tell me what you know about the army.' I told him what I knew."

Then Araqit seized her with her own hands, bound the woman with her hair, which was long, and tied her to the tent ropes, for she dared not deliver her to anyone before night came. Then she called the fairies and said to them, "Do me this favor tonight. Go to those 400 princes; perhaps you will be able to rescue two or three of them.

*Qaymun decided to deliver Alexander to Arsalankhan. But it so happened that the slave girl who attended Alexander in Qaymun's house was from Rum. Alexander decided to make his escape through her. He asked her to tell him her life story.*

The slave girl said, "I belonged to a merchant, and I left Rum the day Philip bequeathed his throne to his daughter's son. On that day there was great rejoicing in Rum. And this was some ten years ago." Alexander said to her, "I am Alexander, Philip's grandson," and he spoke to her of Rum. When the slave girl learned what had happened to the King, she prostrated herself and curtsied. The King said to her, "If you do me a service, I will take you to Rum." "I am your slave in all that you command," she answered. "It is two parasangs from here to my camping-ground," said the King. "I need someone to take a letter there and return." The girl agreed. She obtained an inkpot and a piece of paper, and took them to the King. The King wrote to Araqit, saying, "Let the fairies come to such and such a place and castle. When night comes I shall wait on top of the castle until you arrive. You will see me from the air yourself." Then he said to the Rumi slave girl, "You must go in such a way that none will know. Take this letter. Go to the camping-ground and ask for Araqit's quarters and do not deliver that letter before you see her and are sure that she is Araqit."

The slave girl replied, "O King, I have seen Araqit, the Queen of the fairies, many times and I know her by sight." She placed the letter under her heelpiece and left the castle, pretending that she was going to wash some clothes. The gatekeepers did not stop her, for she always went to do the washing.

After she left through the gate, she took to the road and in one hour reached the camping-ground. She continued on her way until she came to Araqit's quarters. She entered and bowed before Araqit, giving her the letter.

When Araqit saw the King's handwriting, she cried out and swooned. The entire army was summoned and the letter was read to them. The chiefs rejoiced, but they did not reveal it [?].

When night came, Araqit dispatched the vanguard and told the Sage and Piruz of Tus to be cautious. She and the fairies started for the area where the castle was located; by the time they reached it, it was dark. The King was standing on top of the castle. A light shining in the castle guided the fairies and they landed at once. Some of the fairies had flown over that castle before. Then when Araqit landed and saw the King, she threw herself to the ground before him. The fairies all did the same and they said to the King, "We must find a way to help you escape." I have yet many things to do here," said the King.

Araqit gave him his sword and a set of armor, and he said to her, "Let two fairies stay here to take messages to you when necessary. Tomorrow beat the battle drums, for Arsalankhan will not come to battle. But you should start the war and assign Piruz of Tus to protect the rear of the army, for the Zangi cavalry, 50,000 in number, will arrive from the sea in two or three days. Protect the army and be watchful. Station the fairy army to keep watch upon the seashore, so that when the Zangis come ashore, the fairies will bring news to you."

*Araqit told Alexander all that had happened in his absence. Meanwhile, Qaymun confessed to Arsalankhan that Alexander was at his house and promised to surrender him. But by the time Qaymun returned to his house, Alexander was gone. Arsalankhan imprisoned Qaymun.*

## The Return of Alexander to his Camping-Ground and the End of His Story with Arsalankhan

*Alexander made his escape and returned to his camp. Meanwhile, the conflict between the followers of Shahmalik and Arsalankhan led to a war. The supporters of Shahmalik freed Alexander's princes.*

*The cupbearer's wife was punished by death.*

*Afterward, fifty ships belonging to the Zangis arrived. The angel appeared to Alexander and told him that he would fight the enemy on the water. Alexander prayed to God to make the water solid under his feet, and he and 400 men rode to the sea and fought the ships. Many of the Zangis were killed, and the rest fled.*

## How Tarzak, Prince Qaymun, Qaymaz, and Ayaz Fared after They Accepted the Faith

*Some of Arsalankhan's followers accepted Islam and joined Alexander, who rewarded them generously.*

*Arsalankhan confronted Araqit in battle and fled to the fort, seriously wounded. Alexander invited him to accept the faith, or else face him in combat the next day. Arsalankhan asked for a two-week truce until he had recovered.*

*The angel appeared to Alexander and gave him the good tidings of victory.*

## The Arrival of Jundul the Zangi, What Occurred between Him and Alexander, and Shahmalik's Escape to the Zangis

*Jundul, the King of the Zangis, called his dispersed troops together and ordered them to fight against Alexander on their own, rather than as allies* of the Turks. There was a battle between them and Alexander; many more were killed on both sides.

Meanwhile, Shahmalik, who had deceived Alexander into believing that he had converted to Islam, escaped and joined the Zangis.

Shahmalik fought his brother, Arsalankhan, and defeated him. His army grew numerous and he became strong. When Alexander heard of this, he was distressed. Araqit went to Zubaydah and asked her to pray for their victory.

## How Araqit and the Fairies Attacked Shahmalik's Army and Captured Shahmalik

The story goes that when night came, the devout maiden rose and prayed to God. She wept and pleaded, saying, "O God! Grant Araqit victory over the infidel Turks."

Meanwhile Araqit and 1,400 fairies armed themselves and entered Shahmalik's camping-ground. Crying "victory to King Alexander," they put the enemy to the sword. The Zangis and the infidel Turks saw heads being slashed off bodies, but they could see not one striking at them with a weapon. Araqit went straight to Shahmalik's tent, captured him, tied his hands and neck, and put him in a halter. She said to him, "You evil infidel! Your trouble was all settled, but you brought yourself to misfortune again. Now the King of the Earth knows what to do with you."

Some of the Zangis were slain and some escaped. The chief, Jundul, fled to the sea, followed by 40,000 Zangis, and they made their escape. Araqit killed as many Turks as she could; she captured no one except Shahmalik.

And the second night was Araqit's turn with King Alexander; but when he sent for her, she was nowhere to be found. The fairies too had disappeared, but Araqit had taken no man with her. Alexander grew very worried. He said to himself, "There is no war or surprise attack. I wonder where she is." Fear so overcame him that there was a danger that he would slay himself. The King and the princes were all downhearted. The princes said to the King, "Perhaps the King had displeased her and for that reason she went away." But the King said that it was not so. Then the men mounted, each group choosing a different direction. The King, distracted by anxiety, was unaware of his surroundings.

It was night. Alexander rode toward the city of the enemy. Half a parasang from the garden, he found Araqit, who after that evening's battle had gone to the cloister to bid the maiden farewell and had covered twenty parasangs in an hour. When the King saw her he almost swooned for joy. He said to her, "Where have you been?" "I have brought Shahmalik," she replied. The King inquired into the circumstances. Araqit told him all that had occurred. She dismounted and brought Shahmalik before the King, who said, "You wretched villain! Have you not had your fill of deceit and treachery? Do you aim to deceive God Himself? The evil results of your treachery will surely return to you." He took Shahmalik from Araqit and brought him to his camp. The clamor of drums and cheers rose from the camping-ground. The men rejoiced over Shahmalik's captivity and the defeat of his army. Then Shahmalik was brought before Alexander's throne. The King said to Shahmalik, "You wretched apostate! You had turned to God and saved yourself from hell. Why did you throw yourself in hell a second time?" Shahmalik replied, "I never accepted the faith, and I never will. For an old faith is better than a new one. I will never renounce an old faith. It is true that I escaped from your hand through deceit, but you did not capture me manfully either; rather, this fairy woman caught me."

The King was enraged. He ordered his men to take Shahmalik to the top of the fort and hang him. And thus this nuisance was ended. Back in his resting-place, he called Araqit and said to her, "O Queen of Queens! You have performed great deeds, and auspicious victories have been won at your hand. But none of your victories and battles was equal to the capturing of this heathen, for he was a formidable enemy and he had mocked God and lied to Him."

News was brought to Arsalankhan that Araqit, single-handed, had defeated Shahmalik's army, captured Shahmalik himself, and dispersed his troops. Arsalankhan was more happy than can be described. His love for Araqit increased, but he could do nothing. He ordered his troops to mount and said to them, "Kill those of Shahmalik's army whom you find guilty of treason, and take those whom you cannot kill as captives. Call back the Zangis, but if they do not come, let them go. For none of them will escape Alexander." Then he sent a messenger to Alexander, saying, "Once more you called upon the fairies and captured my brother through treachery. Now he is defeated, but we remain. Let us meet tomorrow. Our armies standing face to face, you and I shall do combat. Let fortune favor whom she will, and thus end this confusion."

When Alexander's men heard this, they raised their voices and said, "Where there are 400,000 soldiers, why should the King fight in his own person and try the field with such an unworthy adversary?" But the King sent a messenger to Arsalankhan, saying, "Make sure you come to the field yourself, for I will be there."

Arsalankhan was not yet well and had made this challenge for the sake of honor. He wanted to find out about his brother and learn what had become of him. And King Alexander instructed his men to send the messenger back by the road that led to the fort. Thus the messenger saw Shahmalik hanging from a tree by his feet at the top of the fort, and he was afraid. On his return, he told Arsalankhan all the circumstances and gave him the answer to his message. Arsalankhan said, "He sends Araqit and when I see her, I cannot move a limb. What can I do with this fairy woman? She has made me helpless. But I think it is wise to send someone to the rising place of the sun and to summon the Elephant-ears to fight them, tear them limb from limb, and rescue us." "Be it as you say," the men replied. Then Arsalankhan said to the messenger, "Go to the King of the Elephant-ears and inform him of these circumstances. Say to him, 'Alexander intends to fight you. Give us aid and help us drive him away.'" Then he said, "What news from my brother?" "He was hung by his feet on top of the fort," replied the messenger. When Arsalankhan heard this he threw his headgear to the ground. His soldiers did the same, following his example, and they mourned for seven days.

*Following the angel's instructions, Alexander removed all the valuables from the fort. Meanwhile, entering the fort through a secret passage, the Zangis were surprised by Alexander's men, who killed them all except for a few who took the news to Arsalankhan.*

## Alexander's Battle with the Elephant-Ears and Arsalankhan, His Displeasure with Araqit, and How He Cast Her Away

The story goes that King Alexander decided to destroy the fort but an angel appeared to him and told him to wait three more days. The King waited until the three days were passed. On the fourth day, all the Zangis were slain and Jundul's head was placed beside the fort. One day the King said to the fairies, "We have received no news from Arsalankhan and we are ignorant of his intentions. Let us send the troops to besiege his city, and end this trouble also." "The King is to be obeyed," said the soldiers, "but it would be better to send a messenger and know his mind." The King said, "I have sent too many messengers. He is not important enough to require so many messengers. Let us take the army, pitch tents outside the city, and fight. Whatever God has decreed will come to pass." The men could do nothing but obey the King. Alexander chose 200,000 worthy horsemen from the Iranians and the Rumis. He appointed the Sage as the chief of the Rumis and Piruz of Tus as the chief of the Iranians. He said to them, "Pitch tents within two parasangs' distance from the city, and if the enemy comes from the city to fight you, fight back. But if they do not come forward, besiege the city and let no one enter it. I myself will follow you." Having said this, he dispatched the men.

Araqit went to the top of the fort to find out the circumstances. The King pondered upon the words of the angel who had said to him, "Do not destroy the fort." Formerly, that instruction from the angel had resulted in the defeat of the Zangis. This time the King did not know the reason for what the angel had said. "God knows best, for he knows all mysteries," he said. He spent three days and three nights with Araqit. He talked to her of many things and he said, "I fear that death will take me by surprise." "Say not so, O King," said Araqit. "For you are still young and shall live for many years."

On the fourth day the King said, "We must follow the troops; it is not wise to leave them there." And the King prepared to depart with 100,000 cavalry, and he let 100,000 soldiers stay with Araqit. He left the garden, the fort, the treasure house, and the women in Araqit's charge. But when he descended from the fort, he found the army retreating in defeat. The Sage and Piruz of Tus were among them, driving the elephants fast.

"What is it?" the King inquired. "Do not ask, O King," they replied. "Fifteen hundred of our men were slain. The enemy is pursuing us. Thousands of our camels and mules remain behind, dead. The enemy will arrive here tomorrow. Arsalankhan is following them with thousands of horsemen." "Whom is he following?" asked the King. "The Elephant-ears," they replied.[75] "What are they?" he asked. "They are tall as the tamarisk tree, and have two ears like the ears of an elephant. They use neither mattress nor covers, but spread one ear under and one ear over their body when they sleep. We had pitched our tents when Arsalankhan's messenger arrived and said, 'Tomorrow is the day of the battle.' The next morning we were all in the camping-ground when suddenly the Elephant-ears swarmed in like so many serpents or worms. They fought with their teeth and claws; teeth like a boar's tusks, and claws like the lion's paws. Our elephants, being frightened, jumped among the beasts. The Iranians shot at them with arrows and put many of them [the elephants?] to death. But the beasts did not stop from running. We fled, and Arsalankhan followed us."

When the King heard this, he ordered that the women, the treasure house, and the sheep and beasts be carried into the fort. They stationed the elephants and the troops in the garden. The army was equally divided between the garden and the fort.

Then King Alexander asked Araqit what was to be done. Araqit laughed, saying, "O King, these came to fight me many times; there is no creature as mischievous as they in the world. Their number is known to God only. If you kill a thousand times thousand of them now, there will be ten times more in an hour." "That is who they are," said the Sage. "They came in such a great number that the face of the earth was darkened with them." Lady Araqit knew how to fight them, but she wanted to see what the King would do.

When the Elephant-ears arrived, the King was on the top of the fort and the soldiers were partly on the fort and partly in the garden. Suddenly the Elephant-ears came into view, tearing the ground with their claws. They tried to climb the garden wall but halfway up they would fall down again and could do nothing. Meanwhile, from the garden and the top of the fort the Iranians hit them with arrows and killed many of them. When night came, they covered themselves between their ears. The arrows had no effect on their ears. Araqit watched the King, laughing. King Alexander said to her, "These are your neighbors; you know better how to deal with them." Then Araqit asked for 1,000 bottles filled with naphtha. They set the bottles on fire and hurled them at the Elephant-ears; the flames rose high. The Elephant-ears can be destroyed in no other way but by fire. And when the fire reached them, some were burned and some turned to flee. Araqit instructed the fairies to hurl ignited bottles at them from the air. The King and the army watched, amazed. The King pursued those who fled, with the elephants.

On their way, the Elephant-ears came upon Arsalankhan, who found them all half-burned, retreating. He realized that this was the fairies' doing, and heard the clamor of Alexander's army at their back. When Arsalankhan saw the Elephant-ears in that state, he became afraid of them. And they all turned to him, saying, "You deceived us. You surrendered us to the fairies in order to seize our land." They set upon his army and destroyed many of his men and beasts.

Then Arsalankhan saw King Alexander approaching with his troops and he was forced to fight Alexander. The Elephant-ears went away after killing a great number from Arsalankhan's army. But some 100,000 Elephant-ears had perished. Then the armies of King Alexander and Arsalankhan engaged in battle, and many were killed on both sides until more troops came to King Alexander's aid; they vanquished Arsalankhan's army and put them to flight. But since Alexander's soldiers were afraid of the Elephant-ears, they did not pursue the runaways from Arsalankhan's army. Instead, they all returned to the fort.

Earlier, when the two armies confronted each other, Arsalankhan, moved by his desire for Araqit, decided to go to the gate of the garden, hoping to seize her. Thus, while Alexander was fighting his army, Arsalankhan turned away and came to the garden with 50,000 horsemen. Araqit, who was on the fort with the soldiers, thought the horsemen belonged to the King. But when she and the soldiers looked closely, they saw Arsalankhan. Araqit immediately armed herself and descended from the fort with 100,000 horsemen accompanied by the fairies. A terrible fight followed but Arsalankhan dared not go before Araqit; he stood at a distance. King Alexander knew nothing of this, and, thinking that Arsalankhan had taken to flight, he camped four parasangs from the garden and rested. At the garden gate, the battle between Arsalankhan and Araqit lasted until the time for evening prayers. Finally Arsalankhan addressed her, saying, "O Queen of the Earth, hear one word from me. Then we will do combat if you want, or return if you will." When he had spoken thus, Araqit went before him. On that day she was not wearing a veil, and her face shone like the moon and the sun. When Arsalankhan saw her, he trembled all over. His eyes filled with tears and he said, "O Lady, beware! I can no longer bear your love. Come to my rescue. Why have you set your heart on this foreign King? For tomorrow he will return, and if you do not go with him, he will abandon you. But if you do as I say, you will continue to rule this land and I will be your slave, attending your will before your throne. Leave the garden and the fort this instant. Go with me, and this very day you will ascend the throne as the sovereign of this land. From here to your own land all shall be under your rule. I will make all obey you, and I myself will be as your slave. I will call back all the dispersed fairies, and the whole world will be run according to your desire."

When Araqit heard these words she was perplexed; for fairies are tenderhearted, and women can be easily beguiled. "He is right," she said to herself. But she made no answer to him, turned her horse, and rode off.

The Sage, who was in the center of the troops, was informed that Arsalankhan had tried to win Araqit, who was softened so that she did not fight him but turned her horse and rode away. "Where did Arsalankhan go?" asked the Sage. "He returned," they answered. "Go after him and waste no time, for I have already sent a horseman to King Alexander, and the King is nearby." The men left Araqit and pursued Arsalankhan. Araqit was angered. "How dare they pursue him when I refrained from battle today?" she said. She sent the fairies to tell the troops to return, but the men did not obey her.

Arsalankhan was joyful, for Araqit had listened to his words, and cheerfulness had brought courage to his heart. Yet he dared not stay, for fear of the King; therefore he galloped away with his army. When the King's army reached Arsalankhan, the fairies told them to return. "We will not return until we bring the head of this infidel," the men said.

And the Sage said to the fairies, "It was Araqit, who pitied Arsalankhan for his love, not us. For many years did King Alexander rule without Araqit and all was well." When the fairies heard this from the Sage, they deserted the army. The Sage and the men attacked. Arsalankhan returned, realizing what had happened. There was a great battle and in the end Arsalankhan vanquished the Sage. The King's troops retreated in defeat. Arsalankhan returned the same way he had come and went to his camping-ground.

And when the host and the Sage returned, Araqit, who was standing at the garden gate, said to the Sage, "You have grown bold and you say what you will." The Sage answered harshly: "You have turned to deceit and treason once more. Every day you have a new desire and a new passion. It is not you who is to blame but the King who has set his heart upon you and trusts you. I will put an end to all this today." When Araqit heard this, she was enraged, both because of her sense of honor and because of Alexander. The Sage rode and passed her by. Araqit followed from behind and with her own hands pulled him down from the saddle. She delivered Aristotle to the fairies to take him to the fort and put him in chains. The men tried to rescue the Sage and began to fight the fairies. The fairy who held the Sage wanted to enter the fort, but Alexander's men rescued the Sage and slew the fairy. How could fairies withstand all those men?

*The angel appeared to Alexander and told him that Araqit was at fault, and that as punishment for her deed, God had deprived the fairies of the ability to fly. The angel commanded him to forswear Araqit's company.*

*Araqit took refuge in Zubaydah's cloister.*

## Araqit's Sojourn at Zubaydah's Cloister and What Occurred between Her and King Alexander and Arsalankhan

*While Araqit was in the cloister, Alexander defeated Arsalankhan. The angel told Alexander that God was punishing Araqit, who in vainglory had claimed that whatever Alexander had accomplished was because of her. For victory is granted by God and not won by man. Araqit promised Arsalankhan to fight on his side. In disguise she faced Alexander in combat. After some fighting Alexander snatched her from the saddle and was about to throw her to the ground when she revealed her identity. Araqit was carried to the fort, where she begged Alexander either to kill her or to forgive her. Later, Araqit asked the pious maiden, Zubaydah, for help. The latter advised her to repent from what she had said out of vanity. Araqit repented and prayed to God day and night.*

Alexander had pitched camp in the Haft Anbur Garden in triumph. He would spend one night with Qatil's bride, one night with Qaymun's daughter, and the rest of the week with his concubines. One evening he thought to himself, "I wish the devout Zubaydah were my wife. But the angel has said to me, 'You will not take to wife the daughters of kings any more.'"[76] Then he thought, "Zubaydah is not of the seed of kings; she is a pious woman. If she becomes my wife, I will gain the kingdom of heaven as well as this world." After he mused thus he called the Sage and said to him, "You must go to Zubaydah as my messenger and ask her in marriage for me. There are many roads to the cloister. Take the road which would lead you there without taking you near the city. That maiden has a face the like of which cannot be found in this world and is perhaps to be sought in heaven." "The King is to be obeyed," said the Sage, rising and setting out for the maiden's retreat.

That night, Zubaydah dreamed that they said to her, "You must take a husband, for a young, chaste woman who has no husband is perforce tempted by the devil." And that night she thought to herself, "I wish King Alexander would ask me in marriage." In the morning the Sage came to her and spoke of the King's inclinations and of marriage. Zubaydah rejoiced and bowed with her forehead to the ground. She gave her word to marry the King, but she said, "I have conditions that the King will have to accept. I wish to spend the night in prayer. Two nights a week I will be at the King's service, and I will spend five nights praying to God. I demand that the King esteem no woman above me, favor me above all, and do whatever I say, for I say nothing but what would please God." The Sage returned and delivered her message to the King, who accepted her conditions.

*Alexander married Zubaydah. After Araqit was pardoned by God, the angel informed Alexander that he could be reconciled with Araqit. Alexander sent a* howdah *for her, brought her to the garden, and was reconciled with her.*

The King's wives were never jealous of one another, and if they were, they would never reveal their jealousy, except for Zubaydah and Araqit, who became enemies; and the King knew about their enmity. Araqit had been with the King two nights a week, but Alexander increased it to three nights. And two nights a week it was Zubaydah's turn, and two nights the turn of other women. And the King would add the days to the nights also. And it is said in legends that if Alexander had intercourse fewer than twelve times in one night, the next morning he would be faint and weak. And this is the way it was. And Zubaydah and Araqit would quarrel, and the King would judge between them.

Alexander wanted to start the battle with Arsalankhan, but his son, born to him by Araqit, passed away. He became sad and heavyhearted, for he had no other son. He wished to have a son worthy to become king. The King mourned for three days. But Araqit thought nothing of the death of the baby, for fairies love their husbands more than their children.

*Arsalankhan, who did not know that Alexander and Araqit were reconciled, sent a sorcerer to fetch her. The sorcerer, disguised as a fairy, entered Araqit's chamber and told her that Arsalankhan had gone to Alexander's tent to slay him. Araqit followed the sorcerer. . . .*\*

*Alexander decided to go hunting. Arsalankhan's spies informed him of this and he went to Alexander's hunting-place.*

## How Alexander Was Captured by Arsalankhan, and How Araqit and the Army Rescued Him

*Chasing a deer, Alexander was separated from his army and captured by Arsalankhan, but later Araqit rescued him. Arsalankhan was seriously wounded.*

*Meanwhile 30,000 soldiers from the army of the Turks came to Alexander and accepted Islam.*

The next day the angel came to Alexander and before the King asked him anything, the angel said, "O Alexander, you went from one end of the world to the other, you shed blood justly and unjustly, and you did

---

\*One leaf is missing from the manuscript.

many good deeds; but none of your wars against the infidels and none of your victories was better than the destruction of the giants and the Zangis.[77] You must now finish the war with the infidel Turks; then you will have accomplished everything." "You had said to me that I would remain here no more than five months. Now four months have passed, and if Arsalankhan enters the fort our task will become difficult and will take longer," said Alexander. The angel answered, "The fort of the Zangis, the garden, and the victory over Shahmalik were won in four months. The war against Arsalankhan will end in two or three days, for two or three days remain before you conquer the city. Then a woman will appear who will incite the city to rebel against you and you will lose it again. There are many wonders in store for you. It is not wise to leave this region before you have given this land to believers to rule. You will not stay long in the rising-place of the sun, but will cross that land in two days, for there is none to block your way. It is here in Arsalankhan's dominion that you will suffer. However, victory will be yours in the end, and order will be restored. Then you will go to Jabalsa[78] and see those wonders, and you will go as far as Bayn al-Saddayn, and do much good."

When the King heard this, his hope for life increased and he rejoiced. Then he said to the angel, "Shall we permit him to enter the fort?" "Yes," said the angel. "Little is left of his life; the nuisance he has caused will end before long. One more trial is ahead of you and many more wonders. But the trials will end in rich rewards, and with the wonders there will be good tidings for the Hereafter."

The King said no more. The angel disappeared and Alexander allowed Arsalankhan to enter the fort. There were twenty-four gates around the city.

## How Arsalankhan Was Captured and Killed by Araqit, and the City Conquered

*In the final battle between the two armies Arsalankhan was captured and killed by Araqit. Following his victory, the citizens asked Alexander to give them amnesty, enter their city, and ascend the throne.*

*Congratulating Alexander on his victory, the angel instructed him to remain in that land until the citizens accepted Islam.*

*Alexander divided the land among several rulers and brought justice to that region.*

One day the King mounted and went to Zubaydah's cloister. He said his prayer, weeping and pleading before God. Then a mysterious voice called upon him, saying, "O Alexander! Have you not had your fill of this world? You have conquered the whole world; you are in a paradise of blessings: the city, the garden, and the fort are all filled with silver and gold. What more do you want? Greed has made you restless. Stay and hasten not, for many years you will sleep in the grave." When the King heard these words, he stayed in the land and from every part kings and princes came to his presence and gave him riches and rare, precious gifts. And the King remained there, waiting.

One night the King was in the garden with Araqit beside him; they were both sound asleep. Suddenly the fairies came and said to Araqit, "O Lady! This is no time for sleep, for Yaqutmalik, your uncle's daughter, has come with 100,000 fairies to fight the King. She claims that she seeks to avenge the blood of her father, Ruvid. She has entered the city and seized the throne. Her troops have killed whoever they found and the majority of the citizens have sworn allegiance to them. Our troops have fled from the city." The King was astounded. He looked at Araqit, who had turned pale and was trembling with fear. "What is it with you?" asked the King. "O King," she said, "I knew of this before. Death is more pleasant to me than these tidings. I wish it were thousands of infidel Turks and not these fairies."

There were several things she feared. One was that Yaqutmalik far exceeded her in beauty: her father was a fairy but her mother was human, and she favored human beings. Moreover, she was so strong that in battle ten like Araqit were no match for her. Most of all, Araqit feared her because she knew that Yaqutmalik desired King Alexander. She also feared that Yaqutmalik would blame her for having sacrificed her kingship to love. Again, she wondered if there were a battle between Yaqutmalik and the King, who would come to her aid.

Yaqutmalik was exquisitely beautiful and graceful. She had given hope to 100,000 princes, but had gratified no one and remained a sealed virgin. And she was younger than Araqit. Alexander was perplexed.

By God's grace we shall live rightfully and prosper.

# The Events Concerning Araquit, King Alexander, Yaqutmalik, and the Fairies

*Yaqutmalik entered the city with her vast army. The two armies engaged in battle, and Alexander killed seventy men from her army in combat.*

*In reality, Yaqutmalik had come after Alexander. She had heard much about him and hoped that the King would marry her. But she pretended to have come to avenge the death of her father so that people would not blame her.*

*On the second day of the battle, Alexander defeated Yaqutmalik's mother and captured her. She was exchanged for the King's wives who had been detained by Yaqutmalik after she conquered the city.*

*In the third battle, Yaqutmalik encountered Araqit in combat.*

"Welcome!" said Araqit to Yaqutmalik. "I wonder what I have done to you that you have left your land and come to win my dominion and my husband. What do you mean by this?" Yaqutmalik was offended by these words. She said to Araqit, "You shameless woman! This land belonged to me and my husband. What has come over you that you have given up a seventy-year-old sovereignty in order to follow your sweetheart? You gave your name and kingship to your sweetheart, and today you have come to the field to fight with me in order to please him. I wonder what this man does that you have become so captivated and infatuated with him." Araqit replied, "I am not infatuated with him. He won my kingdom and my kingship by the sword. My life too was in danger; I could not give up my life just because I had lost my kingdom. A woman cannot help but take a husband, and in the entire world there is no husband better than he. Today, praised be God, he is the King of the East and the West. What mischief has come over you, that you have left your home and come here? Have you any doubt that you and 10,000 like you are no match for him?" "I seek to avenge the blood of my father and my husband," Yaqutmalik replied. Then they attacked each other and struggled long. They fought until it was time for the evening prayer, but neither gained victory. When the drums signaled that it was time for rest, the two women withdrew from battle and they marveled at each other. Yaqutmalik sent a fairy to Araqit as messenger, saying, "You shameless woman! See what you have done. You dared confront me and fight with me! Now wait for your reward."

*The angel appeared to Alexander and told him that he would conquer Yaqutmalik in the end, but that victory would not be won without effort.*

*In order to intimidate Alexander, Yaqutmalik made her vast army parade in the field. When Alexander saw the size of her army he was afraid that the Turks among his men would be too frightened to fight. He sent a fairy to draw the magic circle around Yaqutmalik's army. The enemy was thus imprisoned within the circle. Then Alexander challenged Yaqutmalik to combat.*

Araqit attacked Yaqutmalik's army with 1,400 fairies in the name of God, and nearly 10,000 of the enemy were killed within the magic circle. Araqit's fairies fought, uttering the name of God.

Yaqutmalik realized that what they did was by virtue of that name. She uttered the name, and having made her escape from the magic circle, fled to the city. Araqit attacked the right wing of the enemy and broke their lines. Storytellers claim that on that day 80,000 men and fairies were slain. The rest of the fairies fled to the city and shut the gates, and when Yaqutmalik came to the city, she summoned the nobles and the chiefs of the army, and she said, "It is useless to fight them; we cannot withstand that army. They call us fairies because we can change appearance 1,000 times in an hour, travel the waters without a boat, or fly in the air. Let us contrive a scheme and capture this man. Then we will do to him what we must."

She called the chief of the fairies and asked, "How can we capture Alexander?" The chief replied, "I will assume Araqit's appearance and lure the King out of his camping-ground. You must be ready there. Then I will surrender him to you." "I will go with you," said a fairy to the chief. "I will make you the chief of the army," Yaqutmalik said to him, "if you carry out this scheme." When night came, Yaqutmalik sent 1,000 fairies with him and he told them to wait for him in a certain place until he returned. Then he assumed Araqit's appearance and went to King Alexander's quarters. He found the King sleeping beside Araqit. Therefore he changed his scheme, assumed Zubaydah's appearance and clothing, and returned to find Alexander awake, preparing to say his prayers. And Lady Araqit was with the King. The fairy entered, disguised as Zubaydah. When Alexander saw the fairy he said, "What is it, O Zubaydah?" "O King, it is a secret matter. Rise and come with me, but come alone. Lady Araqit will take offense, for I am taking you when it is her turn. But a grave matter has occurred." The King rose. He held her by the hand and they walked for a brief while. Araqit took the sword and followed to see where she was taking the King. By chance, she uttered the name of God and the fairy resumed his real appearance. "You villain! Where are you taking the King?" she cried and with one blow cut off the fairy's head. Then Araqit said to the King, "These fairies are crafty and cunning, and they can do mighty deeds, especially my uncle's daughter, who can assume any appearance she wants. They are not like me, who gave up treachery and cunning, kingdom, kingship, and home, all for the King, only to be reproached by fairy and man alike. But I gave up all in order to serve the King. Giants, fairies, and mankind are all created by God. All my deeds were done in the name of God, and as long as God is on our side the schemes of the fairies will do us no harm."

Then the King said, "Now Yaqutmalik is in the city while we are in the field. She is comfortable and at ease, while we must hasten to leave. I wonder what we should do." Then he sent a messenger to Lady Yaqutmalik again, saying, "We have waited too long. Bring your army and let us fight. You have lingered in the city too long. How dare you plot to deceive me? The giants, the fairies, the Davalpayan, and the Elephant-ears were all destroyed and brought to ruin through me. Now it is your turn. I intended to let you pass; I thought you would return if treated with leniency, and would leave this territory alone. But you refuse to obey me. Now I will give you three days. If you withdraw from the city, well and good; if not, I will bring you and your army to ruin." The messenger delivered the message.

When Yaqutmalik heard the message, she said, "He thinks nothing of me." She answered, "You are wrong to put me and my army in the same order with them. For I am not the kind who would become infatuated with you and abandon kingdom and kingship. I have no grudge against you; I want to revenge myself upon Araqit. Surrender her to me and leave in peace."

When the King heard her answer he said, "This is a foul woman. We shall send her no more messengers. It is the citizens who are to blame because they swore allegiance to her. For if there were two factions and they disagreed, they would not have sworn allegiance." The citizens included some Muslims and some infidels who pretended to have accepted the faith for fear of the King's sword. The heathens, who had the upper hand, had sworn allegiance to Yaqutmalik.

In his anger the King ordered the men to mount their horses, saying, "I will do to this fairy woman today what shall be remembered as long as this world lasts." But he was distressed and hoped that what Araqit had predicted would not come true. Then the King and the army mounted and they went to the city and found the gates open. Each group went to a different gate and they killed all those who were at the city gates. Yaqutmalik was asleep in the palace. The King entered the palace and sat upon the throne. His men were scattered throughout the city and some remained outside the gates. The city was big and had twenty-four gates; the distance from one gate to the next was one parasang.

When Yaqutmalik learned what had happened she hid under the ground; of her fairies, 10,000 had perished. Meanwhile, Alexander ascended the throne. Yaqutmalik went to join the fairies and when she realized that the King was at ease and felt secure, she flew and with her army returned to the city. But the King drew the magic circle around himself. They wanted to attack the King, but were prevented by the circle. They continued coming forward and returning until they grew weary. And they wondered, saying, "Is this man Solomon, who put a spell on the giants and the fairies?"

And King Alexander ordered his men to shoot at the fairies with arrows until they retreated. Yaqutmalik's army left the city for Zubaydah's cloister. Those who had survived gathered there and were joined by Yaqutmalik. She found the cloister pleasant and she said, "It was our fault not to have come here from the first."

When the King learned that she had left, he dealt with the affairs of the city. The supporters of the King and the believers were all in prison, for they had opposed Yaqutmalik. The King set them all free. One thousand of his opponents were beheaded, their bodies were suspended from the gates, and their houses were plundered. The King established justice in that land, and he sent the princes to the gates. And the King . . .*

---

*The manuscript breaks off here.

# A Glossary of Characters' Names

‘ANBAR: Son of Rāfi‘ the Zangī, captured by Arāqīt.
ARĀQĪT: Fairy queen who fought Alexander and eventually became his wife.
ARSALĀNKHĀN: Succeeded his brother, Shahmalik, fell in love with Arāqīt, and died at her hand.
ARASṬAṬĀLĪS (Aristotle): Alexander's minister.
AYĀZ: Arsalānkhān's second messenger to Alexander.
ĀZĀDBAKHT: King of Kashmir, defeated by Alexander.
BARQAṬĪSAH: Alexander's wife and the daughter of the King of Egypt.
BUQRĀQUZ: Shahmalik's son, pardoned by Alexander at first but eventually killed by him.
CUPBEARER'S WIFE: Shahmalik's messenger and later Alexander's spy.
DĀRĀB (Darius): King of Iran, defeated by Alexander, his elder half-brother.
FARRUKHBAKHT: Āzādbakht's brother, made Kashmir's ruler by Alexander.
FILĪNŪS: Aristotle's son.
FĪLQŪS (Philip): Alexander's grandfather who pretends Alexander is his son.
FŪR (Porus): King of India, beheaded at Alexander's command.
GHĪLĀN: Fairy taken captive by Alexander.
ILYĀS SON OF MUẒAR: Chief of Mecca.
ISKANDAR (Alexander): Hero of the romance, the King of Rūm (Greece or Macedonia) and the Conqueror of the World. He is Dārāb's elder half-brother.
JĀNŪSIBĀR: One of Dārāb's two assassins.
JUNDUL: King of the Zangīs, killed by Alexander.
KAYD: Indian king who makes peace with Alexander.
KASANDAR: King of Oman, who accepts Islam.
KHIDR: Prophet who guides Alexander in his journey to the Land of Darkness.
LAND: Qātil's messenger and later Alexander's spy.
MĀHĀFARĪN: Āzādbakhat's daughter and Alexander's wife.
MĀHYĀR: One of Dārāb's two assassins.
MANKŪS: King of the Zinj, captured by Alexander.
MUNẒAR: King of Yemen.
NĀHĪD: Porus's daughter and Alexander's wife.
PĪRŪZ OF ṬŪS: One of the Persian princes in Alexander's army.

QARĀKHĀN: King of Transoxania.
QĪDĀFAH (Candace): Queen of Andalusia.
QAYMĀZ: Arsalānkhān's messenger to Alexander.
QAYMŪN: One of Arsalānkhān's princes who shelters Alexander (when he is taken captive) and gives him his daughter.
RĀFIʿ: Brother of Qātil, killed in war against Alexander.
RUSHANAK (Roxana): Dārāb's wife.
RUVĪD: Arāqīt's uncle imprisoned by Alexander.
SHAHMALIK: King of Ṭaghmāj, captured by Arāqīt after a long period of war and hanged.
SINDAH: Giant captured by Alexander.
SITĀRAH: Alexander's wife and the daughter of the King of Egypt.
SUHAYL: Daughter of the King of Yemen, in love with Alexander after she sees him in a dream.
ṬAFQĀJ: Relative of Shahmalik, in love with Arāqīt and eventually killed by her.
ṬAMGHĀJ: King of Divas
ṬARZAK: One of Arsalankhān's princes who joins Alexander.
ṬĪNŪSH: Candace's son and the King of Egypt's son-in-law.
TŪRĀNMALIK: Shahmalik's brother, captured with his son in combat by Alexander's wife.
YĀQŪTMALIK: Arāqīt's cousin who attacks Alexander and is in love with him.
ZUBAYDAH: Pious maiden whom Alexander marries.

# APPENDIX I

# Persian Alexander - Romances

## Sources

THE MEDIEVAL KNOWLEDGE of Alexander was derived from three sources: historical accounts of the life of Alexander, such as those written by Quintus Curtius, Justin, and Orosius; material belonging to the Pseudo-Callisthenes tradition which, while retaining a good deal of historical truth, made Alexander the hero of many legendary accounts and fabulous adventures; and the fabulous accounts of the life of Alexander in which historical truth is almost entirely overshadowed by fabulous and fantastic adventures ascribed to the hero.

The Pseudo-Callisthenes, an anonymous Greek Alexander-romance believed to have been written between 200 B.C. and A.D. 300, has four main branches known as the $\alpha$, $\beta$, $\gamma$, and *$\delta$ recensions. Persian Alexander-romances belong to the *$\delta$ recension.[1] Although no Greek manuscript is known for this recension, that such a text once existed is evidenced by the preface of Archpresbyter Leo of Naples to his Latin translation *Nativitas et Victoria Alexandri Magni Regis*, where Leo indicates that his translation is being made from a Greek source.[2] Leo's version, which was done about A.D. 950, was enlarged at some time in the eleventh century through the addition of materials from *Commonitorium Palladii*,[3] *Dindimus de Bragmanibus*,[4] *Collatio Alexandri Cum Dindimo per Litteras facta*,[5] and *Epistola Alexandri ad Aristotelem*.[6] This enlarged version is known as *Historia de Preliis I*$^1$. From this the I$^2$ *Historia de Preliis* was made with interpolations from Orosius's *Historia adversum paganos libri septem*, Pseudo-Methodius for Gog and Magog, *Pseudo-Epiphanius* for the bones of Jeremiah, Josephus for the visit to

Jerusalem, Valerius Maximus, and further extracts from *Epistola ad Aristotelem* and the Brahman texts.[7] *Leo's text is the ultimate source of most romances of Alexander written in the Middle Ages in Europe.*

In the East, a Pahlavi translation of the *δ became the source of Syriac, Persian, Arabic, and Ethiopic romances. The Pahlavi text is now lost, but the sixth-century Syriac translation of it is evidence that it was a close rendition of the Greek manuscript.[8] For example, it preserved the Pseudo-Callisthenes account of Alexander's birth, which was replaced with a Persian account in most Persian and Arabic histories and romances. The Syriac version was translated into Arabic in the ninth century. The Arabic version, now lost, was the source of the Ethiopic version done between the fourteenth and the sixteenth century.[9]

While the Pseudo-Callisthenes tradition in the West has been the subject of numerous studies, the Persian Pseudo-Callisthenes and fabulous Alexander-romances form a relatively unexplored area in the scholarship of Alexander literature. I have therefore provided summaries of the Persian Alexander-romances and attempted to establish the position of these texts in the *δ recension. Furthermore, the Appendix will briefly note the mention of Alexander in pre-Islamic Persian writings and in material written about Alexander in Persian and Arabic in the Islamic era in sources other than romances. These nonfiction materials influenced the portrait of Alexander in Persian literature.

The Persian romances of Alexander by Firdawsī, Nizāmī, Jāmī, Ṭarsūsī, and the anonymous *Iskandarnāmah*, written between the eleventh and the fifteenth century, differ greatly in their fidelity to the Pseudo-Callisthenes. Firdawsī's version is a fairly faithful rendition of the *δ recension, and, in the main, corresponds to the Syriac text. Nizāmī and Jāmī, under the influence of the tradition presented in the work of Hunayn ibn Ishāq (see pp. 177, 219), move farther from the *δ text. Finally, in the version of Ṭarsūsī and in *Iskandarnāmah*, we deal with fabulous accounts of Alexander. Persian and Islamic folklore and legendry as well as the Koran and other Arabic sources have contributed to these versions. Here Alexander is celebrated not only as a king and conqueror but also as a sage and prophet. A summary of the Persian versions mentioned above will be given here, and a comparative study of

# APPENDIX I. PERSIAN ALEXANDER-ROMANCES

these romances with the pseudo-Callisthenes,[10] the Syriac, and the Ethiopic versions will be carried out in the notes.

## Firdawsī's Version

In Firdawsī's *Shāhnāmah* (Book of Kings: A.D. 1010), the reigns of Dārāb, his son Dārā (Darius), and Alexander form a metrical version of the *δ Pseudo-Callisthenes, some 3,000 dictichs long.[11]

In the section on the reign of Dārāb, Firdawsī gives an account of the war between Dārāb and Philip, the peace between the two kings (pp. 22–25),[12] and the marriage of Dārāb and Philip's daughter, Nāhīd. Noticing that his bride had a foul breath, Dārāb sent her back to her father, ignorant that she was pregnant. Philip kept her pregnancy secret, and when she gave birth, he pretended that he was the father and the child was born to him by a concubine.[13] At the time of Alexander's birth a mare gave birth to a foal with a body like that of a lion. Philip took this as an auspicious sign (pp. 26–27).[14] Alexander grew into a wise and intelligent youth, receiving the education that suited a king (p. 27).[15]

In Iran, Dārā, Dārāb's son by a second wife, became king after the death of his father (pp. 27–28), and in Macedonia Alexander succeeded Philip. Alexander followed Aristotle's wise counsel in all he did (pp. 35–36).[16]

When Alexander's reign was established in Rūm, Dārā sent his messengers to him, demanding tribute. Alexander refused to pay the tribute that Philip used to send Dārāb annually (p. 36).[17] He began his expedition around the world, went to Egypt, and defeated the king of that land (pp. 36–37).[18] Hearing of this event, Dārā marched toward Rūm with his army (p. 37).

Disguised as a messenger, Alexander visited Dārā and told him that Alexander did not mean to fight him; the purpose of his expedition was only to see the world. "Are you not Alexander?" asked Dārā, suspecting the messenger. But Alexander insisted that he was only a messenger. While drinking wine in Dārā's presence, Alexander put the empty gold cups in his breast. Asked why, he explained that this was the custom in

Rūm. In the course of the banquet the messenger who had been sent to Alexander in Rūm recognized him, but Alexander escaped before they could capture him (pp. 38–41).[19]

Alexander defeated Dārā in three battles and the latter fled to Kerman. Alexander went to Persepolis, giving the Iranians amnesty (pp. 42–48).[20] He took Dārā's family captive and refused to make peace with him (pp. 49–50).[21]

Dārā wrote to Porus, the king of India, for aid (p. 51). This angered Alexander and he began another battle, in the course of which Dārā was stabbed by two of his own ministers who hoped to be rewarded by Alexander (pp. 50–52).[22] Alexander placed the head of the dying Dārā in his lap and wept, confessing that he was Dārā's brother. Dārā asked him to marry his daughter Rushanak (Roxana), hoping that she might bear a son who would rekindle the sacred fire of Zoroaster and preserve the customs of the Persians. Alexander agreed (pp. 50–55).[23]

After Dārā's burial, Alexander put the assassins to death (p. 56).[24] He went to Isfahan, assuring Dārā's family of his protection. In his letter to the nobles of Iran, he called himself a Kiyānīd king (i.e., a king of the same dynasty as Dārā), and promised to rule with justice (pp. 57–59). He made fair promises to the Persians, assuring them that he would hear all who sought justice from him (p. 85).[25] Then he wrote to Dārā's wife and daughter. Dārā's wife wished him well; now Alexander was their Dārā, she said. Alexander's mother visited Dārā's wife and daughter and offered them gifts. Later, Alexander married Rushanak, was pleased with her, and loved her dearly (pp. 87–91).[26]

"Thus says the Pahlavi writer," says Firdawsī, starting the long episode of Kayd, the king of India, who had ten dreams, the first of which foretold Alexander's arrival. The interpreter advised Kayd to give Alexander the four wonderful things he had: his daughter, his physician, his philosopher, and a cup the contents of which would never decrease (pp. 91–97). When Alexander called Kayd to his presence, the latter sent him the four wonderful things and they made peace.[27] Alexander married Kayd's daughter according to the Christian faith.[28] He tested the other gifts and was pleased with them (pp. 104–10).

Alexander was very fond of women. His physician therefore warned him that overindulgence precipitated old age, and made him a medicine, because he had grown very weak. Later, seeing that Alexander was sleeping alone, he threw away the medicine, explaining that since Alexander was not sleeping with women he no longer needed the medicine (p. 108).[29]

Alexander wrote to Porus and called him to his presence.[30] When Porus refused to obey him, he marched toward India. But his men, who were weary of war, were unwilling to follow him. Alexander admonished them (pp. 111–14).[31] In the battle with Porus, Alexander's men lost heart when they saw the elephants in the Indian army. Alexander built horses and horsemen out of iron, filled them with naphtha, and, when the elephants approached, set the iron horses on fire, causing the elephants to retreat. Alexander killed Porus in single combat (pp. 115–17).[32]

Afterward, Alexander went to the pilgrimage of the Ka'bah and the House of God, built by the prophet Abraham. He restored the position of the chief of Mecca to the true heir and went to Jiddah, where he built ships (pp. 119–21).[33] In Egypt, Alexander made peace with the King, and stayed there for a year (pp. 121–22). Meanwhile, Candace, the Queen of Andalusia, sent a painter to Egypt, and he painted Alexander's portrait for her.

Alexander wrote to Candace and called her to his presence. When she refused to come, Alexander marched toward Andalusia and on his way fought and killed King Faryār, the father-in-law of Candace's son. The son and his wife were taken captive. Alexander instructed a minister to pretend that he was Alexander, and sentence Candace's son to death. Alexander would then beg the minister to pardon the son. The minister would do so, and then send Alexander as a messenger to Candace.

This was done. But Candace recognized Alexander, and when he delivered his message, demanding that she either obey Alexander or prepare for war, she replied, "You are very brave, Alexander. You act as your own messenger." Upon Alexander's denial, she showed him his portrait. Finding himself in her power, Alexander was angry and embarrassed. But Candace did not reveal his identity to her court. Alone with Candace, he swore by the Christian faith never to trouble her or her sons again. Candace sent many gifts to his camp (pp. 123–43).[34]

Continuing his expedition, Alexander visited the unworldly Brahmans and asked them many questions. They called Alexander a slave of avarice and admonished him for having shed much blood. When Alexander told them to request something from him, they asked for immortality. "I have no power against death," said Alexander. "Why, then, since you are but a mortal, have you caused the world so much suffering?" they asked. Alexander replied that he had only fulfilled God's will (pp. 143–47).[35] He then came upon an endless sea and a region where men veiled their faces. The speech of the people was strange, and they fed upon fish (p. 148).[36]

Sailing upon the sea, Alexander saw a great mountain emerge from the water. Some of his men rowed toward it in a boat and discovered it to be an enormous fish. The fish dived into the water, causing the boat to sink (p. 147). Afterward, Alexander reached a pleasant meadow where his men rested. At night they were set upon by snakes, scorpions, boars, and lions (pp. 148–49).

Crossing this region, Alexander reached the land of Habash and fought its gigantic, black inhabitants. At night, however, his men were attacked by wolves, and this caused Alexander to leave in haste (pp. 149–50).[37] He then reached the land of the Narmpāyān and killed many of them in battle (p. 150).[38] In the land of the Arabs he received many gifts from the inhabitants and killed the dragon that plagued them (pp. 151–52).[39]

On a high mountain Alexander found a dead body upon a throne and a voice warned him that his death was near (pp. 152–53). Alexander went to Harūm (Amazon) and wrote a letter to the chief of that land, calling her to his presence (pp. 153–54). The chief of the Amazons sent him a letter about the land and customs of the Amazons (pp. 154–55). On their way to meet the Amazons the soldiers crossed a region where many of them died of cold, and an area where they seemed to pass through fire (pp. 156–57). The Amazons gave Alexander many gifts (p. 157).[40]

Then Alexander went toward the West, meeting a people who had red hair and yellow skin. An old man told him of the spring where the sun set, and of the Land of Darkness and the Water of Life. Alexander visited the spring where the sun set. Searching for the Water of Life, Alexander entered the Land of Darkness, guided by the prophet Khidr. But the two were separated and only Khidr found the Water and drank of it. Alexander reached a mountain where he was addressed by two birds. He climbed the mountain and saw the angel Isrāfīl, who admonished him for his cupidity. Alexander said that it was his fate to go around the world and see the open and the hidden. He joined his men, and they left the Land of Darkness, crossing a gravel of rubies on their way (pp. 159-62).[41] In the East, Alexander built a barrier against Gog and Magog (pp. 163-65).[42]

Alexander came upon a house made of ruby on a mountain. Inside, he found a saltwater spring and a dead creature on a throne. A mysterious voice warned Alexander that his death was near and ordered him to return (p. 166). His death was also prophesied by two talking trees which told him that he would die after he had ruled for fourteen years and that he would never return to Rūm (pp. 167-69).[43]

Disguised as a messenger, Alexander went to the Emperor of China, and, after receiving many gifts, returned to his men (pp. 169-74). In Sind, the inhabitants fought Alexander and almost all were slain by him (p. 157). Later, Alexander reached Yemen, where the King went to his presence and they made peace (pp. 175-76).

Alexander decided to kill the Persian princes because he feared that they would attack Rūm after his death. But following Aristotle's counsel, he divided the land among them (pp. 178-80).[44] In Babylon a woman gave birth to a monstrous child, half-man, half-beast; the event was interpreted as an omen of Alexander's death (pp. 180-81).[45] Alexander wrote to his mother, begging her not to grieve over his death (p. 181). "If Roxana bears a boy," he said, "he shall be my heir. But if she bears a girl, give her in marriage to Philip's son. Send my other wife, Kayd's daughter, to India with all her dowry" (pp. 181-83).[46]

Alexander was buried in Alexandria (pp. 183-85). The Persian and Greek sages moralized upon his coffin (pp. 187-89).[47]

## Niẓāmī's Version

Niẓāmī's metrical version of the Alexander story (A.D. 1191) is in two parts: *Sharafnāmah*, which gives the account of Alexander as a king and a warrior, and *Iqbālnāmah yā Khiradnāmah-yi Iskandarī*, which celebrates him as a sage and a prophet.⁴⁸ Niẓāmī's version contains more interpolations than Firdawsī's. In the beginning of the poem Niẓāmī declares that he will write of Alexander first as a king and conqueror, then as a sage, and finally as a prophet (*Sharafnāmah*, pp. 50–54). From the legends of Alexander, he informs the reader, he has chosen what is credible and changed the order of the episodes. Since the various versions of the story of Alexander did not agree, he made selections from each source, drawing upon new versions of the history of Alexander, and Jewish, Christian, and Pahlavi sources (pp. 54–55). In Niẓāmī's retelling of the story, didactic and lyrical passages alternate with episodes relating to Alexander. These nonnarrative passages are omitted from the following summary.

Philip, who was a just king, was defeated by Dārā and agreed to pay an annual tribute. Alexander refused to pay the tribute when he succeeded Philip (pp. 80–81).

Some claim that Alexander was the son of a poor woman who died giving birth to him, and that Philip found and adopted him. Firdawsī made Alexander the son of Dārāb. None of these stories is true. Alexander was the son of Philip (pp. 81–83). At his birth, astrologers cast his horoscope and foretold that he would conquer the whole world. Philip appointed Aristotle's father to be Alexander's teacher. Aristotle, who was Alexander's classmate, would teach him whatever he learned from his father. When Alexander succeeded Philip, he followed Aristotle's counsel in all he did and ruled with justice (pp. 84–89).

The Egyptians resorted to Alexander to protect them against the Zangīs (black citizens of Zinj). Alexander sent a messenger to the chief of the Zangīs, who killed the messenger and drank his blood. To intimidate the Zangīs, Alexander ate the blackened head of a sheep, pretending that it was the head of a Zangī. In the battle with the Zangīs, seventy men from Alexander's army were killed in single combat, until Alexander entered the field. He slew many Zangīs in single combat and defeated the enemy. At his command the Egyptians who had joined forces with the Zangīs were sold as slaves (pp. 95–138).⁴⁹

Alexander built Alexandria in Egypt and showed kindness to the

# APPENDIX I. PERSIAN ALEXANDER-ROMANCES  175

Egyptians.⁵⁰ He returned to Rūm, and sent gifts to Dārā from the booty. The latter accepted the gifts but, being fearful and envious of Alexander, did not thank him as he should have (pp. 136–39).

Some time after this, Dārā's messengers asked Alexander for tribute. When Alexander refused to pay the tribute, Dārā sent him a ball and a rod, implying that Alexander was still a child, and some sesame seeds, symbolic of his vast army. Alexander gave a favorable interpretation to the gifts (pp. 160–61).⁵¹

When the Persians heard that Alexander intended to fight Dārā they rejoiced, because Dārā was an oppressive king (p. 170). A counselor told Dārā that according to a prophecy, a king from Rūm would end the Kiyānīd rule. He advised Dārā to make peace with Alexander, but Dārā rejected his counsel (pp. 171–83). He wrote to Alexander again, calling him a child and asking for tribute (pp. 184–89). Alexander swore by the faith of Abraham that he would destroy the Zoroastrian temples.⁵² He advised Dārā not to seek war (pp. 189–97). But war proved inevitable, and, on the second day of battle two of Dārā's men stabbed Dārā with Alexander's agreement. Yet, regretting what he had done, Alexander wept over the dying Dārā. Dārā asked him to spare the lives of the Persian princes, punish his assassins, and marry Roxana (pp. 204–20).

Alexander became king, gained possession of Dārā's treasures, and sent messengers to the nobles, calling them to obey him. Later, he put the assassins to death (pp. 227–28). Alexander was eager to learn the history of Iran and its kings and heroes (pp. 229–37).⁵³ But being a follower of the faith of Abraham, he destroyed the temples of the fire worshippers and abolished the new-year festivities in which maidens, one day each year, could do as they pleased (pp. 238–40). In Isfahan Alexander came upon a Zoroastrian temple guarded by a maiden in the form of a dragon. A sage who accompanied Alexander made the maiden's talisman ineffective. Alexander gave the maiden to him to be his wife (pp. 241–45).

Alexander sent rich gifts to Dārā's family and married Roxana (pp. 245–56). He ascended the throne in Persepolis and in an address told his subjects that he was sent by God to call them to the true faith. One among those present asked Alexander for a silver coin. Alexander ordered him to ask for a gift worthy of a king. The man asked for the whole world. "This time you asked for more than you deserve," said Alexander (pp. 258–63).[54]

Before setting out on his expedition Alexander divided Iran among several princes. He sent Roxana and Aristotle to Rūm. At his command, many Persian books were sent to Rūm to be translated. In Rūm, Roxana gave birth to a boy whom they called Iskandarūs (pp. 265–69).

Alexander went to Arabia and visited the House of God in Mecca (pp. 271–72). After visiting Yemen and Iraq he went to Armenia to abolish the worship of fire (pp. 273–74). From there he went to Bardaʿ, formerly called Harūm,[55] ruled by Nūshābah (Candace), a beautiful and wise queen who had thousands of slaves and a large army. She lived with women in a place where men were not allowed.

Nūshābah sent Alexander provisions; when he went to her as a messenger, she recognized him, because she had his portrait. She told Alexander that he had better not fight her because there was no honor in defeating a woman; and if she defeated him, he would be disgraced. When they sat down to eat, she placed a plate full of gold and rubies before him. "Bring us some food, for these are but stones," said Alexander.[56] "Why, then, have you caused so many wars for these stones?" asked Nūshābah. Alexander replied that she deserved more blame than himself: he had jewels only in his crown, while she had so many that she filled her dishes with them. The two signed a peace treaty (pp. 277–308).

From there Alexander went to Sarīr fort to sit upon Kaykhusraw's throne and drink from Jamshīd's cup. He visited Kaykhusraw's tomb (pp. 325–41), and defeated a ruler who had rebelled against him in Iran (pp. 343–50). He next visited India[57] and China. In China the Emperor went to him as a messenger. Alone with Alexander, he revealed his identity and they made peace. The Emperor gave Alexander many wonderful gifts—among them a hunting bird, a horse, and a maiden (pp. 407–16).[58]

Having built many cities in Transoxania, Alexander was about to return to Rūm when he was informed that the Russians had taken Nūshābah captive and destroyed her kingdom. He fought the Russians in seven battles, defeated them, and rescued Nūshābah (pp. 477–83).[59]

# APPENDIX I. PERSIAN ALEXANDER-ROMANCES 177

Next, Alexander went on a journey to the Land of Darkness.[60] Here, he heard the voice of an angel admonishing him for being unsatisfied even after conquering the whole world. The angel gave him a stone which, when weighed, proved to be equal to a bit of dust. This signified that only the grave could cure Alexander's greed (pp. 498–516).[61]

Alexander reached a city where people would not die; instead, they would hear their names called from a mountain, would climb the mountain, and disappear (pp. 517–20).

When Alexander returned to Rūm, the whole world was ruled under rulers established by him. Then God appointed him as a prophet and he started a second journey, this time to the mountains and the wildernesses of the earth (pp. 520–24).

The second book of Niẓāmī, *Iqbālnāmah yā Khiradnāmah*, belongs to the genre represented in Ḥunayn ibn Isḥāq's ninth-century *Kitāb nawādir al-falāsifah wa-al-ḥukamā' wa ādāb al-muʿallimīn wa-al-qudamā'*[62] and Mubashshir ibn Fatik's eleventh-century *Mukhtār al-ḥikam wa maḥāsin al-kilam*,[63] which gave accounts of the lives of philosophers and a collection of their wise sayings.[64] Popular with Arab writers, the genre perhaps originated from the Greek, but no Greek text is extant. In Mubashshir's work, where Alexander is treated as one of the philosophers, a section on his life (pp. 243–51) is followed by a collection of his wise sayings (pp. 243–51). Following this tradition in *Iqbālnāmah*, Niẓāmī presents Alexander as a sage in the company of sages, as we shall see in the following summary.

Alexander announced that in his court a man's status would depend on the degree of his learning. The Greeks were thus encouraged to compete for knowledge, and they gained fame for their learning. Alexander was always accompanied by fighting men, sorcerers, orators, sages, devout men, and prophets (pp. 38–41).

There was much rivalry among the philosophers in Alexander's court. Once, being jealous of Hermes, the philosophers rejected his right sayings. Hermes cursed them, causing them to die. Alexander heard of this and praised Hermes (pp. 82–85).

One day, in the presence of Alexander and the philosophers, Aristotle claimed to be above all learned men. Plato, who was more learned than Aristotle, was displeased. He built an instrument which, when played, would render man and beast unconscious. A different tune played on the instrument would bring them back to consciousness. Aristotle attempted to do the same but failed and had to acknowledge Plato's supremacy (pp. 86-92).

Alexander invited Socrates to visit him. The philosopher, who led an ascetic life, refused to go, explaining that being a servant of God, he was Alexander's master; whereas if he went to Alexander, he would become Alexander's subject. When Alexander visited him, Socrates admonished him for his avarice. Alexander asked Socrates to impart to him of his wisdom, and Socrates did so (pp. 97-108).[65]

A philosopher who was a fire worshipper came to Alexander from India, agreeing to forgo the worship of fire if Alexander could answer his questions on the Creator, life after death, and the like. Alexander answered the questions and the Indian turned to God (pp. 108-20).

Alexander met with seven philosophers: Aristotle, Balīnās (Appolonios), Socrates, Plato, Vālis, Farfūriūs (Porphyrios), and Hermes. He asked them about the creation of the world. Each of the seven sages gave a theory of creation. The theories of Alexander and Niẓāmī are given last (pp. 120-34). Having learned about God's creation, Alexander sought God himself. God chose Alexander as a prophet[66] and instructed him to go around the world and call the people to the way of God (pp. 135-40). When Alexander asked Aristotle, Socrates, and Plato to give him counsel on his mission, they each gave him a book of wisdom (pp. 141-64). Alexander made his son heir to the throne, and Alexander's mother ruled in his absence.

He went to Alexandria with a great army, and built a tower and a magic mirror in that city. In Jerusalem Alexander fought an enemy of God who persecuted the believers.[67] He then reached the sea that surrounded the earth. From there he went to the river Nile, and later reached a cliff but could not climb it, because anyone who attempted to do so would laugh and fly away like a bird (pp. 172-77).

Alexander reached the Garden of Iram built by Shattād and met tribes that lived in caves and fed upon whatever they could get from hunting.[68]

# APPENDIX I. PERSIAN ALEXANDER-ROMANCES 179

He was told of a people who lived 500 years without getting old (pp. 182–88), and came upon a tribe who worshipped the dried-up human skull. Alexander converted them to the way of God (p. 189).

Alexander went to India and destroyed the temples of the idolaters. In China he converted the Emperor. Continuing on his voyage, Alexander saw the sirens whose voice would make a man unconscious (pp. 202–5). He crossed the China Sea, and, reaching the point beyond which man could not go, he went to the North and built the barrier against Gog and Magog (pp. 224–26). He visited the land of the people who had no need to lock their houses, because they were all righteous (pp. 227–32).

Alexander heard a voice ordering him to return, and warning that little was left of his life. Shortly afterward, he became ill near Babylon; because he thought that he had been poisoned, all cures failed (pp. 236–38).[69] He made his will and wrote a letter to his mother, begging her not to grieve over his death. He instructed her to give a banquet and ask that only those who had never experienced sorrow eat of the food. Alexander knew that they all would refrain from food and she would realize that she was not alone in suffering the death of a beloved (pp. 247–57).[70] Alexander's son, Iskandarūs, refused to become king. An account of the remainder of each philosopher's life concludes *Iqbālnāmah*.

## Jāmī's Version

Jāmī's *Khiradnāmah-yi Iskandarī* (Book of Alexander's Wisdom: A.D. 1485–91) is an imitation of Niẓāmī's *Iqbālnāmah*. In this version materials on Alexander alternate with moral tales not related to him. In the following summary, these non-Alexander tales have beem omitted.

Philip entrusted Alexander to Aristotle to teach him all learning and to breed in him the love of justice. Through the knowledge of God's creation, Alexander came to know God himself (pp. 930–32). Philip tested Alexander, was satisfied with his learning, and made him his heir. At Philip's request, Artistotle wrote a book about the secrets of kingship for Alexander (pp. 933–34).[71]

After Philip's death, Alexander addressed the people, saying that he was one like themselves, not superior to them, and asking them to choose themselves a ruler. They chose Alexander (pp. 937–38).

At Alexander's command, the wise sayings of the philosophers were written in gold. Aristotle, Plato, and Socrates each wrote him a book of wisdom (pp. 938–49).

Alexander invited Socrates to his palace, and, when Socrates rejected the invitation, Alexander visited him and asked the philosopher to make a request from him. Socrates asked him to step out of his sun.[72] Socrates' wise sayings follow this episode (pp. 949–51). An account of the books of wisdom of Buqrāt (Hippocrates), Pythagoras, Isqilīnūs, and Hermes follows (pp. 953–63). After these books were written, Alexander set out on his expedition to Ethiopia, fought Dārā, and visited India, China, Russia, Khvarazm, and the Land of Darkness. He called the people to the way of God, built many cities, and made a barrier against Gog and Magog. Alexander himself was a sage, and on his expedition he was accompanied by sages and prophets (pp. 964–65). He wrote a book of wisdom which, among his wise sayings, included his answer when Dārā requested him to marry his daughter. "If I marry Roxana," Alexander said, "I will love her so much that I will be ruled by her. Then people will say that Alexander won the world from Dārā only to surrender it to Dārā's daughter" (pp. 966–68).

Alexander's statement is followed by stories on the wiles of women, and counsel to young men to remain single and be cautious against becoming enslaved to women (pp. 969–70).[73] The romance continues as follows.

In China, the Emperor sent Alexander a maiden, a slave, and a garment. By these gifts he meant to say that all one needed in the world was a garment to wear, a woman to sleep with, and a slave to serve one, and that Alexander could get no more than these even if he conquered the whole world. Alexander made peace with the Emperor (pp. 972–74).

He then wrote to his mother and to Aristotle. Upon his request, Aristotle sent him a letter full of wise sayings (pp. 980–82). Alexander visited the Brahmans (pp. 982–83). He reached a righteous people who had no king and no need for locks, because there were no thieves among them. They had dug graves at their doors to remind them of death (pp. 984-88).⁷⁴

Alexander visited a prince who had abandoned kingship and lived in a graveyard, pondering upon the skulls of the dead. He told Alexander that he had tried to tell the skull of a king from that of a beggar but had failed (pp. 987-89). Reaching the sea Alexander walked over the water as one would walk on land (p. 989).⁷⁵ He reached the Qāf mountain and conversed with an angel.

It had been prophesied that Alexander would die in a land made of iron under a sky made of gold. It came to pass one day, that when the army was crossing a hot region, Alexander's nose bled. A soldier spread an iron armor on the ground for Alexander to lie upon, while another held a golden shield over Alexander to protect him from the sun. Alexander realized that his death was near.

He wrote to his mother and gave instructions for his burial. The philosophers, ten in number, moralized upon his death (pp. 997-1002). Alexander's body was carried to Alexandria (pp. 1002-9).

## Ṭarsūsī's Version

The twelfth-century *Dārābnāmah* by Ṭarsūsī is a long prose romance (1,159 pages in the two-volume printed text)⁷⁶ dealing with the lives of Bahman, Dārāb, Dārā, and Alexander. The sections that concern us here are the least two. Ṭarsūsī gives the Persian version of Alexander's birth, with the difference that in his account Nāhīd, Philip's daughter, gives birth to Alexander in Aristotle's cloister, without Philip's knowledge. She leaves the baby and is later married to the King of Barbar, Fīrūzshāh. The childhood of Alexander (I:391-422) is unlike the account in the Pseudo-Callisthenes. We are told that from Aristotle he learned to interpret dreams and this lore opened the courts of Philip and Fīrūzshāh to him. Fīrūzshāh decided to put Alexander to death. But, Nāhīd, who had recognized Alexander to be her son, told him of his ancestry. Finding the two together, Fīrūzshāh suspected them of adultery. Mother and son escaped to Philip, who made Alexander his heir. Later, Philip and Nāhīd were killed by Philip's sons, and, as a result of several plots, all the princes were slain. Consequently, Alexander became king at the people's request and fought and slew Fīrūzshāh. From this point the romance in its outline vaguely resembles the Pseudo-Callisthenes.

News was brought to Dārā that Alexander claimed to be Dārāb's son. Dārā said that the marriage between his father and Philip's daughter was never consummated. While Alexander discussed Dārā's answer with Aristotle a quarrel developed between them. Aristotle prayed that Alexander lose all his learning. His prayer was heard and Alexander could no longer interpret dreams.

After exchanging letters, Dārā and Alexander finally met in battle. Two of Dārā's ministers stabbed him with the knowledge and agreement of Alexander. Before he died, Dārā asked Alexander to marry his daughter, Būrāndukht. At first, Būrāndukht refused to marry Alexander, who had caused her father's death. But after a series of battles against Alexander (I:457–561; II:1–92), she consented to be his wife. Having ruled for three years, Alexander decided to see the world. He appointed Būrāndukht to rule in his absence.[77]

Alexander went to India to abolish idolatry, but was attacked by cannibal Indians and lost most of his men. Consequently, when Kaydāvar (Kayd) and Porus united against him, Alexander failed to defeat them and called Būrāndukht to his aid (II: 142). She reached India after many adventures (II: 143–228), and with her aid Alexander defeated the Indians and slew Porus. The Indians accepted Islam (II: 228).

In the land of the cannibal Zangīs, Alexander and his men were taken captive, and many of the men were killed and devoured. But Būrāndukht saved Alexander and they put the Zangīs to the sword (II: 253–73). After this adventure, they set sail and came ashore in the land of the cannibal Indians, whom they slew because they refused the faith (II: 274–80). The sage Buqrāt joined Alexander on his expedition. Alexander then went on a pilgrimage to Adam's tomb, where the descendants of Adam gave him a grain of wheat weighing twenty-four pounds. Adam ate of this wheat and was expelled from paradise for his transgression.[78] He had told his sons to keep the wheat for Alexander, the Dhul-Qarnain. Wheat grains were reduced in size as a result of man's evildoings.

After sailing into a dangerous sea, Alexander came ashore in a region where the inhabitants fed upon fish and worshipped the thunder. They killed many of Alexander's men. Buqrāt caused the land and its inhabitants to sink under the sea (II: 303–24). Later, Alexander reached an island inhabited by bearded women with both female and male genitals.[79] From there he went to an island inhabited by people with hounds' heads.[80] Leaving this region behind, many of Alexander's soldiers were killed by men with eagles' claws who came from the sea (pp. 325–59). Next, they came upon a land inhabited by women so desirous of men that they wore phallic replicas on their foreheads. Rare gems were left on their shore by oxen that came from the sea (II: 361–78).

Envy among the sages who accompanied Alexander led to many untoward incidents. Plato caused one of the sages to die, and, as a result, was expelled by Alexander. Later, however, he was asked to return. After more adventures Alexander met the sage Luqmān, who was 2,500 years old (II: 396–416).

Alexander rescued a youth from a magic castle where he had been left by fairies to die. The fairies demanded the youth, because he had killed a fairy child while it was disguised as a dove. Alexander begged them to pardon the youth. They did so, and Alexander protected them against their enemies, the giants (II:451–55).[81]

While fighting the giants Alexander was carried by one of them to the Qāf mountain, where he met the prophet Khidr and his brother Ilyās. He visited the valley inhabited by those who had attained salvation. An angel who looked like Muhammed delivered a sermon and told Alexander that Muhammed would come 1,000 years later. The angel took Alexander back to his army in a wink.

Alexander defeated the giants and employed them to perform various tasks for him (II: 458–75). He visited many lands and went to the pilgrimage of Ka'bah.[82] Khidr and Ilyās and the sage Luqmān accompanied him on his journey. Khidr told him that there were forty prophets among his soldiers. In Egypt Alexander built a bridge over the Nile (II: 523–30). In Sayvatān, Balīnās built a tower in the water and Plato constructed a magic mirror upon it (II: 531–34). Among other marvels in this region, Alexander came upon two islands that would alternately vanish under the water, and saw gigantic spiders, flies, and gnats. He then reached the coast where the sand wept. The sage Luqmān explained that the sand was what remained of the tribe of 'Ād. The wind had carried them around the earth, smashing them against one another, turning them into little crumbs. From there Alexander went to the land of Narmpāyān (II: 549–72).[83]

Alexander visited an island where the people were naked.[84] After more adventures he descended into the sea in a diving bell in order to see the creatures of the deep (II: 572–79).[85] After building the barrier against Gog and Magog (II: 582–83) and visiting the Land of Darkness (II: 584–91), he reached a mountain where the angel Irmā'īl told him that the wonders God had created were too many for him to see. He gave Alexander a stone.[86]

Khidr and Ilyās brought Alexander the news that God had given him power over the wind, the fire, the water, and all animals (II: 594).[87]

Alexander died of illness on his way to Jerusalem and was buried in that city. Būrāndukht died a year later (II: 594–97).

Common features of the romances compared above show the close relationship of the texts. None seems, however, to have descended from any of the other texts. It is difficult to establish the line of descent of the Ethiopic and the Persian romances with certainty for several reasons. First, at least two significant versions, the Pahlavi and the Arabic (perhaps more than one Arabic romance) are lost. Second, an excessive amount of secondary materials—added to the texts for nationalistic or religious reasons—and the influence of local folklore and legendry would produce differences between the texts even if they were translated from or based on a single source. Third, the Persian and the Ethiopic writers did not treat their romances as mere translations, and it is not always possible to tell whether certain differences between the texts indicate differences in the original sources used, or are the result of changes produced by the authors. Figure 1 attempts to show the nature and the extent of the interpolations in the texts studied and the relationship among these texts.[88]

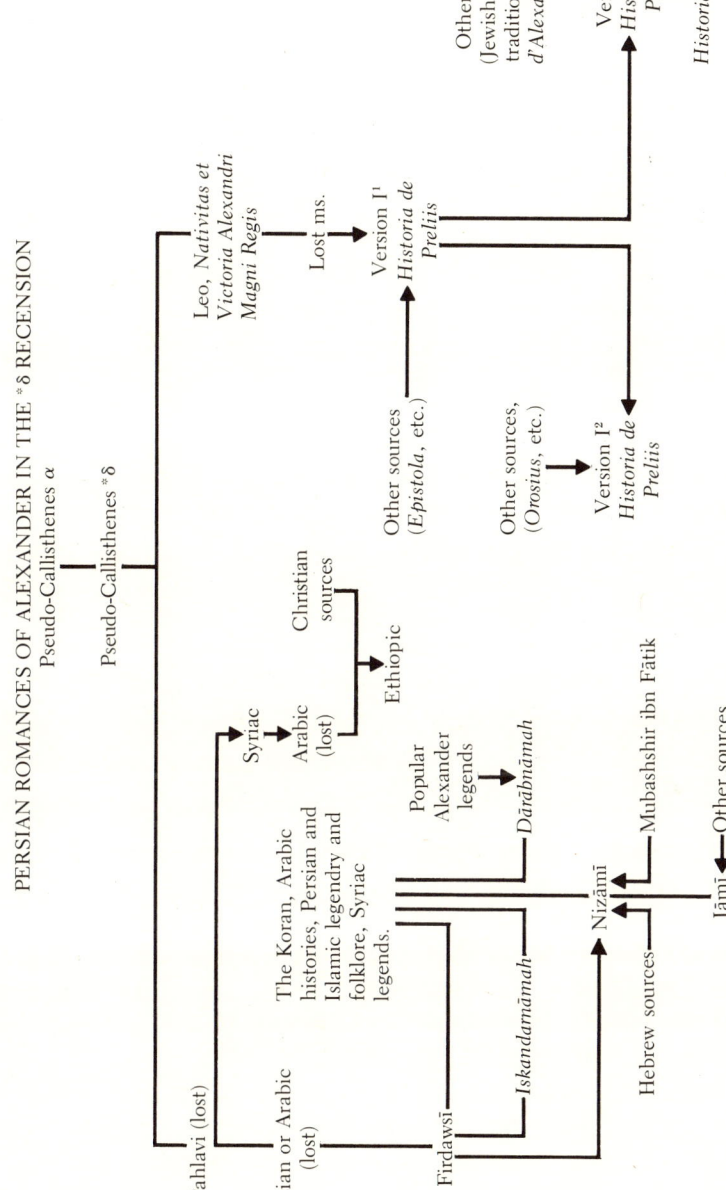

# APPENDIX II

# Alexander in Pahlavi Literature

PAHLAVI LITERATURE, produced between the third and the tenth centuries in Pahlavi (Middle Persian), is almost entirely theological and liturgical. It was written by Zoroastrians in the Pahlavi script, which they continued to use even after the Arab conquest (A.D. 643) had resulted in the adoption of the Arabic script by the Iranians.

The portrait of Alexander in Pahlavi literature is entirely different from that presented in the works of Muslim writers of Persian and Arab descent, who for their histories and romances of Alexander drew upon foreign sources. By contrast, the Zoroastrians drew from their own experiences and they never forgave Alexander, who according to their tradition burned their sacred books, slaughtered their priests, and destroyed their temples.

Alexander could not become the hero of a Pahlavi romance, for a romance hero must be idealized and glorified by his maker and no Zoroastrian could write about Alexander in that vein. Thus the mention of Alexander in Pahlavi writing is limited to brief, unfavorable remarks in works primarily dealing with subjects other than Alexander. (The Lost Pahlavi translation of the Pseudo-Callisthenes, where Alexander is a celebrated hero, was probably the work of an Armenian who did not share the Zoroastrians' negative view of Alexander.) In the Islamic era, however, the Pseudo-Callisthenes and other nonnative material became the source of Persian romances and histories of Alexander. Here, Alexander was converted into a Persian prince, a mighty king, a Muslim, a sage, and even a prophet—a hero of mythic proportions.

This portrait of Alexander sharply contrasts with his image in Pahlavi literature, where he is generally dismissed as a cursed enemy of God and an agent of Ahrīman (the principle of evil in Zoroastrianism).

The following is a reference to Alexander in *Nāmah-yi Tansar*[1] (The

Book of Tansar, A.D. 557–70) in a passage describing the period of religious decadence that followed Alexander's conquest of Iran:

Alexander burned 12,000 oxen hides [scrolls?] from our religion in Persepolis. Part of the religion had remained in people's memories, but they only remembered the stories and legends; they did not know the laws. Then even those stories and legends . . . vanished from the memory of man, so that not a single sign of its truth remained. (p. 11)

The Pahlavi text of *Nāmah-yi Tansar* is lost, but it has come down to us through the Arabic translation of Ibn al-Muqaffa', of which Ibn al-Isfandiyār made a Persian translation at the beginning of the thirteenth century. The latter is the text I have used. In the introduction to his Arabic translation of *Nāmah-yi Tansar*, Ibn al-Muqaffa' explains that Alexander divided the kingdom of Iran among ninety independent rulers known as Mulūk al-Ṭawā'if (tribal kings), for he feared that if ruled by a single ruler, the Iranians would rebel against him. According to Arab historians, the rule of Mulūk al-Ṭawā'if was ended by the first king of the Sassanian dynasty (A.D. 229–652), Ardashīr, the son of Bābak. After fourteen years of war, Ardashīr succeeded in uniting the kingdom of Iran of which he became king. In Pahlavi literature Ardashīr is celebrated as the king who revived the national life and faith crushed by Alexander. Referring to Ardashīr's intention, Tansar remarks, "He will not rest until he has avenged Dārā upon the descendants of Alexander [i.e., the Romans, who in Ardashīr's day ruled Greece] . . . and rebuilt the cities that Alexander destroyed . . ." (p. 42).

Similarly, *Kārnāmag-i Ardashīr-i Bābagān*[2] (The Book of the Deeds of Ardashīr the Son of Bābak, a Pahlavi romance of about A.D. 600) makes Ardashīr a direct descendant of Dārā and gives an account of his efforts to create national unity. The passage of interest to us is a reference made to Alexander by two brothers who give shelter to Ardashīr when he is separated from his army. Seeing that he is worried and restless they say:

Be not so sad and sorrowful, for Ohrmazd [the supreme deity of Ancient Iran] and the Amshāspandān [the seven highest angels in Zoroastrianism] will redress this wrong and will not leave this evildoer [i.e., Ardashīr's enemy] alone. For God who was displeased with Ẓaḥḥāk, Afrāsiyāb the Tūranī, and the Rūmī Alexander[3] completely destroyed them and wiped them from the earth in spite of their power. And the whole world knows this. (p. 41)

Here Alexander's name is coupled with the Iranians' greatest national enemies, Ẓaḥḥāk and Afrāsiyāb, the struggle against whom is the subject of many episodes in Persian national epics.[4]

*Ardāvīrāfnāmag*[5] (The Book of Ardāvīrāf), a Pahlavi text attributed to the ninth century, makes Alexander an agent of Ahrīman, the principle of evil and the source of ignorance, injustice, and darkness in Zoroastrianism:

It is said that once the holy Zoroaster proclaimed a religion which was given him by Ahūrāmazdā [the supreme deity of the Zoroastrians], and made it prevalent in the world. For 300 years the religion was pure, and men were believers. Then the accursed Ahrīman, in order to make man lose faith in this religion, enticed the Rūmī Alexander who resided in Egypt[6] to wage war against Iran and sack and destroy it. He slew the nobles of Iran and destroyed the seat of kingship.

And this religion, like Avesta and Zend, was written in gold on oxen hides which were placed in the archives of Istakhr [Persepolis]. And the evil, accursed, miserable, evildoer Ahrīman enticed the Rūmī Alexander who resided in Egypt, so that he burned the scrolls. And he slew the desturs, the judges, the hīrbuds, the mūbids,[7] and the learned men of Iran. And he caused enmity and strife among the nobles and the rulers of the country, and himself went and fell in hell. (p. 1)

In *Zand Ākāsīh, Iranian or Greater Bundahišn*,[8] which was completed in the eleventh or the twelfth century but the bulk of which belonged to a much earlier period, we are given an account of Alexander's conquest in Chapter 33, entitled, "As regards the calamities which befell Irânshahr, in each millenium":

Then during the reign of Dârâê son of Dârâê, the Emperor Alexander came to Irânshahr, hying from Arûm, killed king Dârâê, destroyed all *the* famil*ies* of rulers, magi, and public-*men* of Irânshahr, extinguished *an* immense number *of sacred*-fires, seized *the* commentary *of the* Revelation of Mazdâ-worship, and sent it to Arûm, burned *the* Avesta, and divided Irânshahr among ninety petty rulers. (pp. 275–77)

The negative view of Alexander in Pahlavi religious literature is also found in Iranian folklore. James Darmesteter gives a parody of the Persian version of the birth of Alexander which makes Alexander the son of a Persian king and the brother of Dārā. The parody of the birth of Alexander was told to Gabriel du Chinon, who visited Iran about 1650, by the Zoroastrians of Isfahan.[9] Like the version of the birth of Alexander in the *Shāhnāmah*,[10] the story begins with an account of the peace treaty between Philip and Dārā, and the latter's intention to marry Philip's daughter. But soon it takes a different turn:

Ce roi ayant donc envoyé sa fille à ce Dârâb, le diable en devint aussi amoureux; et s'étant transformé en un tourbillon de vent, et d'une couleur aussi noire qu'on le dépeint, la fille fut enveloppée dans ce tourbillon; ce qui la rendit fort noire, et son ventre fort enflé. Elle fut conduite en cet état devant Dârâb, roi de Gaures, qui perdit tout l'amour qu'il avait pour elle, la voyant en cet horrible état. Il la renvoya à son père, et aussitôt elle enfanta un monstre de l'enfer, qui avait une figure hideuse, et surtout les oreilles d'âne. Ce fils fut nommé Alexandre, et vint ensuite en cette belle forme faire un horrible ravage dans toute l'Asie, où il s'assujettit tous les pays, par une force qui n'eût pas été appréhendée d'eux, si elle n'eût été plus qu'humaine.

As Darmesteter observes, here the two horns of Alexander are transformed into the two ears of a donkey. Chadrin, who visited Iran some twenty years after Gabriel du Chinon, gives the following account of the attitude of the Zoroastrians toward Alexander:

Je n'ai rien trouvé de plus sensé dans les enseignements des Guèbres que le mal qu'ils disent d'Alexandre le Grand. Au lieu de l'admirer et de révérer son nom, comme font tant d'autres peuples, ils le méprisent, le détestent et le maudissent, le regardant comme un pirate, comme un brigand, comme un homme sans justice et sans cervelle, né pour troubler l'ordre du monde et détruire un partie du genre humain.[11]

The Zoroastrians maintained this view of Alexander during centuries when, as we shall see below, a completely different portrait of Alexander was presented in the works of Persian historians, poets, and romance writers.

# APPENDIX III

# Alexander in the Works of Persian and Arab Historians of the Islamic Era

PERSIAN AND Arab historians of the Islamic era drew their knowledge of Alexander from the Pseudo-Callisthenes (perhaps through the lost ninth-century Arabic believed to have been translated from the Syriac version), Syriac material,[1] the Koran and Arabic legends of the Dhul-Qarnain,[2] and to a minor extent Persian sources.[3]

There is no basic difference between these so-called historical accounts and the material found in the romances. The accounts of the life of Alexander in the histories follow the Pseudo-Callisthenes in the main and resemble short romances. The heroic exploits recounted in these histories can be more easily identified with the adventures of Alexander in romances and legends than with the actual events of his life. F. Speigel observes: "Es kann uns dies bei der Kritiklosigkeit der orientalischen Historiker und des Mittelalters überhaupt gar nicht auffalen . . . [weil] auch occidentalische Scribenten die Alexandersage für wahre Geschichte annahmen."[4]

The works examined here belong to the ninth to thirteenth centuries. The summaries given demonstrate the extent and the nature of the

# APPENDIX III. PERSIAN AND ARAB HISTORIES

material available to the authors of Persian and Arabic Alexander-romances. As we shall see, unlike the Pahlavi writers, most Persian and Arab historians glorify the figure of Alexander and justify his war against Darius.

## Al-Dīnāwarī's Version

The life of Alexander in Abū Ḥanīfah al-Dīnāwarī[5] (d. 894–5) resembles Firdawsī's version in the *Shāhnāmah*. Al-Dīnāwarī's account is summarized below.

In the war between Philip and Dārāb ibn Bahman, Philip was defeated. He agreed to pay an annual tribute of 100,000 golden eggs, and gave his daughter in marriage to Dārāb ibn Bahman. The latter ruled for twelve years. After his death, his son Dārāb succeeded to the throne. He was a contemporary of Alexander.

Scholars differ as to Alexander's ancestry. The people of Pars believe that he was the son of Dārāb ibn Bahman and Philip's daughter. Dārāb ibn Bahman, having found an unpleasant odor in Philip's daughter, had her cured with an herb called "al-Sandar." Ignorant that she was pregnant, he sent her back to Greece. A son was born to Philip's daughter, and she called him al-Iskandar, after the name of the herb.[6] Alexander grew into an intelligent youth and his grandfather, Philip, made him his heir. When Alexander became king, his intention was to regain the kingdom of his father, Dārāb ibn Bahman, from his brother, Dārāb. Dārāb, who was an arrogant king, wrote a letter to Alexander, demanding the tribute that Philip used to pay. Alexander replied that the hen that laid the golden eggs had died.[7]

Alexander was an oppressive king until Aristotle, a philosopher who believed in God, paid him a visit and warned him that God destroys tyrants. Alexander, angered, imprisoned Aristotle. But soon he had a change of heart; he sent for Aristotle and listened to his counsel. Aristotle ordered him to gather his soldiers and his subjects, renounce idolatry in their presence, and call them to turn to God, who is one and has no partner. Alexander did so.[8]

In the war between Alexander and Dārāb, the latter was stabbed by two of his own men. Putting the head of the dying Dārāb in his lap,[9] Alexander confessed that he was Dārāb's brother. Dārāb asked Alexander to marry his daughter, Rushanak. Alexander promised to do so.[10] He asked Dārāb to reveal the names of the assassins, but Dārāb died before answering.

Alexander punished the assassins. He wrote to his mother and he married Rushanak.[11] He then went to India and fought Porus, the king of India, and killed him in single combat.[12]

After an expedition to Sudan and Yemen, Alexander went to the Arabian Peninsula. The inhabitants of Mecca at that time were the Khuzā'ah tribe. Alexander expelled the Khuzā'ah from Mecca, and gave Ka'bah to Naẓur ibn Kannānah.[13] Having performed the hajj, Alexander gave away many gifts and left for North Africa.[14]

He wrote to Qandāqah (Candace), the queen of Ethiopia, of whose wisdom and prudence he had heard much. Alexander visited Candace, and there are many stories about this visit.[15] He made peace with her and went toward the Land of Darkness which is in the North.[16] He then turned toward Greece, building two cities on his way.

Learning of Alexander's intention to go to the rising-place of the sun, his ministers warned him that the region was close to Baḥr al-Akhẓar,[17] whose water was like pus; no one could go near it. Alexander said that he would go, even if he were to go by himself.[18]

He left Greece, moving toward the rising-place of the sun. He crossed the lands of the Slavs, the Khazars, and Turkistan. In China, disguised as Fīnāvūs, a messenger, he went to the King of China.[19] The latter surrendered to Alexander and sent him many gifts. From China Alexander went to the nation whose story God has given in the Koran.[20] Then he visited the land of the people whose men and women would meet three days a year. If they wanted to marry, they would do so in those three days. If a woman bore a boy, she would send him to his father; if she bore a girl, she would keep her.[21]

Alexander visited Eastern Iran. He built many cities. He intended to go to Jerusalem and Syria, but he feared that the nations whose kings he had killed and whose riches he had plundered would rebel in his absence. Therefore he decided to slay the nobles of Iran. But following Aristotle's counsel, he divided Iran among tribal princes.[22]

Alexander died in Jerusalem.[23] His body was placed in a gold coffin.[24] He built twelve cities around the world.

## Al-Ṭabarī's Version

In his history, Abū Ja'far Muhammad ibn Jarīr al-Ṭabarī (A.D. 839–923) has compiled a series of accounts on Alexander from various sources.[25] According to one account, Dārāb was an oppressive king who killed many of his nobles and was harsh to the commoners among his subjects. Therefore, when Alexander attacked Iran many of the Iranian nobles joined him. Dārāb was slain by two of his own subjects, who took the head to Alexander in expectation of a reward. But Alexander punished the assassins. He married Dārāb's daughter and went to India and the East. After this expedition he intended to go to Alexandria, but died before reaching it. His body was placed in a gold coffin.

From a second source, al-Ṭabarī renders the account of a peace treaty between Philip and Dārāb's father. Upon Alexander's refusal to send the tribute, Dārāb scorns him by sending him a ball and a rod to play with, and a container full of sesame seeds, representing the number of the Persian army. Alexander says that the ball symbolizes the world, and the rod signifies that he will conquer the world. He sends Dārāb a small amount of mustard seeds, saying that his soldiers were few but strong.[26] The story of the war between Alexander and Dārāb is similar to Dīnawarī's version.

A third account gives the Persian version of the birth of Alexander. In a fourth source used by al-Ṭabarī, Alexander himself bargains with the assassins to kill Dārāb. However, he places the head of the dying Dārāb in his lap, and, weeping, confesses that he is Dārāb's brother. Later he punishes the assassins.[27]

According to al-Ṭabarī, Alexander ordered that Persian books on science, astrology, and philosophy be translated into Greek. He destroyed the cities of Iran and set rulers of his own in the land. Having visited India, China, Tibet, and the Land of Darkness, he returned to Babylon, where he died at the age of thirty-six.[28] His son, Iskandarūs, refused to succeed to the throne and chose to devote himself to the worship of God.[29]

## Al-Mas'ūdī's Version

Al-Mas'ūdī, who wrote about A.D. 943, does not mention the Persian version of Alexander's birth.[30] He devotes much space to the account of Alexander's expedition to India, China, Tibet, and Turkistan. To the histories of al-Ṭabarī and al-Dīnāwarī, al-Mas'ūdī adds the moralizing of the philosophers, twenty-nine in number, upon Alexander's coffin. Their sayings are followed by the comments of Alexander's mother and wife.[31] According to al-Mas'ūdī, Alexander asked Ptolemy to write to Olympias, give her the news of his death, and ask her to proclaim a banquet to which the herald invited those who had never experienced the death of a beloved. Seeing that no one came to the banquet, she realized that not a single person had escaped this pain.[32] At her command, Alexander's body was removed from the gold coffin and placed in a marble one, for she knew that future kings would not leave the gold coffin undisturbed.

To the Pseudo-Callisthenes version of Alexander's Indian adventures, al-Mas'ūdī adds the episode of the Indian king, Kand (in the *Shāhnāmah*, Kayd), who obeyed Alexander and in order to prevent a war sent him four wonderful presents: his daughter who was unique in beauty, a philosopher who knew all things, a physician who cured all ailments, and a cup whose contents would never decrease.[33]

In his account of the building of Alexandria (I: 410–21), al-Mas'ūdī records an episode reminiscent of Alexander's submarine adventures in the diving bell found in talmudic literature.[34] According to al-Mas'ūdī, when Alexandria was under construction, strange creatures came from the sea and caused much damage. Alexander and two men descended into the sea inside a chest. Through the windows of the chest, they saw the animals who had interfered with the building of the city and the two men drew their picture. Alexander ordered craftsmen to build images of those animals from the pictures and placed the images on the shore. When the animals came from the water and saw those images, they went back to sea, never to return.[35]

Al-Mas'ūdī also gives the story of the Tower of Alexandria built by Alexander. After Alexander's death the magic mirror in the tower was used by Egyptian kings to protect their coasts against invasions from Greece. If any ship approached the coasts, it would be seen in the mirror.

## Other Accounts

Contrary to histories examined above, the account of Darius and Alexander in the history of Ḥamzah ibn al-Ḥasan al-Iṣfahānī (A.D. 893–970) is very brief.[36] Writing from the Persian point of view, he states that "having killed Dārāb, Alexander besieged the cities of Iran, did much evil, and exceeded all bounds in bloodshed. He gathered the nobles of Iran, 7,000 in number, and each day he would have twenty-one of these captives slain." According to this source, Alexander died on his way to Babylon. "It is said that he built twelve cities," says al-Isfahānī, "but this statement has no basis in truth, for he was a destroyer and not a builder (p. 29)."

Abū 'Alī Muḥammad al-Bal'amī,[37] who in A.D. 936 translated al-Ṭabarī's history into Persian, elaborated upon the version of the life of Alexander in his original, changing it into a short Alexander-romance. He gives the Persian version of Alexander's birth and a detailed account of the expeditions and wars of Alexander.

Al-Bīrūnī seems to be the only historian who deals with Alexander's wars in Greece before he started his conquests abroad.[38] He credits Alexander with the building of the barrier against Gog and Magog, and follows the Pseudo-Callisthenes version of Alexander's expeditions closely. He mentions Alexander's journey to Baḥr al-Akhẓar and Egypt, the building of Alexandria, the journey to Syria and Jerusalem (where he offers sacrifice at the temple), the expeditions to Armenia and Darband (in Caucasus), and the victory over the Copts. He refers to the Persian version of Alexander's birth, but says that it was invented by the

Iranians out of enmity. In a second book, *India*,[39] he refers to the story of Nectanebus.

In Ibn al-Balkhī's twelfth-century Persian history, *Fārsnāmah*,[40] Alexander is a wise, learned, and generous king who attacks Iran because he is incited by Dārāb's harsh messages. Ibn al-Balkhī clears Alexander of all blame, saying that he brought justice to the world, and did more good than can be described.

The Pseudo-Callisthenes version of Alexander's birth, absent from most Persian and Arabic romances and histories, is mentioned in the anonymous Persian history *Mujmal al-tawārīkh wa-al-qiṣaṣ*[41] (A.D. 1130). "There are many stories about Alexander's ancestry," the author says. "It is said in the *Iskandarnāmah*[42] that Bakhtyānūs [a corrupt form of Nectanebus], the King of Egypt, who was a sorcerer, went to Greece after he lost his kingdom, and through magic, slept with Philip's daughter al-Mufīd and begot Alexander. (Al-Mufīd is the Arabicized form of Olympias, name of Philip's wife. In the Pseudo-Callisthenes, Nectanebus sleeps with Philip's wife.)

The account of Alexander in Ibn al-Athīr follows al-Ṭabarī almost word for word, except for the episode of Alexander's expedition to China.[43] In Ibn al-Athīr's version it is the Emperor of China, who, disguised as a messenger, visits Alexander. The latter is so impressed with the wisdom of the King of China that he makes peace with him.

## Dhul-Qarnain and Alexander

Most histories mentioned above identify Alexander with the Dhul-Qarnain of the Koran, giving the story of his journey to the rising-place and the setting-place of the sun, and attributing the building of the barrier against Gog and Magog to him. The basis of this information is the following passage in the Koran, 18: 82ff.:

The Jews will ask thee concerning Dhu'lkarnein. Answer, I will rehearse unto you an account of him. We made him powerful in the earth, and we gave him means to *accomplish* everything *he pleased*. And he followed *his* way, until he came to the place where the sun setteth; *and* he found it to set in a spring of black mud; and he found near the same a certain people. And we said, O Dhu'lkarnein, either punish *this people*, or use gentleness towards them. He answered, Whosoever *of them* shall commit injustice, we will surely punish him *in this world*; afterwards shall he return unto his LORD, and he shall punish him with a severe punishment. But whosoever believeth; and doth that which is right, shall receive the most excellent reward, and we will give him in command that which is easy. Then he continued *his* way, until he came to the place where the sun riseth; *and* he found it to rise on certain people, unto whom we had not given anything wherewith to shelter themselves therefrom. Thus *it was*; and we comprehended with our knowledge the *forces* which were with him. And he prosecuted *his* journey *from south to north*, until he came between the two mountains; beneath which he found certain people, who could scarce understand what was said. *And* they said, O Dhu'lkarnein, verily Gog and Magog waste the land; shall we therefore pay the tribute, on condition that thou build a rampart between us and them? He answered, The *power* wherewith my LORD hath strengthened me, is better *than your tribute:* but assist me strenuously, and I will set a strong wall between you and them. Bring me iron in large pieces, until it fill up *the space* between the two sides *of these mountains*. And he said *to the workmen*, Blow *with your bellows*, until it makes *the iron red hot as* fire. *And* he said *further*, Bring me molten brass, that I may pour upon it. Wherefore, *when this wall was finished*, Gog and Magog could not scale it, neither could they dig through it. *And Dhu'lkarnein* said, This *is* a mercy from my LORD: but when the prediction of my LORD shall come *to be fulfilled*, he shall reduce *the wall* to dust; and the prediction of my LORD is true.[44]

The name "Alexander" does not occur in this passage; and the origin of the epithet "Dhul-Qarnain" ("the two-horned") is not explained here. Yet, commentators of the Koran in general identify Dhul-Qarnain as Alexander the Great.[45] Most Persian and Arab writers and historians of Alexander-materials make an attempt to explain why Alexander was called the Dhul-Qarnain, but the diversity of their explanations leads us to conclude that none of them knew the significance or the origin of the epithet.[46] In Arabic the word *qirn* means a "horn," "summit," "the first visible part of the sun," and "century." Based on these meanings, it has been argued that Alexander was called Dhul-Qarnain (the owner of two *qirns*) because he had visited the East and the West; because he entered the darkness and the light; because he had two plaits of hair; because both his parents were of noble birth; or because his life lasted from one century into the next. The author of *Iskandarnāmah* gives Alexander a pair of real horns which he playfully exposes in the presence of the king of Turkistan.[47]

In addition to having to define "Dhul-Qarnain," writers who identified Dhul-Qarnain with Alexander had another problem to solve. In the Koran, 18, the same chapter where Dhul-Qarnain is mentioned, there is a story about Moses and an unnamed old man, who is identified by commentators as Khidr. In some legends Khidr is said to be a contemporary of Abraham. According to legends of Alexander, Khidr served as Alexander's guide in his journey to the Land of Darkness. Since this would set Alexander's time close to the time of Abraham and Moses, some writers came to the conclusion that there were two Dhul-Qarnains—one a contemporary of Khidr, the other, who is mentioned in the Koran, Alexander the Great.[48]

There have been writers, however, who believed that the Dhul-Qarnain of the Koran was a king of Yemen. An important source to be studied in this respect is the account of the life of Ṣaʻb Dhul-Qarnain in *al-Tījān*, written by Ibn Hishām (d. A.D. 829).[49] The book belongs to the ninth century; its material on Dhul-Qarnain, however, is quoted from Wahb ibn Munabbih (A.D. 654–732), who, in turn, used earlier materials as his source. In the *al-Tījān* there are two episodes which, except for the Arabic and the Persian, are not found in any branch of the Pseudo-Callisthenes. These are the account of Dhul-Qarnain's pilgrimage to Mecca, and the celebrating of his character as a prophet. Both of these episodes are attributed to Alexander in Islamic romances and histories.[50] A summary of the *al-Tījān* follows.

Wahb, inquiring about the identity of the Dhul-Qarnain of the Koran, was told that he was Ṣaʻb Dhu-marāthid, a Ḥamīrī king of Yemen and a believer in the faith of Abraham.[51] He built two towers and the gate against Gog and Magog. Wahb asked, further, whether Alexander was the Dhul-Qarnain whom God has mentioned in the Koran.[52] He was told that Alexander was called the Dhul-Qarnain because he had built two towers, one in Alexandria and one in Greece. However, he was not identical with the Dhul-Qarnain of the Koran. Ṣaʻb Dhul-Qarnain met Abraham and lived before Alexander, whose lifetime was close to that of Jesus.[53]

## APPENDIX III. PERSIAN AND ARAB HISTORIES

According to Wahb, Ṣaʻb was an oppressive king until he was shown the joys of heaven and the horrors of hell in a dream. He was told that the former was the reward of those who humbled themselves to God, and the latter the reward of the arrogant. The dream changed Ṣaʻb, and made him humble before God. Ṣaʻb had three more dreams, but no one in his court could interpret them. An old man told him of a prophet in Jerusalem who was a descendant of Abraham and who would interpret Ṣaʻb's dreams.

Ṣaʻb went toward Jerusalem with an army vaster than that of any king before him. Later he visited Mecca and entered Kaʻbah barefoot. From there he went to Jerusalem, where he met the prophet Musá al-Khidr.[54] The prophet addressed Ṣaʻb as Dhul-Qarnain, the first time that Ṣaʻb was thus addressed. The prophet explained the meaning of the epithet: Ṣaʻb was the possessor of the two horns of the sun.

He also interpreted Dhul-Qarnain's dream. In his first dream Hell was shown him as a warning, and Heaven was shown him, for it was promised him. The second dream, in which Dhul-Qarnain ascended into the sky and returned to earth followed by the stars and carrying the sun and the moon in his hands, signified that all the kings and the rulers of the earth would surrender to him. The third dream, in which Dhul-Qarnain devoured the earth and drank the waters of the seas, meant that he would possess the whole earth and all that was upon it[55] and that he would cross all the seas.[56] In his fourth dream Dhul-Qarnain had seen that man and jinn came to him and were in his power. He caused them to be carried by the winds to various regions of the earth. He saw also that animals, insects, and birds were in his power. The dream signified that all living creatures would be in his power, and that he would rule the winds and transfer the jinn from one place to another.[57]

After this Dhul-Qarnain saw in a dream that the earth was dark as night until the sun rose from the West, and he went toward the sun and followed it until he reached a land covered with stars and he walked upon that land. According to Khidr's interpretation, in this dream Dhul-Qarnain was ordered to go toward the West, where he would reach the valley of the rubies.

Dhul-Qarnain and his army marched toward the West, and Musá al-Khidr went with them. On his way Dhul-Qarnain slew those who deserved death. He transferred people from one land to another. He conquered Ethiopia and went to Sudan, crossed the land of a people who were mute, and reached a people who had blue eyes. He reached a tribe whose ears were like the ears of camels, and a people whose ears reached to their chins. He conquered Andalusia and reached Baḥr al-Muḥīt.[58] He intended to cross the sea, but the wind blew against him. Dhul-Qarnain caused the wind to stop, and he sailed the sea until he reached the muddy spring where the sun sets.[59] He continued his journey until he was told by Khidr[60] that it was not granted him to go any farther. They entered the Land of Darkness and they walked on slippery ground. Dhul-Qarnain said to his men that they were in the land where those who took from it would regret it as well as those who did not. The land was covered with rubies. Those men who took rubies regretted that they had not taken more; and those who did not take any regretted that they had none.[61]

Then they reached a rock, which Dhul-Qarnain attempted to climb and could not, for the rock shook beneath him. But Khidr climbed the rock until he disappeared from sight. A voice commanded Khidr to drink from the Spring of the Water of Life. Having done so, Khidr returned, telling Dhul-Qarnain that it was not granted him to drink of the water of life, and that Dhul-Qarnain had reached the limit that man and jinn could reach. Dhul-Qarnain heard a voice commanding him to go to the land where people did not know God, to impart to them the knowledge of God, and to call upon them to worship Him.[62]

Having visited several lands, Dhul-Qarnain went to Iran. He slew those who did not turn to God. He visited the tribes of Jabalqā and Jabalsā and presented them with the faith.[63] Moving toward the East, he passed the rising-place of the sun, crossed a land covered with ice, and reached the land of the angels. An angel admonished Dhul-Qarnain, for it had been granted him to see the land of man and jinn and yet he wanted more. The angel showed him Isrāfīl, ready to blow his trumpet,[64] and gave him a stone and a bunch of grapes.[65] He told Dhul-Qarnain to weigh the stone, eat of the grapes, and give some also to his men. Dhul-Qarnain and his men ate of the grapes and yet the grapes did not decrease. He weighed the stone and found that it outweighed everything. Khidr informed him that the stone symbolized Dhul-Qarnain's eye, which was not satisfied by anything. Khidr then covered the stone with dust, and thereby the weight of the stone was diminished. Dhul-Qarnain reached the region between the Two Mountains where he built the barrier against Gog and Magog. He found a people who had no locks to their doors, no judges, and no princes.[66] Having crossed the land of the Khazars, China, Sind, and India, he went to Babylon, where he died. After his death, Khidr disappeared.

Most of the stories attributed to Dhul-Qarnain in the *al-Tījān* occur in the romances of Alexander. The episode of the building of the gate against Gog and Magog is found in the "Christian Legend Concerning Alexander," and in the poetic version of Jacob of Serugh which was written not later than A.D. 521. The Koran was written over a century after this version.

According to Nöldeke, "The Christian Legend" was the source of the Koran, 18: 82ff.[67] Thus it seems likely that Wahb's tales of Ṣa'b Dhul-Qarnain were taken from the legends of Alexander. The possibility that Wahb used a source that was earlier than both the "Christian Legend" and the Koran is eliminated by the fact that Wahb's stories have characteristics peculiar to the Islamic era. For example, Dhul-Qarnain is said to be a follower of the "faith of Abraham," which was the prototype of Judaism and Islam. This concept was invented by Muhammed, who, through associating Islam with Abraham, created a place for Islam in religious history.[68]

It is likely that Sa'b Dhul-Qarnain was substituted for Alexander by Muslims who were disturbed to see a heathen king so highly esteemed in the Koran. It should be mentioned, however, that Muslims regarded Alexander highly. Even in *al-Tījān* itself Alexander is referred to as "a righteous man and a sage" (p. 310).

While it is difficult to resolve the problem presented by the stories in the *al-Tījān*, it is easy to see the far-reaching effects of such stories and the passage in the Koran; for Arab and Persian historians and romance writers attributed these stories to Alexander and celebrated his character as a believer, a Muslim, a fighter for religion, and a prophet.

# Afterword

THE PERSIAN ROMANCES of Alexander range from the Pseudo-Callisthenes (pseudohistorical) to the fabulous. Although closely related to the Pseudo-Callisthenes, they possess qualities peculiar to themselves, because of the nationality and the religion of the writers and compilers, and the influence of local folklore and lengendry.

None of the versions of the Alexander-romance studied here has outstanding literary merit. The explanation for this failure lies in the nature of the Alexander-material itself rather than in the performance of the writers. A linear story of Alexander composed of a series of wars, adventures, and expeditions to strange lands lacks the potential to be the raw material of a great work of art. Here and there we are given insight into the character of the hero—his good qualities like his courage, and his weaknesses like his avarice. The main interest of the narrative is not, however, the personality of the protagonist, but the adventures and the wonders of strange lands. The story never reaches a climax. The plot moves from one episode to the next until the story ends with the death of the protagonist. Alexander does not meet his death as a result of a tragic mistake or his "tragic flaw"; the death is caused by poisoning or simply by sickness.

The writers of Persian Alexander-romances have not deviated from this basic pattern. They changed the details and the episodes, often making them more fantastic, but preserved the episodic plot structure, merely repeating the episodes without reflecting upon them. Their main interest was in narrating the events in the story rather than in examining the human factors responsible for them.

Even the version of Firdawsī, in my opinion the most effective of the romances discussed in Appendix I, fails to reach the level of a great literary work. True, some passages in the poem have the quality of greatness—for example, the section where Alexander meets the dying Dārā. Dārā reflects upon mutability, and Alexander realizes that his own greatness is vulnerable. This section is among the best of Firdawsī and a great piece of poetry. But this tone of deep tragic involvement cannot be sustained in a poem that is basically a series of adventures.

The version of Niẓāmī, as a result of excessive interpolation of non-Alexander materials, lacks unity. Niẓāmī retells a series of actions without exploring the feelings and emotions of the performers of these deeds. This same defect is also characteristic of the Syriac and The Ethiopic texts.

## INTRODUCTION

1. Kroll, ed. (one recension), *Historia Alexandri Magni* (Berlin, 1926).
2. *Res Gestae Alexandri Macedonis*, ed. B. Kübler (Leipzig, 1888).
3. Pfister, *Der Alexanderroman des Archipresbyters Leo*.
4. For edition and information see Appendix I, where the *δ recension and the Pahlavi, Syriac, Arabic, Ethiopic, and Persian romances are discussed.
5. Donath, *Die Alexandersage in Talmud und Midrasch*; Lévi, "La Légende d'Alexandre dans le Talmud," 2 (1881) 2; 293–300, 7:78–93; Gaster, "An Old Hebrew Romance of Alexander," pp. 485–549; Bonfils, *The Book of the Gests of Alexander of Macedon*; Reich, *Tales of Alexander the Macedonian*.
6. Iraj Afshar, ed., Persian Texts Series, no. 17 (Tehran, 1964).
7. A microfilm of this manuscript is available in the library of Tehran University.
8. *Iskandarnāmah*, "Introduction," p. 23.
9. *Ibid.*, p. 22.
10. Bahar, *Sabkshināsī*, 2:133; Safa, *Ḥimāsah'sarā'ī dar Īrān*, p. 90.

## ISKANDARNĀMAH

1. According to the story of Dārāb in the *Shāhnāmah*, Bahman, the Kiyānīd king, lay with his own daughter Humāy and she became pregnant. He died before Humāy gave birth, making her his heir. Humāy concealed her pregnancy, and when the baby was born put him in a chest and placed the chest in the river. The chest was recovered by a man whose newborn infant had just died. He adopted the child, and, since he had found it in the water, called him Dārāb ("in water").

Dārāb subsequently discovered his ancestry and became king. He defeated Philip, whose daughter he then married. Of this union Alexander was born. Historical elements enter the biography of Dārāb's second son, Dārā. Dārā can be identified with Darius III, who was defeated by Alexander. See *Shāhnāmah-yi Firdawsī*, ed. E. Bertels (Moscow, 1963–71), 6:354–406. Subsequent references are to this edition.

2. Dhul-Qarnain, meaning the "two-horned," is Alexander's title in the Koran 18:82ff. See above, pp. 196-97.
3. Greece or Macedonia.
4. The names of the murderers correspond to those in the *Shāhnāmah*. In most Pseudo-Callisthenes texts, however, the murderers are called Bessos and Ariobarzanes.
5. Roxana is the name of Darius's wife and not, as in most Alexander-romances, of his daughter. The daughter, whom Alexander married, was called Estatira. While our text uses the correct name for Darius's wife, it makes no mention of Alexander's marriage to Darius's daughter at her father's request.
6. Isfandiyār was the father of Bahman and the great-grandfather of Dārāb in the legendary Kiyānīd dynasty.
7. The fact that Darius's wife died in childbirth is apparently historically authentic, but the incident is not mentioned in other Alexander-romances. See Plutarch, *Lives*, 7:311.
8. The phrase called *takbīr*, meaning "God is very great."
9. A Muslim who wages war against infidels.
10. In the Islamic tradition Jamshīd was considered the first idolater. See Muhammad ibn al-Jarīr al-Tabarī, *Tarjumah-yi tafsīr-i Ṭabarī*, ed. H. Yaghma'i (Tehran, 1961), 1:35-36. This book, a commentary on the Koran, will hereafter be cited as the *Tafsīr*.
11. In other versions of Alexander-romance Porus is killed in single combat by Alexander.
12. A unit of measure equivalent to 5,919 meters.
13. The meanings of these words are as follows: *ruhbān* is a monk; *aḥbār* is the plural of *ḥibr*, the name given by the Jews to their learned man; *'ulamā* is the plural of 'Ālim, "a learned man." The author uses these three words as synonyms.
14. The word *bargushādan* is used to mean both "to conquer" and "to make potent."
15. Perhaps what is meant is the hair growing on Māhafarīn's face, for later the old woman instructs her to clean her forehead with a dagger.
16. The story of Adam in Islamic tradition (See the Koran, 2:30ff.; 15:26) is based on Hebrew sources. The story of Adam's tomb was familiar in Islamic legendry. *Tafsīr*, 2:399-400, gives the following account: "When Adam was expelled from paradise he landed on the earth on a mountain in Ceylon. It was on this mountain that God accepted his repentance. The tomb of Adam and Eve was on this mountain until the Deluge. Then God told Noah to remove the bones of Adam and Eve from the tomb. At God's behest, Noah buried the bones in Jerusalem when the water had subsided" (translation mine).
According to al-Bal'amī, *Tarjumah va taklimah-yi tārīkh-i Ṭabarī*, p. 85, after the Fall Adam landed on the ground in Ceylon, Eve in Mecca, Satan in a city called Misān, and the serpent in Isfahan.

Alexander's pilgrimage to Adam's tomb occurs in Tarsūsī, *Dārābnāmah*, 2:291-301.

17. The personage who will appear before the end of time. The characteristics attributed to him in Islamic tradition combine features from Christ's sermon to his disciples (Matt. 24; Mark 13) with some elements from Apocalypse of St. John of Patmos (7:7; 12; 13; 20:5-18). Dajjāl is not mentioned in the Koran.

18. According to al-Bal'amī, "For 200 years Adam wept upon that mountain over his sins. From his tears trees and medicinal herbs grew. . . . Then God accepted his repentance and Adam wept for joy. For 100 years he wept out of joy and gratitude. From these tears . . . sprang flowers and sweet-smelling herbs" (*Tārīkh*, pp. 87, 89).

*Mandeville's Travels*, ed. M. C. Seymour (Oxford, 1967), p. 145, gives a similar account: [In the isle of Silha (Ceylon)] "is a gret mountayne, and in mydd place of the mount is a gret lake in a fulle faire pleyn and there is gret plentee of water. And thei of the contree seyn that Adam and Eue wepten vpon that mount an c. yeer whan thei weren dryuen out of Paradys. And that water thei seyn is of here teres. . . . And in the botme of that lake men fynden many precious stones and grete perles."

19. The journey to the Land of Gold does not occur in any other text of the *δ recension except for a reference in the Ethiopic text (see below, p. 213 n. 9), to the mountains of gold in China, p. 179. See also *Mandeville's Travels*, pp. 218-19.

20. According to the *Shāhnāmah*, 1:51-78, Ẓaḥḥāk came from Arabia. He was enticed by Ahrīman (the embodiment of evil) to slay his father. Later, Ahrīman appeared to him as a handsome youth. He kissed Ẓaḥḥāk's shoulders, and from his touch sprang two serpents on Ẓaḥḥāk's shoulders. The serpents had to be fed with human brains. When Ẓaḥḥāk became the king of Iran, each day two men were killed and their brains were fed to the serpents. This was Ahrīman's plot to destroy mankind. Ẓaḥḥāk ruled 1,000 years. His rule was ended by Firaydūn, who chained Ẓaḥḥāk in a cave on a mountaintop and left him there to die.

21. In the *Tafsīr*, 1:11, al-Ṭabarī says that the great name of God is mentioned in the opening chapter of the Koran. Later he gives the epithets "al-Raḥmān" and "al-Raḥīm" (the compassionate, the merciful) as two of the great names of God (p. 18). He who utters them with sincerity, says al-Tabarī, will go to heaven. The names of God were believed to be ninety-nine.

22. *Davālpāyān*, "the rope-legged," were apparently familiar figures in Islamic legendry. Al-Tabarī in the *Tafsīr*, 1:19, speaks of a tribe called Māsūkh, "the metamorphosed," and describes them as lacking shankbones. They cling to people, then kill and devour them. They are not human, says al-Ṭabarī, for they have been metamorphosed. They are believed to dwell in the East. See also below, p. 215 n. 38.

23. Tūrāniyāns are among the Persians' greatest enemies in their national

epics. Afrāsiyāb the Tūrānī murdered Sīyāvush, an Iranian prince, through treachery. The Iranians united to avenge Sīyāvush and a long period of war followed. Here Alexander, as if a Persian king in the Shāhnāmah, is harassed by the threat from Tūrān.

24. Persian Alexander-romances and Persian and Arabic histories dealing with Alexander are the only sources that mention Alexander's journey to Mecca and his pilgrimage to Kaʻbah.

25. Ilyās son of Kharā', later called Ilyās son of Muẓar, was a real person. Al-Ziriklī, *Al-Aʻlām*, vol. 1, identifies him as a descendant of the Prophet.

26. Mīnā, Muzdalifah, and ʻArafāt are places near Mecca visited by the pilgrims of the Kaʻbah. Muzdalifah, where the pilgrims spend the night on their way to Mīnā, is halfway between Mīnā and ʻArafāt.

27. Zamzam is a well in Mecca; Maqām-i Ibrāhīm (Abraham's place) is mentioned in the Koran, 2:125. In the *Tafsīr*, 1:105, al-Ṭabarī explains that Maqām-i Ibrāhīm was a rock upon which Abraham stood while building the Kaʻbah, and that Abraham's footprints are to be seen on the rock. According to the Koran, 2:127, Abraham and Ishmael laid the foundations of Kaʻbah.

28. Legends associating Abraham with the Kaʻbah created a basis for the pilgrimage to Mecca in religious history. Abraham is a significant figure in Islam. His religion, called the faith of Abraham, is the prototype of Judaism and Islam. See the Koran, 2:135; 3:95.

29. In the history written by al-Dīnāwarī (above, pp. 191–93), we are told that Alexander expelled from Mecca the Khazāʻah tribe, which had usurped the position of the chief of Mecca. This episode occurs in other Persian romances of Alexander as well.

30. The story is told in the *Shāhnāmah*, 7:156–64. In Firdawsī's version the king is Ardashīr, son of Bābak, who slew Ardavān and married his daughter.

31. This paragraph reflects the popularity of Alexander-romances at the time the present romance was written. Alexander himself refers to the Alexander book as if it were a chronicle recording the events of his journey and expedition.

32. This tale belongs to a type of story in which the heroine is persecuted, separated from her family, made to suffer exile, but finally is reunited with her husband and children. See Schlauch, *Chaucer's Constance and Accused Queens*.

33. There is a parallel for this paragraph in the Ethiopic, p. 205, but it does not occur in the Greek. Cf. Pseudo-Callisthenes, *The Life of Alexander of Macedon*, translated and edited by E. A. Haight (New York, Longmans, Green, 1955).

34. This story is a summary of the anonymous Persian romance *Bakhtiyārnāmah*, generally considered as part of the Sindbad cycle. See W. A. Clouston, trans., *Bakhtyār Nāma (Lanarkshire, 1833)*.

35. Legends and stories about Khidr (I have preferred the familiar spelling to transliteration) are primarily associated with the Koran, 18:60–82. This section of

the Koran tells the story of Moses and his servant, who while on a journey lost a fish that they were carrying. The fish found its way into the water and swam away. While looking for the fish, they met a servant of God. Moses begged to follow the servant of God; the servant agreed on the condition that Moses remain patient and ask no question no matter what. Moses, however, failed the test of patience and was dismissed from the company of the servant of God.

In the Koran the name of the servant of God is not mentioned, but the majority of the commentators identify him with Khidr. The Koranic story may be traced to the Gilgamesh epic, the Alexander-romance, and the Jewish legend of Elijah and Rabbi Joshua ben Levi. See A. Jellinek, *Bet ha-Midrasch* (Leipzig, 1853), 5:133–35.

Elements of the Koranic story also appear in the romances of Alexander. Alexander looks for the Water of Life guided by an old man, in most versions called Khidr. Also, in most versions it is through a salted fish coming to life that the spring is discovered. In all versions, however, Alexander returns from the journey without having drunk from the Water of Life.

36. According to tradition, the prophet Ilyās (Elijah) cured Alīsa', the son of a widow. The youth, who is the Yīsa' of our text, became Elijah's disciple. The story of Ilyās is related in the Koran, 36:123–30.

37. Persian and Arabic collections of legends of prophets were compiled by many writers. The earliest such collection is believed to be by Wahb ibn al-Munabbih (A.D. 654–732), who knew the ancient books, early legends, fables, myths, and sagas. He also compiled the legends of Dhul-Qarnain. See above, pp. 198ff.

In *Iskandarnāmah* Wahb is mentioned as the source of the episodes of Alexander and the Zangīs, Alexander and the fairies, and the legends of Solomon and David. In *Qiṣaṣ al-anbīyā'* (Legends of Prophets) by Ibrāhīm ibn al-Manṣūr (Tehran, 1961), many stories are related from Wahb.

38. In *Tafsīr*, 1:193–94, we are told that the Jews asked Muhammed twenty-eight questions. One question was about Jābalqā and Jabalsā. The prophet described them as two cities, one in the East and one in the West, both joining the mountain of Qāf. Each city had 12,000 gates and each gate was guarded by 1,000 men. The land was lighted by the mountain of Qāf. The inhabitants were all male and they fed upon grass.

39. The Qāf mountain is described in the *Tafsīr*, 1:192–93, as a mountain of green emerald, joining the first heaven. The color of the sky is said to be from the green light emanating from this mountain; otherwise the sky would be white.

40. See *Shāhnāmah*, 4:8–31; 5:8–64.

41. According to Islamic tradition, on Resurrection Day, the Archangel Isrāfīl, at God's command, will blow the trumpet and arouse the dead from the grave. See *Tafsīr*, 2:323.

42. The Koran, 18:82ff. In the romance the first sentence of the passage from the Koran is in Arabic and the rest of the passage in Persian.

43. The Green Sea or Daryā-yi Akhẓar is the Indian Ocean. The hardships Alexander undergoes while crossing the sea are reminiscent of the account of his journey to the Foetid Sea in "The Syriac Legend Concerning Alexander," in E. A. Budge, *The History of Alexander the Great Being the Syriac Version of the Pseudo-Callisthenes* (Cambridge, 1889), pp. 145ff.

44. Abū Saʿīd Khargūshī (b. A.D. 1016) was skilled in religious jurisprudence and wrote many books on that subject as well as on other topics such as the interpretation of dreams. See al-Ziriklī, *al-Aʿlām*.

45. Coins made of gold from North Africa.

46. A kind of gold or silver coin.

47. The story is mentioned in *Qiṣaṣ al-anbiyāʾ* of Ibrāhīm ibn Manṣūr al-Nayshābūrī, pp. 286–87.

48. Hailed as the Iranians' greatest king in *Shāhnāmah* and early religious writings, Kaykhusraw is said to be immortal.

49. The king's granddaughter is hereafter mistakenly referred to as the king's daughter. For an analogue see the story of Suzanna and the Elders in the Apocryphal Gospel.

50. See note 23 above.

51. The paradise of Ganges was variously located in Turkistan and in China.

52. The question Alexander asks Aristotle is identical with one of the twenty-eight questions the Jews asked Muhammed. The answer, which was brought to Muhammed by Gabriel, is the same as that in our text. See *Tafsīr*, 1:27.

53. Persian form of the Arabic "Zinj," meaning an African black.

54. The story is recorded among legends of Solomon in Ginzberg, *The Legends of the Jews*, 4:138–41.

55. For this motif see Thompson, *Motif Index to Folk Literature*, K978 and *K511.

56. On Alexander's horns see above, pp. 197ff..

57. A conjuror's circle (Manzal) drawn on the ground.

58. Two sources seem to have contributed to Alexander's adventures in the fairyland. In *al-Tijān* (see above, p. 198ff), Dhul-Qarnain is given power over the fairies. The motif entered the Alexander-romance, for some writers identified Dhul-Qarnain with Alexander.

In *Qiṣaṣ al-anbiyāʾ* of Ibrāhīm ibn Manṣūr, in a section dealing with legends of Solomon (pp. 281–310), we are told that Solomon prayed to God to make him the sole ruler of the world. His petition was granted and God gave him power over the fairies, the demons, the wind, the waters, and all animals. The legends of Solomon and David (*Qiṣaṣ al-anbiyāʾ*, pp. 264–81) were popular among Muslims. In the *Iskandarnāmah* an old man tells Alexander the legends of Solomon and David, some of which are claimed to be drawn from Wahb ibn al-Munabbih's collection of legends. Many of these stories are also found among the legends of Solomon in Ginzberg, *The Legends of the Jews*.

59. The figure of Arāqīt, the fairy queen, owes much to the portrait of the

Queen of Sheba in legends of Solomon. In *Iskandarnāmah*, we are told that both Arāqīt and the Queen of Sheba were born of a human mother and a fairy father. Further, Shahmalik's daughter tells Alexander that Arāqīt has hairy legs (p. 85). In *Qiṣaṣ al-anbīyā'* (p. 302), a woman who envies the Queen of Sheba, whom Solomon intends to marry, tells him that she has very hairy legs. Solomon orders the jinn to remove the hair from the Queen's legs. They do so, and Solomon marries her. In Ginzberg, *Legends of the Jews*, 4:145, Solomon tricks the Queen of Sheba into walking on a mirror and sees her hairy legs.

In Islamic legendry, Solomon marries the Queen of Sheba; in *Iskandarnāmah*, Alexander marries the fairy queen, Arāqīt.

60. Tying the toes together had the magical effect of making Alexander unable to free himself.

61. At this point in the story, Ruvīd is nowhere near Alexander's camp. The events mentioned here take place later. See p. 94 of the text.

62. The prophet Hūd appeared among the Arab tribe of 'Ād. His story is told in the Koran, 7, 11, 26, 49. Ṣāliḥ was a prophet sent to the Arab tribe of Thamūd. See the Koran, 7:73; 11:61; 26:141.

63. According to *al-Tījān*, Dhul-Qarnain transferred the jinn from one region to another. See above, p. 199.

64. In *Qiṣaṣ al-Anbiyā'*, p. 271, David is said to have had ninety-nine wives. He would sleep with all of them every night and would spend the day in prayer.

65. Cf. Dan. 2:31ff.

66. A unit of measure equivalent to forty-one inches.

67. Notwithstanding this statement, Alexander later marries the pious maiden, Zubaydah.

68. I do not know the meaning or the pronunciation of this word.

69. For comment on this section see p. 3.

70. Ya'jūj va Ma'jūj, Gog and Magog (cf. Gen. 10:2; Ezekiel 38, 39) are outstanding figures in biblical and Islamic eschatalogy. In both sources they are said to live in the Northeast. They are the tribes who will burst forth from their isolation in the Last Days. The Koran, 18:82ff.; 21:96ff., is the source of the tradition in Arabic and Persian writings. In the Koran, Gog and Magog are connected with the events that occur at the end of time and with the barrier built by Dhul-Qarnain in the rising-place of the sun.

The appearances of Gog and Magog is described differently in different sources. To my knowledge, the Arabic and the Persian sources are the only ones that describe them as having large ears, which they use as mattress and cover when they sleep.

According to al-Ṭabarī's *Tafsīr*, 1:195–96, Muhammed, taken to Gog and Magog by Gabriel, offered to convert them to Islam. They refused to accept Islam, and for this reason they were doomed to Hell. They want to break the barrier built by Dhul-Qarnain, but they will not succeed until one of them becomes Muslim. Then they will seize the world until the Messiah appears.

Gog and Magog also appear in *Mandeville's Travels*, p. 192. For more information see A. R. Anderson, *Alexander's Gate, Gog and Magog and the Enclosed Nations*.

71. Both Khidr (literally, "the green") and Ilyās (literally, "the myrtle") are considered to be immortal. According to Islamic legends Muhammed gave Khidr and Ilyās respectively the duty to aid traveling Muslims in the desert and in the sea.

72. She does not surrender Shahmalik to Alexander in this chapter.

73. The region where Dhul-Qarnain built the barrier against Gog and Magog. See the Koran, 18:92–93.

74. Shahmalik's daughter is at this point dead.

75. Gog and Magog. See above, n. 70.

76. This does not occur in the text. Perhaps the remark was recorded in a leaf that is missing from the manuscript.

77. For the attitude toward blacks in Islamic literature see Lewis, *Race and Color in Islam*.

78. On Jābalsā see above, n. 38.

## APPENDIX I

1. The *δ recension was probably based on an α type manuscript of the Pseudo-Callisthenes. For the *δ recension and its derivatives see Magoun, *Gests of King Alexander of Macedon*, pp. 38–62; Cary, *The Medieval Alexander*, pp. 11, 38–61; Ross, *Alexander Historiatus*, pp. 45–65.

2. Pfister, *Der Alexanderroman des Archpresbyters Leo*.

3. This work is an essay about the Indians and especially about the Brahmans. For its earliest version see C. Müller, ed., Pseudo-Callisthenes in *Arriani Anabasis et Indica* (Paris, 1877), bk. III, chs. 7–16, hereafter cited as Müller. See also Magoun, *Gests of King Alexander*, p. 44, nn. 3–5 and p. 45, nn. 1–4; Cary, *The Medieval Alexander*, pp. 12–13, 43.

4. This work, in which Alexander is unfavorably compared with the Indians, reflects the Cynic attack against Alexander. It occurs in Müller, bk. III, chs. 11–12. See also Magoun, *Gests of King Alexander*, p. 45, nn. 5–8; Cary, *The Medieval Alexander*, pp. 13, 43.

5. This work consists of letters supposed to have been exchanged between Alexander and Dindimus, the king of the Brahmans. The text exists in three forms. See Magoun, *Gests of King Alexander*, pp. 46–47; Cary, *The Medieval Alexander*, pp. 13–14.

6. Müller bk. III, ch. 17, gives the text of the letter supposed to have been written by Alexander to Aristotle about the wonders of India.

7. The source of this paragraph is Ross, *Alexander Historiatus*, p. 53.

8. Edition and English translation: *The History of Alexander the Great, Being the Syriac Version of the Pseudo-Callisthenes*, hereafter cited as *Syriac*.

9. English translation: *The Life and Exploits of Alexander the Great, Being a Series of Translations of the Ethiopic Histories of Alexander by Pseudo-Callisthenes*, hereafter cited as *Ethiopic*.

10. Edition: Pseudo Callisthenes, *The Life of Alexander of Macedon*, hereafter cited as Haight; also Müller.

11. My summary of this version is based on *Shāhnāmah-yi Firdawsī* 7:6–112. For the reader's convenience, references are given to the English translation: A. G. Warner and E. Warner, trans., *The Sháhnáma of Firdausí*, vol. 4 (London, 1905–25). This translation is accompanied by excellent notes and introductory comments.

12. Firdawsī's account is very close to al-Dīnawarī, see above, pp. 191ff.

13. In this Persian version of his birth, Alexander is made the elder brother of Darius and given a right to the Persian throne. To further justify his war against Darius, some romance writers portray Darius as a tyrant whose subjects welcomed Alexander as their liberator. Only after Persianizing Alexander could Persian romance writers celebrate him as the hero of their story. See Tarsūsī, *Dārābnāmah-yi Tarsūsī*, 1:387–91, from now on cited as *Dārābnāmah*; *Iskandarnāmah*, pp. 9–11. This account replaces the story of Nectanebus in Haight, bk I, chs. 1–12; Müller, bk. I, chs. 1–12; *Syriac*, bk. I, chs. 1–12; *Ethiopic*, pp. 1–29.

14. This is the only mention of Bucephalus in Persian Alexander-romances. In Haight, pp. 13–14, and *Ethiopic*, pp. 19, 37, the horse is given a more vital role. See A. R. Anderson, "Bucephalus and His Legend."

15. Haight; *Syriac*, bk. I, ch. 13; *Ethiopic*, p. 32; Niẓāmī, *Sharafnāmah*, pp. 85–88; *Iskandarnāmah*, p. 10; Jāmī, "Khiradnāmah-yi Iskandarī," pp. 930–32.

16. This account roughly corresponds to the *Ethiopic*, pp. 39ff.; al-Dīnawarī, see above, p. 191.

17. In Haight; Müller; *Syriac*, bk. I, ch. 23; *Ethiopic*, p. 34, the messenger comes in Philip's lifetime and is interviewed by Alexander. The golden eggs are mentioned in *Syriac* (p. 31), and in Niẓāmī, *Shrafnāmah* (p. 157), but not in Haight or *Ethiopic*.

18. The Persian romances and the *Ethiopic* correspond in omitting the events prior to the expedition to Egypt found in Haight and *Syriac*, bk. I, chs. 24–34.

19. Müller, bk. II, chs. 14–15; Haight, bk. II, chs. 14–16.

20. In the *Syriac*, bk. II, ch. 9, only one battle is mentioned.

21. Müller, bk. II, ch. 17; Haight, bk. II, ch. 10; *Syriac*, slightly different from the Greek, pp. 76–77; *Ethiopic*, p. 84.

22. Dārā's letter to Porus is longer in Müller, bk. II, ch. 19; Haight, bk. II, ch. 12; *Syriac*, bk. II, ch. 11, *Ethiopic*, pp. 88–99.

23. In the *Ethiopic*, pp. 89–90, and in Niẓāmī, *Sharafnāmah*, p. 214, Alexander himself bargains with the assassins to kill Dārā. In all versions, however, Alexander is moved to compassion by Dārā's death. Dārā's wish that a son born from the union of Alexander and Roxana would preserve the religion and the customs of the Persians is peculiar to *Shāhnāmah*.

In the *Ethiopic*, Alexander himself asks Dārā to give him his daughter in marriage.

24. In Haight, pp. 91–92; *Syriac*, pp. 83–84; *Ethiopic*, pp. 98–100; Niẓāmī, *Sharafnāmah*, p. 228; *Dārābnāmah*, p. 464; Alexander asks the assassins to come forward that he may exalt them above all men. When they do so, he has them hanged.

25. Haight, bk. II, ch. 21; *Syriac*, bk. II, ch. 21, *Ethiopic*, pp. 97–98; Niẓāmī, *Sharafnāmah*, pp. 256–61.

26. Müller; and Haight, bk. II, ch. 22; *Syriac*, bk. II, ch. 14; *Ethiopic*, pp. 101–7; Niẓāmī, *Sharafnāmah*, pp. 246–57; *Iskandarnāmah* does not record the episode.

27. The account of Kayd is given by Mas'ūdī (see above, p. 194). The ten dreams and their interpretation, however, are peculiar to Firdawsī. The source for both was perhaps a Pahlavi text. Kayd's episode occurs in Niẓāmī, *Sharafnāmah*, pp. 356–62.

28. Firdawsī's source for the romance was perhaps a version done by a Christian writer who made Alexander a Christian.

29. The episode is not found in any other text. Alexander, however, is characterized as being very fond of women in *Iskandarnāmah*, where Aristotle advises him to be more moderate. This portrait of the hero contrasts with the chaste Alexander of most Western Christian romances of Alexander.

30. In Haight, pp. 97–98, and *Syriac*, bk. III, ch. 2, it is Porus who writes to Alexander first. The *Ethiopic*, pp. 112–16, agrees with Firdawsī's version.

31. Haight and *Syriac*, bk. II, ch. I; *Ethiopic*, pp. 107–10.

32. Müller; Haight; and *Syriac*, bk. III, chs. 3–4; *Ethiopic*, pp. 119–25; Niẓāmī, *Sharafnāmah*, p. 336; *Iskandarnāmah*, pp. 19–20.

33. Found in Niẓāmī, *Sharafnāmah*, pp. 271–72; *Dārābnāmah*, 2:502–22; *Iskandarnāmah*, pp. 39–40, this account is of Islamic origin and is not found in the Greek, Syriac, or Ethiopic versions.

34. This section corresponds to Müller, and Haight, bk. III, chs. 18–24; *Syriac*, bk. III, chs. 8–14; *Ethiopic*, pp. 188–212; Niẓāmī, *Sharafnāmah*, pp. 227–308, *Iskandarnāmah*, pp. 48–52. There are differences in detail. The account of King Faryār is peculiar to Firdawsī. In the Greek the scene of the story is the kingdom of Semiramis.

35. Haight, bk. III, chs. 5–7; Müller and *Syriac*, bk. III, chs. 5–6; Jāmī, pp. 980–82. In the above texts the episode of the Brahmans occurs after the war with Porus.

36. Haight, bk. III, ch. 7; *Dārābnāmah*, 2:310. At this point Alexander's adventures become more fantastic. In the $\alpha$ recension they form the text of a letter written by Alexander to Aristotle placed between the Brahman and the Candace episodes. Müller, bk. III, ch. 17; Haight, bk. III, chs. 17–18, *Syriac*, bk. III, ch. 7, *Ethiopic*, pp. 141–89.

37. *Dārābnāmah*, II:253–73; *Iskandarnāmah*, p.106ff.

38. In his explanatory notes to the *Sháhnáma*, Warner declares (6:71) that Narmpāyān are mentioned in Pliny's *Nat Hist.*, bk. V, sec. 46, as "Himantopodes quidam quibus serpendo ingredi natura sit."
39. The episode of the dragon occurs only in the *Syriac*, p.107, and *Ethiopic*, p. 166. These versions are different in detail.
40. Haight and Müller, bk. III, chs. 25–27; *Syriac*, bk. III, chs. 15–17, *Ethiopic*, pp. 227–28.
41. The episode of the Water of Life does not appear in the α recension. In the *Syriac*, bk. III, ch. 18, there is an account of Alexander's journey in a very dark land but with none of the other features of the episode. In Müller, bk. III, chs. 39–41, Alexander's journey to the Land of Darkness in search of the Water of Life is given. Here Alexander's cook drinks of the water. The episode was interpolated in Jacob of Serugh's metrical romance (in *Syriac*, ll. 130–97). From there it reached Islamic sources. It occurs in the *Ethiopic*, pp. 261–72; Niẓāmī, *Sharafnāmah*, pp. 498–515; Jāmī, p. 963; and *Iskandarnāmah*, pp. 53ff.
42. The episode is not found in the α recension. It occurs in Müller, bk. III, ch. 26; *Ethiopic*, pp. 136–240; Niẓāmī, *Iqbālnāmah*, pp. 224–26; *Dārābnāmah*, 2:582–83.
43. Müller, bk. III, ch. 17; Haight, pp. 107–8; *Syriac*, bk. III, ch. 7; *Ethiopic*, pp. 172–80.
44. This is found only in the Arabic and Persian sources. See above, p. 193.
45. Müller; Haight, bk. III, ch. 30; *Syriac*, bk. III, ch. 19.
46. For Alexander's will see Müller and Haight, bk. III, ch. 33; *Syriac*, bk. III, ch. 22; *Ethiopic*, pp. 344–49.
47. The Pseudo-Callisthenes account of Alexander's death by poisoning does not occur in the Persian romances except in a modified version in Niẓāmī, *Iqbālnāmah*, pp. 254–60.
For Alexander's burial see Müller and Haight, bk. III, ch. 34; *Syriac*, bk. III, ch. 23; *Ethiopic*, pp. 350–51. For the sentences of the philosophers see above, p. 177 and nn. 62, 63, 64. Among the texts examined here only Jāmī, pp. 997–1002, and Firdawsī mention the episode.
48. Edited in 2 vols. by V. Dastgirdi (Tehran, 1937 and 1956).
49. Cf. above, p. 107ff.
50. The episode does not occur in Firdawsī, but exists in Haight, bk I, ch. 32; *Syriac*, bk. I, chs. 32–33; *Ethiopic*, p. 71.
51. Haight and *Syriac*, bk, I, chs. 36, 38; *Ethiopic*, pp. 65–69. Firdawsī omits the episode.
52. The portrait of Alexander as a fighter for Islam is similar to the Dhul-Qarnain in *al-Tījān*, and contrasts with the Christian Alexander of Firdawsī.
53. This motif occurs in *Iskandarnāmah* where Alexander wishes to learn about the Persian kings, because he himself is the son of a Persian king. In Niẓāmī this feature is preserved even though Alexander is said to be the son of Philip.

54. For analogues see Cary, *The Medieval Alexander*, pp. 209–10.
55. Niẓāmī combines features from the Amazon story with the Candace story. Harūm, for example, is the name given to the country of the Amazons in Firdawsī.
56. This is found in the Amazon story in Jewish sources. See Bonfils, *The Book of the Gests of Alexander of Macedon*, p. 16.
57. The episode of Kayd occurs here.
58. In the *Shāhnāmah* it is Alexander who visits the Emperor.
59. Two love scenes between Alexander and the Chinese maiden occur pp. 467–77, 486–98.
60. Slightly different in detail from the version of Firdawsī.
61. See above, pp. 200–1.
62. For the Hebrew version see Loewenthal, *Honein ibn Ishak, Sinnsprüche der Philosophen*.
63. 'Abd al-Raḥmān Barwī, ed. (Madrid, 1958).
64. In the thirteenth century Mubashshir's book was translated into a Spanish version which was translated into Latin, and in 1402 into French by Guillaume de Tignonville. From the French version an English translation was made by Stephen Scrope, *The Dicts and Sayings of the Philosophers*.
65. In a version of the story about Alexander and Diogenes the latter states that Alexander is a servant of his servant. See Cary, *The Medieval Alexander*, pp. 83–85.
66. Cf. *al-Tījān*, above, p. 198ff.
67. This episode is of Jewish origin. See Bonfils, *The Book of Gests of Alexander of Macedon*, pp. 4–11.
68. For the Garden of Iram see *Iskandarnāmah*, p. 93.
69. Cf. above, p. 215, n. 47.
70. Cf. above, p. 215, n. 46.
71. This is perhaps a reference to *Secretum Secretorum*, a book supposed to have been written by Aristotle for Alexander. See Cary, *The Medieval Alexander*, p. 106 ff.
72. For this story, commonly attributed to Diogenes, see *ibid.*, pp. 83–84, 146–49.
73. Cf. section on the wiles of women in *Iskandarnāmah*, p. 44ff.
74. See above, pp. 171–72.
75. See *Iskandarnāmah*, p. 147.
76. Safa ed., Persian Text Series, Nos. 23, 36.
77. Būrāndukht's adventures have been summarized by W. L. Hanaway, "Persian Popular Romances before the Safavid Period."
78. In the Islamic version of the Fall, Adam is forbidden to eat wheat.
79. See *Mandeville's Travels*, ed. M. C. Seymour (Oxford: Oxford University Press, 1967), p. 148.
80. *Ibid.*, pp. 143–44.

81. Alexander gains the service of the fairies and the giants. For this motif in the legends of Solomon see Ginzberg, *Legends of the Jews*, 6:149-54.
82. This episode is longer and more dramatic here than in other sources.
83. See above, p. 215, n. 38.
84. See *Mandeville's Travels*, p. 131.
85. Müller, p. 89; *Ethiopic*, pp. 282-84.
86. The episode of the wonderstone is given here.
87. See *al-Tījān*, above, p. 198ff.
88. The section dealing with Leo's text on the diagram is based on Ross, *Alexander Historiatus*, pp. 52, 60.

## APPENDIX II

1. M. Minavi, ed. (Tehran, 1933). Passages from Pahlavi texts are translated from Modern Persian translations into English by the present author unless otherwise indicated.
2. Translated into Modern Persian and edited by A. Kasravi (Tehran, 1928?).
3. The Byzantine or the Eastern Roman Empire was known as Rūm during the rule of the Sassanian dynasty (A.D. 229-652) and the early Islamic era. The word Rūm was used to mean Greece or Macedonia. Thus, by "the Rūmi Alexander," Alexander the Macedonian or the Greek is meant.
4. See Safa, *Ḥimāsah'sarā'ī dar Īrān*, pp. 451-61, 600-629.
5. Translated into Modern Persian and edited by M. Mu'in (Tehran, 1947).
6. Nöldeke, "Beiträge zur Geschichte des Alexanderromans," p. 34, takes this remark as evidence that the Iranians thought Alexander to be a king of Egypt.
7. Dastūrs, hīrbuds, and mūbids are Zoroastrian ecclesiastical orders.
8. B. T. Anklesaria, Eng. trans. (Bombay, 1956).
9. Gabriel du Chinon, *Relations Nouvelles du Levant* (Lyons, 1671), quoted in Darmesteter, "La Légende d'Alexandre chez les Parses," pp. 246-47.
10. See above, p. 169.
11. Chardin, quoted in Darmesteter, "Légende d'Alexandre," p. 232.

## APPENDIX III

1. See *The History of Alexander the Great Being the Syriac Version of the Pseudo-Callisthenes*, especially "A Christian Legend Concerning Alexander," which follows the text of the Syriac romance (pp. 144-58), and the poetic version of the same legend by Jacob of Serugh (*ibid.*, pp. 163-200), hereafter cited as *Syriac*.
2. See Spiegel, *Die Alexandersage bei den Orientalen*; Nöldeke, "Beiträge zur Geschichte des Alexanderromans"; Weymann, *Die aethiopische und arabische*

*Übersetzung des Pseudocallisthenes;* Pfister, *Alexander der Grosse in den Offenbarungen der Griechen, Juden, Mohammedaner und Christen.*

3. The twelfth-century Persian history, *Mujmal al-tawārīkh wa-al-qiṣaṣ,* p. 10, gives the following account of the fate of Persian books: "When Alexander the Great conquered Iran, he . . . gathered all the learned men and all the books of which he chose some to be translated, sending the translations to Aristotle in Greece. Then he burnt all the books of the Iranians and put all the priests and the learned men to death. No one remained who had a proper knowledge of any science or who would keep the chronicles" (translation mine).

4. Spiegel, *Die Alexandersage bei den Orientalen,* p. 51.

5. *Kitāb al-akhbār al-ṭiwāl,* pp. 31–41.

6. This Persian version of Alexander's birth converted Alexander into an Iranian king and the elder brother of Darius. Thus the war between Darius and Alexander became the war between two brothers belonging to the same royal dynasty and having equal rights to the throne.

The same motive was behind the Egyptian version of the birth of Alexander in the Pseudo-Callisthenes. Here Alexander is the son of Olympias and Nectanebus, an Egyptian king. According to a prophecy, Alexander would free Egypt from subjugation to the Persians.

7. This corresponds to *Syriac,* p. 31; Firdawsī, *The Sháhnáma of Firdausí,* Warner trans., 6:36.

8. Cf. the account of the *al-Tījān,* where Ṣa'b Dhul-Qarnain, an oppressive king, visited by a dream, learns to be humble. See above, p. 199. A similar episode exists in the Ethiopic version of the Pseudo-Callisthenes: *The Life and Exploits of Alexander the Great, Being a Series of Translations of Ethiopic Histories of Alexander by the Pseudo-Callisthenes and Other Writers,* from now on referred to as *Ethiopic.* Here Alexander chooses Aristotle, who is a believer, as his master and his counselor (pp. 39–40). He gathers the people of his palace, who are idolaters, and calls them to worship the true God (pp. 40–41). The episode is not found in the Greek or the *Syriac.*

Oriental accounts of Alexander generally magnify the figure of Aristotle and his role. This tendency goes back ultimately to the motif of the king and the wise minister found frequently in oriental fairytales and romances.

9. This corresponds to Pseudo-Callisthenes, *The Life of Alexander of Macedon,* p. 88, hereafter cited as Haight; *Syriac,* p. 80; *Ethiopic,* p. 91; *Sháhnáma,* 6:53.

10. This corresponds to Haight, pp. 88–89; *Syriac,* pp. 79–81; *Ethiopic,* p. 95; *Sháhnáma,* 6:55.

11. This corresponds to Haight, pp. 92–95; *Syriac,* bk. II, ch. 14, *Ethiopic,* pp. 101–6; *Sháhnáma,* 6:55.

12. This corresponds to Haight, bk. III, ch. 4; *Syriac,* pp. 87–92; *Ethiopic,* pp. 119–24, *Sháhnáma,* 6:112–19.

13. A historical person mentioned in al-Ziriklī's *al-A'lām,* vol. 8. He was a descendant of the Prophet.

14. This episode is found in Arabic sources and their derivatives. See *al-Tījān*, above, p. 199; *Sháhnáma*, 6:119–21; and the translation, above, p. 39ff.
15. This corresponds to Haight, pp. 108–17; *Syriac*, pp. 117–27; *Ethiopic*, pp. 188–211; *Sháhnáma*, 6:124–43.
16. This episode does not appear in the α recension of the Pseudo-Callisthenes, or in the Syriac, but is found in the γ recension of the Pseudo-Callisthenes. See "Pseudo-Callisthenes," in *Arriani Anabasis et Indica*, bk II, chs. 39–49. The episode is also found in the version of Jacob of Serugh in *Syriac*, bk. II, pp. 132–207; *Ethiopic*, pp. 263–77; *Sháhnáma*, 6:159–62.
17. The Green Sea, also called Bahr al-Muḥīṭ. See al-Masʿūdī, *Al-Tanbīh wa-al-ishraf* (Beirut, 1965), p. 68.
18. Cf. "A Christian Legend Concerning Alexander" in *Syriac*, pp. 145–46, 148; *Ethiopic*, p. 219. The episode does not appear in the Greek.
19. In the *Syriac* the episode forms part of Alexander's letter to Aristotle. Here Alexander calls himself Pithaos. See also *Ethiopic*, pp. 172–76, *Sháhnáma*, 7:169–74.
20. Cf. Koran, 18:82ff., where Dhul-Qarnain's journey to the rising place and the setting place of the sun and the account of the building of the barrier against Gog and Magog are given. The episode is the main subject of the "Christian Legend." See *Syriac*, pp. 153–156; *Ethiopic*, pp. 237–241; *Sháhnáma*, 6:163–65.
21. Cf. Alexander's visit to the Amazons, Haight, bk. III, chs. 24–27; *Syriac*, bk. III, ch. 15; *Ethiopic*, pp. 212–15; *Sháhnáma*, 6:153–58.
22. This corresponds to the "History of al-Makin" in the *Ethiopic*, pp. 366–67; and to the account in Pahlavi sources. See above, p. 188.
23. In Persian and Arabic histories Alexander dies of sickness near Babylon or Jerusalem. In Haight, bk. III, chs. 31–32; *Syriac*, p. 135; *Ethiopic*, pp. 340–44, Alexander is poisoned by Cassandar, the son of his enemy, Antipater.
24. In the *Ethiopic*, p. 348, Alexander asks that his body be placed in a gold coffin.
25. *Tārīkh al-rusul wa-al-mulūk*, added title, *Annales* . . . , 2:692–704.
26. Cf. Haight and *Syriac*, bk. I, chs. 36, 38; *Ethiopic*, pp. 35–36, 68.
27. This corresponds to the *Ethiopic*, pp. 89–91. The only Persian sources that have these accounts are Ṭarsūsī, *Dārābnāmah*, I:461, and Nizāmī, see above, p. 175.
28. Alexander was thirty-six when he died.
29. This does not appear in the Greek.
30. *Murūj al-dhahab wa maʿādin al-jawhar*, 1:318–32. Masʿūdī always refers to Alexander as the son of Philip.
31. In the Arabic book of proverbs by Ḥunayn ibn Isḥāq in the ninth century there is a section devoted to the moralizing of philosophers at Alexander's tomb. This section found its way into *Disciplina Clericalis* of Petrus Alfonsi and the I[3] recension of *Historia de Preliis*. The whole is perhaps related to the account of al-Mubashshir ibn Fatik, *Mukhtār al-ḥikam wa maḥāsin al-kilam*. This last version, however, was written in the middle of the eleventh century.

The episode is found in the *Sháhnáma* 6:185–87; "The History of al-Makin," in *Ethiopic*, pp. 376–80; "The History of abū Shākir," ibid., pp. 398–401.

32. The episode is given by Abū Shākir in the *Ethiopic*, p. 398.

33. This episode does not occur in the Greek. It is found in the *Sháhnáma*, 6:98–110, where the source is declared to be Pahlavi. Originally it must have been independent of the legends of Alexander. It occurs in the Alexander-romance of Niẓāmī, whose Kayd episode is much shorter than Firdawsī's.

34. Both the Pseudo-Callisthenes and the talmudic sources may ultimately derive from a common source. See Bonfils. *The Book of the Gests of Alexander of Macedon*, pp. 19–20.

35. The *Midrash Agadah*, edited by S. Buber (Vienna, 1894), vol. II, Nu. xxx, 15, p. 157, tells how Alexander buried the bones of Jeremiah in Alexandria to keep away noxious serpents. The legend occurs first in Pseudo-Epiphanius's *Vitae Prophetarum*, and passes to Petrus Comestor's *Historia Scholastica Patrologiae Cursus Completus, Accurante*, edited by J. P. Migne, Series Latina (Paris, 1908). In Haight the legend occurs in bk. I, ch. 32. See Bonfils, *The Book of the Gests of Alexander of Macedon*, pp. 23–24; Cary, *The Medieval Alexander*, p. 132, Pfister, *Alexander der Grosse in den Offenbarungen der Griechen, Juden, Mohammedaner und Christen*, pp. 45–50.

36. *Tārīkh sinī mulūk al-arẓ wa-al-anbiyā'*.

37. *Tarjumah wa taklimah-yi tārīkh-i Ṭabarī*, pp. 692–720. Al-Balʿamī mentions the war of Alexander with the Zangīs (the Zinj), an episode which occurs in *Iskandarnāmah*—see pp. 75 and 106ff.

38. *Āthār al-bāqīyah ʿan al-qurūn al-khāliyah*, pp. 59–66.

39. Edited by E. C. Sachau (New Delhi, 1964), pp. 96–97. Text in English translation.

40. Edited by G. Le Strange and R. A. Nicholson (London, 1921), pp. 15–16, 55–57.

41. M. T. Bahar, ed.

42. The text mentioned here has not been identified. It must have been an Alexander-romance with the version of the birth as in Pseudo-Callisthenes.

43. *Al-Kāmil fī al-tārīkh*, edited by Carbus J. Tornberg (Beirut, 1965), I:282–92.

44. *The Koran*, pp. 98–99.

45. Abū al-Kalām Āzād, *Dhul-Qarnain yā Kūrush-i Kabīr*, identifies Dhul-Qarnain with Cyrus the Great. The book was originally part of his commentary of the Koran. The passage in the Koran, he argues, was revealed to the Prophet in answer to a question asked him by the Jews. Examining Jewish sources for the identity of the Dhul-Qarnain, Abū al-Kalām Āzād quotes Dan. 8:1–7, 20–21; Isa. 44:25–28; 45:1–4; 46:10-11; and Jer. 2:1-2, and concludes that the Dhul-Qarnain is Cyrus the Great, for he was likened to a two-horned ram in Daniel's dream, and he was highly esteemed by the Jews (p. 25). Further, he observes that Alexander built no wall, and in his deeds did not resemble the Dhul-Qarnain of the Koran.

# NOTES: APPENDIX III 221

Abū al-Kalām Āzād ignores the fact that the passage could have been based on the legendary rather than the historical Alexander, and that Alexander was accepted as a national hero in Jewish tradition. Furthermore, even though the historical Alexander did not build a wall, in Hebrew tradition based upon the account of Josephus, it was believed that Alexander had constructed the Caspian Gate to keep out the northern barbarians. (See Anderson, *Alexander's Gate, Gog and Magog and the Enclosed Nations*). Moreover, Cyrus was never connected with the events of the Last Days anywhere in the Bible. It was in the "Christian Legend Concerning Alexander," (*Syriac*) that the events of the Last Day and the building of the wall were brought together and were attributed to Alexander. In the Koran these events are mentioned in relation to Dhul-Qarnain.

46. See al-Balʻamī, *Tārīkh*, 692–720; *Mujmal al-tawārīkh wa-al-qisas*, p. 31; al-Bīrūnī, *Āthār al-bāqīyah*, pp. 59–65.

For an effective summary of the scholarship on the subject and bibliography see Anderson's "Alexander's Horns" and his *Alexander's Gate*. . . . mentioned above, n. 45.

47. See above, p. 75.

48. See *Mujmal al-tawārīkh*, pp. 31, 204.

49. The Arabic account of *al-Tījān* is quoted by Mark Lidsbarski in "Zu den arabischen Alexandergeschichten," *Zeitschrift für Assyriologie und Verwandte Gebiete* 8 (1893): 263–312. *Al-Tījān* appears in pp. 278–312.

50. *Al-Tījān* is of special interest to us, for the author of the romance translated here indicates Wahb as the source of some of his stories. See above, p. 64.

51. The faith of Abraham was the prototype of Judaism and Islam.

52. The question asked by Wahb shows that some believed that Dhul-Qarnain of the Koran was Alexander.

53. On several other occasions the statement that the Dhul-Qarnain of the Koran was not Alexander is repeated. It seems, however, that the later romance writers and historians ignored the statement and attributed the episodes of the *al-Tījān* to Alexander.

54. Musá is the Arabic form of Moses. Later in the *al-Tījān*, the name of the prophet occurs as Khidr. In most romances of Alexander, Khidr serves as Alexander's guide in his journey to the Land of Darkness.

55. Like Alexander, Ṣaʻb is the ruler of the entire world. Perhaps the character of Solomon was the prototype for this motif. See Reich, *Tales of Alexander the Macedonian*, pp. 9–13.

According to the legends of Solomon in *Qiṣaṣ al-anbiyāʼ* of Abū Isḥāq Ibrāhīm ibn Manṣūr al-Nayshābūrī, edited by H. Yaghmaʼi (Tehran, 1961), pp. 281–83, Solomon prayed to God for seventy nights, begging God to enlarge his dominion. God granted Solomon's request, promising to make him the sole ruler of the world and its inhabitants.

Solomon prayed for seventy more nights and begged that God give him power over the fairies. This request was granted also. Solomon continued praying for more power until the sovereignty over the giants, all the birds and animals, the winds, the waters, and everything under the sun was given him.

56. This corresponds to the portrait of Alexander in the fabulous romances as well as all the branches of the Pseudo-Callisthenes.

57. In *Iskandarnāmah* Alexander demands that the fairies leave the land and return to sea. The fairy element in this romance is ultimately derived from the legends of Solomon. The writer must have had access to a collection of the legends of prophets written by Wahb ibn Munabbih. I was unable to find the text of Wahb's legends. However, Wahb is known to have compiled many collections of legends and tales, and is mentioned as the source of some of the stories in Nayshābūrī's *Qiṣaṣ al-anbiyā'*.

58. See above, p. 219, n. 14.

59. Cf. the passage from the Koran, quoted above, pp. 196–97.

60. Musá al-Khiḍr is hereafter referred to as Khiḍr in the original.

61. This corresponds to the *Ethiopic*, p. 276, and *Sháhnáma*, 6:162.

62. This corresponds with the character of Alexander as a prophet in Niẓāmī's *Iqbālnāmah*. Likewise, in *Iskandarnāmah* Alexander presents Islam to idolaters.

63. In al-Ṭabarī's commentary of the Koran, *Tarjumah-yi tafsīr-i Ṭabarī* edited by H. Yaghma'i (Tehran, 1960–65), 1:33, Muhammed, taken to these tribes by Gabriel, presents them with the faith.

64. This occurs in the *Sháhnáma*, 6:161.

65. This corresponds to the *Ethiopic*, pp. 271–72. The episode of Alexander and the wonderstone is of Hebrew origin and occurs in the Babylonian Talmud. See Cary, *The Medieval Alexander*, pp. 19–21.

In the *Ethiopic* the grapes are given Alexander by a bird. See pp. 275–76.

66. This is reminiscent of the story of Alexander and the Brahmans. See Magoun, *The Gests of Alexander of Macedon*, pp. 44–45; Cary, *The Medieval Alexander*, pp. 12–13.

67. "Wie andre Geschichten" says Nöldeke, "so hat Muhammed natürlich auch diese auf mündlichem Wege erhalten. Vielleicht wusste schon sein Gewährsmann den Namen Alexander nicht mehr, vielleicht hat ihn nur der Prophet nicht behalten. Die characteristische Bezeichnung, 'der Zweigehörnte,' die in der Legende zweimal vorkommt, genügte. Dafür, dass grade sie die Quelle Muhammed's ist, spricht noch ganz besonders die Verbindung des Wallbaues durch den Zweigehörnten mit der Stelle über den Auf-und Untergang der Sonne." ("Beiträge," p. 32).

The two passages referred to above are as follows: (a) Alexander, praying to God says, " . . . thou hast made me horns upon my head, wherewith I might thrust down the kingdoms of the world" (*Syriac*, p. 146). (b) Addressing Alexander, God says, "Behold I have magnified thee upon all kingdoms, and I have made horns of iron grow on thy head" (*ibid.*, p. 156).

# NOTES: APPENDIX III

Both the "Christian Legend Concerning Alexander" and the poetic version of Jacob of Serugh are based upon chs. 37–39 of the second book of Pseudo-Callisthenes, ed. Müller. See Budge's introduction to the *Syriac*, p. lxxvii.

According to the "Christian Legend," Alexander left an inscription on the barrier against Gog and Magog after it was finished. See pp. 154ff. This is not mentioned in the Koran but occurs in the Persian history *Mujmal al-tawārīkh wa-al-qiṣaṣ*, p. 57, where the text of the inscription is given in Arabic. None of the other sources examined above mention the inscription. The following is my translation of it:

In the name of God the mighty, the generous. This barrier was built with the power of God. It will remain as long as God wills, and upon the conclusion of 860 years from this millenium, this barrier will break open in a time when sins are abundant, when all man is concerned with is himself, and when hearts have become hard. Then from this wall these nations shall come forth in such number as only God can count. They will reach the West and eat whatever they come upon of food and fruit. They will even consume the grass and the leaves of trees, and shall drink all the waters they come upon until they will not leave of the water a sip. And when they reach the land of Sābūs [west of Tigris] they will destroy the inhabitants to the last person with the decree and permission of God.

68. On this issue see Guillaume, "The Influence of Judaism on Islam," pp. 129–71, esp. pp. 132, 141.

# Bibliography

Works are listed under their authors and in the case of anonymous works, under their titles.

## PRIMARY SOURCES IN THE ARABIC SCRIPT

*Literary Works*
Firdawsī, Abū al-Qāsim. *Shāhnāmah-yi Firdawsī*. Edited by E. Bertels. 10 vols. Moscow, 1963–71.
*Iskandarnāmah*. Edited by Iraj Afshar. Persian Texts Series, no 17. Tehran, 1964.
Jāmī, 'Abd al-Rahmān. "Khiradnāmah-yi Iskandarī." In *Masnavī-yi haft awrang*, edited by M. Madrasi Gilani. Tehran, 1958.
Nizāmī, Nizām al-Dīn Ilyās. *Sharafnāmah*. Edited by Vahid Dastgirdi. Tehran, 1937.
—— *Iqbālnāmah yā Khiradnāmah*. Edited by Vahid Dastgirdi. Tehran, 1956.
al-Ṭarsūsī, Abū Ṭāhir Muḥammad. *Dārābnāmah-yi Ṭarsūsī*. Edited by Z. Safa. 2 vols. Persian Text Series, nos. 23, 36. Tehran, 1965–68.

*Histories*
Bal'amī, Abū 'Alī Muḥammad. *Tarjumah va taklamah-yi tārīkh-i Ṭabarī*. Edited by M. T. Bahar. Tehran, 1962.
al-Bīrūnī, Abū Rayhān. *Athār al-bāqīyah 'an al-qurūn al-khālīyah*. Translated into Persian by A. Danasirisht. Tehran, 1942.
al-Dīnāwarī, Abū Ḥanīfah. *Kitāb al-akhbār al-ṭiwāl*. Leiden, 1888.
Ibn al-Athīr. *al-Kāmil fī al-tārīkh*. 12 vols. Beirut, 1965–66.
Ibn Hishām. *Kitāb al-Tījān*. In Mark Lidzbarski, "Zu den arabischen Alexandergeschichten," *Zeitschrift für Assyriologie und verwandte Gebiete* 8 (1893):278–312.
al-Iṣfahānī, Ḥamzah ibn al-Ḥasan. *Tārīkh sinī mulūk al-arẓ wa-al-anbīyā'*. Beirut, n. d.

al-Mas'ūdī, Abū al-Hasan 'Alī. *Kitāb al-tanbīh wa-al-ishrāf.* Beirut, 1965.
—— *Murūj al-dhahab wa ma'ādin al-jawhar.* 4 vols. Beirut, 1965–66.
*Mujmal al-tawārīkh wa-al-qiṣaṣ.* Edited M. T. Bahar. Tehran, 1940.
al-Ṭabarī, Abū Ja'far Muḥammad. *Tārīkh al-rusul wa-al-mulūk.* Added title page: *Annales,* edited by J. Barth et al. 15 vols. Beirut, 1962–65.

## PRIMARY SOURCES IN LATIN, ENGLISH, OR ENGLISH TRANSLATION

Bonfils, I. *The Book of the Gests of Alexander of Macedon.* Edited and translated by I. Kazis. Cambridge: The Medieval Academy of America, 1962.
"A Christian Legend Concerning Alexander." In *The History of Alexander the Great Being the Syriac Version of the Pseudo-Callisthenes* (q.v.).
"Epistola Alexandri ad Aristotelem." In *Three Old English Prose Texts,* edited by S. Rypins. Early English Text Society, Original Series 161, pp. 79–100. London, 1924.
Firdawsī, Abū al-Qāsim. *The Sháhnáma of Firdausí.* Translated by A. G. Warner and E. Warner. 9 vols. London, 1905–25.
*Historia Alexandri Magni.* Edited by W. Kroll. Berlin, 1926.
*The History of Alexander the Great, Being the Syriac Version of the Psuedo-Callisthenes.* Translated by E. A. W. Budge. Cambridge, 1889.
Jacob of Serugh. "A Discourse Composed by Mar Jacob upon Alexander. . . ." In *The History of Alexander the Great Being the Syriac Version of the Pseudo-Callisthenes* (q.v.).
Julius Valerius. *Res Gestae Alexandri Macedonis.* Edited by B. Kuebler. Leipzig, 1888.
*The Life and Exploits of Alexander the Great, Being a Series of Translations of the Ethiopic Histories of Alexander by the Pseudo-Callisthenes and Other Writers.* Translated by E. A. W. Budge. London, 1896.
Niẓāmī, Niẓām al-Dīn Abū Muhammad. *The Sikandar Nāma-e Bara, or Book of Alexander the Great.* . . . Translated by H. Wilberforce Clarke. London, 1881.
Pseudo-Callisthenes. *The Life of Alexander of Macedon by Pseudo-Callisthenes.* Translated by E. H. Haight. New York: Longmans, Green, 1955.
"Pseudo-Callisthenes." In *Arriani Anabasis et Indica.* Edited by C. Müller. Paris, 1877.
*Tales of Alexander the Macedonian.* Edited and translated by R. Reich. New York, Ktav. 1972.

## SECONDARY SOURCES

Works in the Arabic script are marked with an asterisk.
*Abū al-Kalām Āzād, Mawlānā. *Dhul-Qarnain yā Kūrush-i Kabīr.* Translated into Persian by M. A. Bastani Parizi. Tehran, 1965.

Anderson, A. R. "Alexander's Horns." *American Philological Association Transactions and Proceedings* 58 (1927):100-122.
—— "Bucephalus and His Legend." *American Journal of Philology* 51 (1930):1-21.
—— *Alexander's Gate, Gog and Magog and Enclosed Nations*. Medieval Academy of American Publications, No. 12, Cambridge, Mass., 1932.
*Ardāvīrāfnāmag. Translated from Pahlavi into Modern Persian and edited M. Mu'in. Tehran, 1947.
Bacher, W. *Nizami's Leben und Werke und der zweite Theil des Nizamischen Alexanderbuches*. . . . Göttingen, 1871.
*Bahar, M. T. *Sabkshināsī*. 2 vols. Tehran, n. d.
*The Bakhtyār Nāma*. Translated by W. A. Clouston, Lanarkshire, 1833.
Berzunza, J. A. *A Tentative Classification of Books, Pamphlets, and Pictures Concerning Alexander the Great and the Alexander Romances*. Privately printed, 1939.
al-Bīrūnī, *Albiruni's India*. Translated and edited by Edward C. Sachau. 2 vols. in 1. New Delhi, 1964.
Cary, George. *The Medieval Alexander*. Cambridge: Cambridge University Press, 1956.
Darmesteter, James. "La Légende d'Alexandre chez les Parses." In *Essais Orientaux*, pp. 227-50. Paris, 1883.
*Dihkhudā, 'Alī Akbar. *Lughatnāmah*, "Iskandar" and "Dhul-Qarnain." Tehran, vols. dated 1952, 1950.
Donath, L. *Die Alexandersage in Talmud und Midrasch*. Fulda, 1873.
Gaster, M. "An Old Hebrew Romance of Alexander." *The Journal of the Royal Asiatic Society* (1897):485-549.
Ginzberg, L. *The Legends of the Jews*. 7 vols. Philadelphia: The Jewish Publication Society of America, 1925-47.
Guillaume, A. "The Influence of Judaism on Islam." In *The Legacy of Israel*, edited by E. A. Revan and C. Singer. Oxford: Oxford University Press, 1953.
Hamilton, G. L. "A New Redaction (I³ᵃ) of the *Historia de Preliis* and the Date of the Redaction I³. *Speculum* 2 (1927):113-64.
Hanaway, W. L. "*Persian Popular Romances before the Safavid Period*." Ph.D. dissertation, Columbia University, 1970.
*Hudūd al-'ālam: The Regions of the World, A Persian Geography*, 982 A.D. trans. V. Minorsky. London, 1937.
*Ibn al-Balkhī, *Fārsnāmah*. Edited by G. Le Strange and R. A. Nicholson. Gibb Memorial Series, n.s., 1. London, 1921.
*Kārnāmag-i Ardashīr-i Bābagān*. Translated into Modern Persian from Pahlavi and edited by A. Kasravi. Tehran, 1928?
The Koran, Translated by George Sale. London, Frederick Warne, n.d.
Lévi, I. "La Légende d'Alexandre dans le Talmud." *Revue des Etudes Juives* 2 (1881):293-300; 7 (1883):78-93.

Lewis, Bernard. *Race and Color in Islam*. New York: Harper and Row, 1971.
Loewenthal, A. *Honein ibn Ishak, Sinnsprüche der Philosophen*. Berlin, 1896.
Magoun, F. P. *Gests of King Alexander of Macedon*. Cambridge, Mass.: Harvard University Press, 1929.
*al-Mubashshir ibn Fātik. *Mukhtār al-ḥikam wa maḥāsin al-kilām*. Edited by 'Abd al-Rahmān Barwī. Madrid, 1958.
*Nayshābūrī, Ibrāhīm ibn Manṣūr. *Qiṣaṣ al anbiyā'*. Edited by H. Yaghma'i. Persian Texts Series, no. 119. Tehran, 1961.
Nöldeke, T. "Beiträge zur Geschichte des Alexanderromans." In *Denkschriften der Kaiserlichen Akademie der Wissenschaften*, Philos.-Hist. Klasse 38 (1890).
—— *Das Iranische Nationalepos*. Berlin, 1920.
Pfister, F. *Der Alexanderroman des Archipresbyters Leo*, Sammlung Mittellat. Texte, vol. 6. Heidelberg, 1913.
—— *Alexander der Grosse in den Offenbarungen der Griechen, Juden, Mohammedaner und Christen*. Berlin, 1956.
Plutarch, *Parallel Lives*. Translated by B. Perrin. 11 vols. London, 1914–26.
Ross, D. J. A. *Alexander Historiatus: A Guide to Medieval Illustrated Alexander Literature*. London, 1963.
*Safa, Z., ed. *Ḥimāsah'sarā'ī dar Īrān*. Tehran, 1954.
Schlauch, M. *Chaucer's Constance and Accused Queens*. New York: New York University Press, 1927.
Scrope, Stephen. *The Dicts and Sayings of the Philosophers*. Edited by C. F. Bühler. Early English Text Society, Original Series 211. London, 1941.
Spiegel, F. *Die Alexandersage bei den Orientalen*. Leipzig, 1851.
*al-Ṭabarī, Abū Ja'far Muhammad ibn al-Jarīr. *Tarjumah-yi Tafsīr-i Ṭabarī*. Edited by H. Yaghma'i. 7 vols. Tehran, 1960–65.
*Tansar, Hirbuzān Hīrbuz. *Nāmah-yi Tansar*. Edited by M. Minavi. Tehran, 1933.
Tavadia, J. C. *Die mittelpersische Sprache und Literatur der Zarathustrier*. Leipzig, 1956.
Thompson, S. *Motif Index of Folk Literature*. 6 vols. Bloomington: Indiana University Press, 1955–58.
Weymann, K. F. *Die aethiopische und arabische Übersetzung des Pseudocallisthenes*. Kirchhain, N. L., 1901.
*Zand-Ākāsih, Iranian or Greater Bundahišn*. Translated into English by Behramgore Tehmuras Anklesaria. Bombay, 1956.
*al-Ziriklī, Khayr al-Dīn. *al-A'lām*. 10 vols. Cairo, 1954.

# Index

'Abd al-Rahman ibn Abi al-Barakat, 3, 115
Abel, 31
Abraham, 40, 171, 198, 201, 208
Abraham, faith of, 74, 175, 198, 201, 208, 221
Abu Sa'id Khargushi, 63, 210
Abu Shakir, 220
'Ad, 93, 106, 211
Adam, 31, 93, 182, 206–7, 216
Adam's tomb, 30–31, 38, 182, 206–7
Afrasiyab (national enemy in Iranian legendry), 38, 54, 94, 104, 188, 208
Afridun (Iranian legendary King), 54, 93
Afshar, I., 3
Ahriman (principle of evil in Zoroastrianism), 187, 188, 207
Ahuramazda, see Ohrmazd
Akhtaf, 120, 126, 136
al-A'lam, 208, 210, 218
Alexander, 1; birth in Persian accounts, 3, 9–10, 168, 188–89, 191, 195, 205, 213, 218; birth in Pseudo-Callisthenes, 168, 174, 196, 215, 218, 220; as a Christian, 170, 171, 214; cupidity of, 20, 22, 48, 50, 59, 93, 159, 173, 176, 177, 200; disguises of, 17–18, 30, 41–42, 48, 67, 169, 171; divine protection of, 17–18, 31–32, 35, 61–62, 67, 73, 90–91, 120–21; dreams of, 101, 113, 135–36; as follower of faith of Abraham, 175, 201; horoscope of, 10, 73, 174; interest in marvels, 3, 30–31, 54–55, 63–65, 120–21, 158, 178–79, 182–84; justice of, 10, 11–12, 13, 21, 33, 36, 37, 66, 104, 159, 196; likened to Solomon, 76, 77, 91, 92, 163, 184, 217, 222; as Muslim king against infidels, 20, 25–26, 30, 43, 65, 97–98, 105, 119, 120, 149, 151, 158–59, 179, 182, 215; Persianization of, 3, 9–10, 66, 145, 168, 181, 215; as prophet and sage, 178–79, 180, 201, 222; as protector of mankind, 94–95, 97, 113; Two-Horned, see Dhul-Qarnain; worries about death, 35, 46, 57, 73, 113–14, 121, 151, 173
Alexander and Diogenes or Socrates, legend of, 180, 216
*Alexander Historiatus*, 217
Alexander histories, *see* al-Bal'ami; Ibn al-Balkhi; al-Dinawari; Justin; al-Mas'udi; Orosius; Quintus Curtius
Alexander-romances, *see* Pseudo-Callisthenes
*Alexanderroman des Archpresbyters Leo, Der*, 2, 205
*Alexandersage bei den Orientalen, Die*, 190, 217
*Alexandersage in Talmud und Midrasch, Die*, 205
Alexander's battles; against Anbar, 114; against Arsalankhan, 152–54, 156, 157–58; against Darab, 12–13, 169–70, 175–76, 182; against Davalpayan, 36–37; against fairies, 79–80, 86–87, 96; against giants, 76, 92–93, 96; against Gog and Magog, 152–53; against Gold Bees, 34–35; against Jundul, 147–48; against King of Egypt, 44; against King of Yemen, 43; against Mankus, 120; against Porus, 18–20, 171; against Qatil, 106, 109–11, 119–20; against Russians, 102; against Shahmalik, 120; against the Turks, 120–21, 126–29; against Yaqutmalik, 161, 162; against Zangis, 106–7, 109–10, 112, 114, 119–20, 147–48, 174, 182

## INDEX

Alexander's expeditions; Amazon, 172, 176, 216, 219; Andalusia, 3, 47, 48, 53, 200; Ceylon, 17, 20, 21, 22, 23, 30, 38, 206; China, 3, 5, 66, 67, 176, 180, 192, 194, 196, 201; Egypt, 3, 5, 43, 44, 169, 171, 174, 183, 188, 196; Ethiopia, 180, 192, 200; India, 3, 63, 99, 170, 176, 182, 192, 193, 194; Iran, 3, 11–13, 169–70, 175, 192; Kashmir, 17, 22, 30, 38; Khvarazm, 180; Land of Darkness, 3, 33, 35, 48, 53, 54, 55, 56–59, 61, 63, 64, 92, 104, 121, 172, 177, 192, 195, 198, 200, 215, 221; Land of Davalpayan, 36–37, 172, 207, 215; Land of fairies, 3, 74–75, 76, 210, 211; Land of giants, 74, 75; Land of Gold, 22, 30, 32–36; Land of Zangis, 34, 78, 98, 103–5, 106–14, 119–20, 121, 131–32, 147–48, 150, 158, 174, 182, 210; Mecca, 39–40, 171, 183, 192, 199, 206, 207, 208; Oman, 15, 16, 17, 18, 20, 37; Russia, 100, 102, 180; Sagha, 53; Yemen, 3, 40, 41, 42, 43, 173, 176, 192

*Alexander's Gate, Gog and Magog and Enclosed Nations*, 212, 221

"Alexander's Horns," 221

Alexander's wives, *see* Araqit; Barqatisah; Burandukht; Kayd's daughter; the King's daughter; Mahafarin; Maiden saved from Zangis; Nahid; Qatil's bride; Qaymun's daughter; Roxana; Shahmalik's daughter; Sitarah; Suhayl; Zubaydah; *see also* Polygamy

Alexandria, 1, 173, 174, 178, 181, 193, 194, 195, 198

Alisa', 209, *see also* Elijah; Yisa'

Allah Akbar, 19, 32, 35, 79, 110, 206

Amazon (also called Harum), 172, 176, 216, 219

Ammon (Egyptian divinity), 1

Amshaspandan (high angels in Zoroastrianism), 188

'Anbar, 112, 113, 114, 165

Andalusia, 3, 47, 48, 53, 200

Anderson, A. R., 212, 213, 221

Apocalypse of St. John of Patmos, 207

Apocryphal Gospel, 210

Arabian Peninsula, 192

'Arafat, 40, 208

Araqit, Fairy Queen, 76, 77, 78, 79; bears a son, 120; betrays Alexander, 153–55; fights Alexander, 77–78, 79, 87–88, 96; fights 'Anbar, 114; fights Arsalankhan, 141, 158; fights the Gog and Magog, 152–53; fights Qatil, 121–22; fights Shahmalik, 148; fights Tafqaj, 131–32; fights the Turks, 121–22; fights Yaqutmalik, 160–61; is likened to Queen of Sheba, 83; is seduced by Shahmalik, 122–26; kidnaps Alexander, 80–82; marries Alexander, 97–98, surrenders to Alexander, 95

Arastatalis, *see* Aristotle

Ardashir (Sassanid King), 187, 208

Ardavan (king mentioned in *Shahnamah*), 208

*Ardavirafnamag*, 188

Ariobarzanes (Darab's assassin), 206, *see also* Janusibar; Mahyar

Aristotle, the Sage, 191, 218; mentioned in *Darabnamah*, 182; in *Iqbalnamah*, 178; in *Iskandarnamah*, 27, 31, 38, 40, 41, 44, 47, 52, 53, 54, 55, 57, 61, 65, 67–69, 73–74, 77, 78, 85, 97, 98, 100, 105, 107, 109, 116, 117, 118, 119, 125, 137, 138, 141, 146, 151, 152, 154–55, 156, 165; in *Khiradnamah*, 179; in *Shahnamah*, 169, 173, 214; in *Sharafnamah*, 174

Armenia, 176, 195

*Arriani Anabasis et Indica*, 212, 219; *see also* Müller

Arsalankhan, 82, 98, 115, 134, 136, 137, 138, 139, 140, 141, 143, 145, 146, 147, 149–51, 152, 155, 157, 158

Arsalankhan's daughter, *see* Shahmalik's daughter

Arthur, 1

*Athar al-baqiyah 'an al-qurun al-khaliyah*, 220, 221

Avesta (sacred writings of Zoroastrians), 188

Ayaz, 147, 165

'Ayn al-Hayat, 111, 113

# INDEX

'Ayn al-Sha'ab, 33
Azad, Abu al-Kalam, 220–21
Azadbakht, 22–23, 24, 25, 28–29, 30, 39, 165

Babil, 41
Babylon, 173, 179, 194, 195, 201, 219
Baghdad, 41
Bahar, M. T., 3
Bahman (Darab's grandfather), 14, 182, 205
Bahr al-Akhzar (also called Bahr al-Muhit), *see* Green Sea
Bahr al-Muhit (also called Bahr al-Akhzar), *see* Green Sea
Bahram, 65
Bahrein, 13
Bakhtiyar, 52
*Bakhtiyarnamah*, 208
Bakhtyanus, *see* Nectanebus
al-Bal'ami, Abu 'Ali Muhammad, 195, 207, 220, 221
Balinas (Appolonios), 178
Barqatisah, 48, 49, 165
Bayn al-Saddayn, 136, 158
"Beiträge zur Geschichte der Alexanderromans," 201, 217, 222
Bessos (Darab's assassin), 206, *see also* Janusibar; Mahyar
*Bet ha-Midrasch*, 209
Bible, 220
Bilqays (Queen of Sheba), 83, 211
Birahnigan, *see* Gog and Magog
al-Biruni, Abu Rayhan, 195–96, 220, 221
Bones of Jeremiah, 167; *see also* Pseudo-Epiphanius
Bonfils, I., 2, 205, 216, 220
*Book of the Gests of Alexander of Macedon, The*, 2, 205, 216, 220
Brahmans, 172, 180–81, 214, 222
Brahman Texts, 168
Bucephalus, 169, 213
"Bucephalus and His Legend," 213
Bukht al-Nasr (King of Syria), 101
Buqraquz (son of Shahmalik), 116–18, 119, 123, 129, 133–35, 165

Buqrat (Hippocrates), 180, 182, 183
Burandukht, 182–84, 216
Byzantine Empire, *see* Rum

Callisthenes, 1
Candace (also called Nushabah and Qandaqah), 48–51, 166, 171, 176, 192, 214, 216
Cary, George, 212, 216, 220, 222
Caspian Gate, 221
Cassandar (son of Antipater), 219
Ceylon, 17, 20, 21, 22, 30, 38, 206
Chardin, 189, 217
Charlemagne, 1
*Chaucer's Constance and Accused Queens*, 208
Chief of Egypt, 44, 45, 46, 52, 53
China, 3, 5, 66, 67, 176, 180, 192, 194, 196, 201
China Sea, 63, 64, 179
"Christian Legend Concerning Alexander, A," 201, 218, 219, 221, 223
Christ's sermon to his disciples, 207
*Collatio Alexandri Cum Dindimo per Litteras facta*, 176, 212
*Commonitorium Palladi*, 176, 212
Copts, 195
Cupbearer's Wife, 123, 125–28, 134, 136, 138–39, 141–45, 165
Cyrus the Great, 220–21

Dajjal, 31, 207
Daniel, 63, 101
Dara, *see* Darab ibn Darab
Darab, son of Bahman (Darab and Alexander's father in Persian legendry), 9–11, 169, 181–82, 191, 193, 205
Darab ibn Darab (also called Dara, Alexander's half brother in Persian legendry), 5, 9, 11–14, 16, 165, 169–70, 174–75, 180, 181, 187, 188, 189, 191–92, 193, 195, 196, 204, 205, 214
Darabgard, 11
*Darabnamah*, 181–84, 185 (fig.), 207, 214, 215, 219

Darab's assassins, *see* Ariobarzanes; Bessos; Janusibar; Mahyar
Darband, 195
Darius (Achaemenid King), 5, 205, 218; *see also* Darab ibn Darab
Darmesteter, J., 189, 217
Davalpayan, 36–37, 172, 207, 215
David, 62, 67, 209, 210, 211
Dhul-Qarnain, 3, 9, 10, 33, 37, 48, 59, 75, 182, 190, 196–201, 209, 210, 211, 215, 219, 220–21, 222–23
*Dhul-Qarnain ya Kurush-i Kabir*, 220–21
*Dicts and Sayings of the Philosophers*, 216; *see also* Hunayn ibn Ishaq; Mubashshir ibn Fatik
al-Dinawari, Abu Hanifah, 191, 193, 194, 213, 218
Dindimus de Bragmanibus, 167, 212
Disciplina Clericalis, 219
Divas, 114
Donath, L., 2, 205

Egypt, 3, 5, 43, 44, 169, 171, 174, 183, 188, 196
Elephant-ears, *see* Gog and Magog
Elijah and Rabbi Joshua ben Levi, legend of, 209
Emperor of China, 67, 69
*Epistola Alexandri ad Aristotelem*, 168, 214
Estatira (Darius's daughter), 206
Ethiopia, 180, 192, 200
Eve, 31, 206, 207

Fabulous Alexander-romances, 2, 168, 169, 222
Fairyland, *see* Land of Fairies
Fairy Queen, *see* Araqit
Farfurius (Porphyrios), 178
Farrukhbakht, 30, 38, 39, 165
*Farsnamah*, 196
Faryar, 171, 214
Filinus, 41, 165
Filqus, *see* Philip
Firaydun (legendary Iranian King), 207
Firdawsi, Abu al-Qasim, 2, 4, 168, 170, 191, 203, 208, 214, 215, 216, 218

Firuzshah, 181
Foetid Sea, 210
Fur, *see* Porus

Gabriel, 70, 210, 211, 222
Gabriel du Chinon, 189, 217
Gaster, Moses, 2, 205
*Ghazi*, 20, 206
Ghilan (a fairy), 89, 165
Gilgamesh epic, 209
Ginzberg, L., 210, 211, 217
Gog and Magog (also called Elephant-ears and Ya'juj wa Ma'juj), 3, 116, 120, 150–53, 167, 173, 179, 180, 195, 196, 198, 201, 211–12, 219, 221, 223
Gold Bees, 31–35
Golden eggs, 9, 170, 191, 213
Greece, 191, 192, 195, 196, 198, 218; *see also* Macedonia; Rum
Green Sea (Indian Ocean, also referred to as Bahr al-Akhzar, Bahr al-Muhit, and Akhzar Sea), 62, 65, 192, 195, 200, 210, 219
Gudarz of Isfahan, 14
Guillaume de Tignonville, 216; *see also Mukhtar al-hikam wa mahasin al-kilam*

Haft Anbur Garden, 111, 112, 113, 118, 120, 122, 128, 156
Haight, E. H., 213, 214, 215, 218, 219, 220
Hanaway, W. L., 216
Harum, *see* Amazon
Hermes, 177, 178, 180
Hijaz, 3
*Himasah'sara'i dar Iran*, 217
*Historia Adversum Paganos libri Septem*, 167
*Historia Alexandri Magni*, 205
*Historia de Preliis I¹*, 167, 185 (fig.)
*Historia de Preliis I²*, 167, 185 (fig.)
*Historia de Preliis I³*, 219, 185 (fig.)
*Historia Scholastica Patrologiae Cursus Completus, Accurante*, 220
"History of Abu Shakir," 220
"History of al-Makin," 219–20
Hud, 93, 211
Hum, 57

INDEX

Humay, 14, 205
Hunayn ibn Ishaq, 177, 216, 219

Ibn al-Athir, 196, 220
Ibn al-Balkhi, 196, 200
Ibn al-Isfandiyar, 187, 217
Ibn al-Muqaffa', 187
Ibn Hisham, 198
Ilyas (Elijah), 55, 56, 121, 183, 209, 212
Ilyas, son of Khara, 39, 208
Ilyas, son of Muzar, 40, 165, 208
India, 3, 63, 99, 170, 176, 182, 192, 193, 194, 201
*India*, 196, 220
*Iqbalnamah ya Khiradnamah*, 174, 177–79, 215, 222
Iram Garden, 93, 178, 216
Iran, 3, 9, 11–13, 38, 169–70, 175, 192
Isfahan, 14, 31, 170, 175, 189, 206
al-Isfahani, Hamzah ibn al-Hasan, 195, 220
Isfandiyar (Kiyanid King), 14, 206
Ishmael, 39, 40, 208
Iskandar, 165, 191; *see also* Alexander
*Iskandarnamah*, 3, 4, 5, 46, 62, 80, 93, 168, 197, 209, 211, 213, 214, 215, 216, 220, 222
Iskandarus, 120, 157, 176
Isqilinus, 180
Israfil (archangel), 59, 173, 200, 209
Istakhr (Persepolis), 13, 97, 175, 187, 188

Jabalqa, 57, 200, 209
Jabalsa, 117, 158, 200, 209, 212
Jacob of Serugh, 201, 215, 217, 219, 223
Jami, 'Abd al-Rahman, 168, 179–81, 213, 214, 215
Jamshid (legendary king), 21, 93, 116, 176, 206
Jamshid, religion of, 21, 116, 206
Janusibar (Darab's assassin), 13, 165, 192, 193, 213; *see also* Ariobarzanes; Bessos; Mahyar
Jellinek, A., 209
Jerusalem, 178, 184, 195, 199, 219
Jesus, 198
Jidda, 31, 171

Josephus, 167–68, 221
Julbab, 99
Julius Valerius, 2, 205
Jundul (King of Zangis), 147–48, 151, 165
Justin, 1, 167

Ka'bah, *see* Mecca
al-Kamil fi al-tarikh, 196, 220
Kand, *see* Kayd
*Karnamg-i Ardashir-i Babagan*, 187, 211
Kasandar, 15, 16, 165
Kashmir, 17, 22, 30, 38
Kayd (also Kand), 17, 20, 21, 30, 38, 165, 170, 182, 194, 214, 216
Kayd's daughter, 30, 41, 170
Kaykavus (legendary king), 54
Kaykhusraw (legendary king), 53, 54, 65, 93, 94, 176, 210
Kayqubad, 54, 93
Kazis, I., 2; *see also Book of the Gests of Alexander of Macedon, The*
Kerman, 12, 13, 14, 36
Khazars (a people), 192, 201, 208
Khidr (a prophet), 55, 56, 57–58, 121, 165, 172, 183, 199, 200, 208, 209, 212
*Khiradnamah-yi Iskandari*, 168, 179–81, 185 (fig.), 213, 214, 215
Khudadad, 52
Khvarazm, 180
King of Egypt, 44, 51
King of Oman (Kasandar), 15, 16, 165
King of Yemen (Munzar), 40–41, 42–43, 165
King's daughter, the (Alexander's wife), 66
*Kitab al-akhbar al-tiwal*, 218
*Kitab nawadir al-falasifah wa-al-hukama*, 177, 216, 219
*Kitab al-tanbih wa-al-ishraf*, 219
Kiyanids (legendary dynasty), 5, 170, 175, 205
Koran, 1, 31, 59, 168, 186, 192, 196–97, 198, 201, 209, 211, 219, 220, 221, 223

Land, 107–11, 112, 113, 117, 119, 131, 166
Land of Darkness, 3, 33, 35, 48, 53, 54, 55, 56–59, 61, 63, 64, 92, 104, 121, 172, 177, 192, 195, 198, 200, 215, 221

Land of Fairies, 3, 74–75, 76, 210, 211
Land of Giants, 74, 75
Land of Gold, 22, 30, 32–36
Land of Habash, 172
"Légende d'Alexandre chez les Parses, La" 189, 217
"Légende d'Alexandre dans le Talmud, La" 2, 205
*Legends of the Jews*, 210, 211, 217
Leo of Naples, Archpresbyter, 2, 167, 205, 217
Levi, I., 2, 205
Lewis, Bernard, 212
*Life of Alexander of Macedon by Pseudo-Callisthenes* (translated by E. H. Haight), 213, 214, 215, 218, 219, 220
*Life and Exploits of Alexander the Great, Being a Series of Translations from Ethiopic*, 2, 168, 169, 184, 204, 207, 209, 213, 214, 215, 217, 218, 219, 220, 222
Loewenthal, A., 216
Luhrasb (legendary king), 57, 66
Luqman, the Sage, 183

Macedonia, 169, 217; *see also* Rum
Machin, 64
Magic circle (manzal), 75, 76, 77, 78, 91, 163, 210
Mahafarin (King of Kashmir's daughter), 22, 25–26, 27–30, 41, 165, 206
Mahjasb, 111
Mahyar (Darab's assassin), 13, 165, 182, 192, 193, 213; *see also* Ariobarzanes; Bessos; Janusibar
Maiden saved from Zangis (Alexander's wife), 75–76
al-Makin, 219–20
*Mandeville's Travels*, 207, 212, 217
Mankus (a Brahman), 26–27
Mankus (a Zangi Chief), 120, 165
Mankus's son, 120, 126, 136
Manuchihr (legendary king), 93
Manzal, *see* Magic circle
Maqam-i Ibrahim, 40, 208
al-Mas'udi, Abu al-Hasan 'Ali, 194, 195, 214, 219

Mecca, 39–40, 171, 183, 192, 199, 206, 207, 208
*Medieval Alexander, The* (George Cary), 212, 216, 220, 222
Mediterranean Sea, 63
Messiah, 101, 211
*Midrash Agadah*, 220
Mina, 40, 208
Misan, 206
Moses, 62, 63, 198, 209, 221
*Motif Index to Folk Literature*, 210
Mountain of Gold, *see* Land of Gold
Mubashshir ibn Fatik, 177, 216, 219
al-Mufid (Arabicized form of Olympias), 196; *see also* Olympias
Muhammed, 201, 209, 210, 211
*Mujmal al-tawarikh wa-al-qisas*, 196, 218, 221, 223
*Mukhtar al-hikam wa mahasin al-kilam*, 177, 216, 219
Mukran, 43
Müller, C., 212, 213, 214, 215, 217
Muluk al-tawa'if (tribal kings), 187, 189, 193
Munzar, 40–41, 42–43, 165
Musá al-Khidr, 199, 222; *see also* Khidr
Muzdalifah, 40, 208

Nafisi, Sa'id, 3
Nahid (Alexander's mother), 9–10, 169, 181
Nahid (Porus's daughter), 22, 29, 30, 165
*Namah-yi Tansar*, 187, 217
Names of God, 35, 63, 76, 79, 81, 87, 89, 90, 107, 207
Narmpayan, *see* Davalpayan
Nasr, son of Qabit, 40
*Nativitas et Victoria Alexandri Magni Regis*, 2, 167, 205, 217
*Natural History* (by Pliny), 215
Nayshaburi, Ibrahim ibn Mansur, 4, 56, 210, 211, 221
Nazur ibn Kannanah, 192
Nectanebus (Egyptian sorcerer king), 1, 196, 213, 218
Nile, 178, 183

# INDEX

Nizami, Nizam al-Din Ilyas, 168, 174, 177, 178, 179, 204, 213, 214, 215, 216, 220, 222
Noah, 93, 206
Nöldeke, Theodore, 201, 217, 222
Nushabah, *see* Candace

Ohrmazd, 188
"Old Hebrew Romance of Alexander, An" 2, 205
Olympias (Alexander's mother), 1, 194, 196; *see also* Nahid
Oman, 15, 16, 17, 18, 20, 37
Orosius, 167

Pahlavi (Middle Persian), 186
Pahlavi literature, 186, 187, 188, 189, 214
Palestine, 43
Paradise of Ganges, 66, 210
Pars, 9, 11, 13, 14, 20, 31, 33, 97
Persepolis, *see* Istakhr
"Persian Popular Romances before the Safavid Period," 216
Petrus Alfonsi, 219
Petrus Comestor, 220
Philip (Alexander's father; in Persian legendry, his grandfather), 1, 9, 10, 145, 169, 174, 179, 189, 191, 193
Piruz of Tus, 146, 151, 152
Plato, 178, 180, 183
Pliny, 215
"Poetic Version of Alexander's Story," 201, 215, 217, 219, 223
Polygamy, 14, 41, 45, 65, 74, 75–76, 98–99, 105, 123, 156–57, 170, 173
Porus (King of India), 16, 17, 18, 19–21, 22, 165, 170, 171, 182, 192, 206, 213, 214
Psalms, 67
*Pseudo-Callisthenes* (a prose biography of Alexander), 1, 167, 185 (fig.), 190, 206, 208, 218, 219, 220, 222; Arabic derivative, 2, 168, 184, 190; Ethiopic derivative, 2, 168, 169, 184, 204, 207, 209, 213, 214, 215, 217, 218, 219, 220, 222; Latin derivatives, 2, 167, 205, 214, 215, 217; Pahlavi derivative, 2, 168, 184, 186; Persian derivatives, 2, 168, 184, 186, 191, 203, 208; Syriac derivatives, 2, 168, 169, 190, 204, 210, 212, 214, 215, 217, 218, 219; *see also* Firdawsi; Iskandarnamah; Jami; Nizami; Tarsusi
Pseudo-Callisthenes recensions, 185 (f.); α, 167, 214, 219; β, 167; γ, 167, 219; *δ, 2, 167, 168, 169, 184, 207, 212
*Pseudo-Epiphanius*, 167, 220
Pseudo-Methodius, 167
Ptolemy, 194
Pythagoras, 180

Qaf Mountain, 57, 59, 182, 183, 209
Qandaqah, *see* Candace
Qarakhan, 82, 166
Qatil, 106, 107, 108, 109, 110, 119–20, 131
Qatil's bride, 103–5, 109, 137
Qaydafah, *see* Candace
Qaymaz, 147, 166
Qaymun, 137, 138, 139, 140, 145, 147, 166
Qaymun's daughter, 156
*Qim* (a horn), 197
*Qisas al-anbiya'*, 4, 56, 210, 211, 221
Queen of Sheba, 83, 211
Quintus Curtius, 1, 167
Qum, 31

Rabbi Joshua ben Levi, 209
*Race and Color in Islam*, 212
Rafi', 112, 166
Reich, R., 2, 221
*Res Gestae Alexandri Macedonis*, 2, 205
Ross, D. J. A., 217
Roxana (also called Rushanak, Darab's wife), 14, 166, 170, 175, 180, 206, 213
Rum (Macedonia or Greece), 9, 10, 13, 14, 16, 17, 25, 37, 38, 41, 50, 63, 87, 90, 99, 113, 123, 145, 173, 175, 177, 217
Rumi slave girl, 145–46
Rumi sorcerers, 77, 88–90
Rushanak, *see* Roxana
Russia, 100, 102, 180
Ruvid, 94, 96, 97, 98, 159, 166, 211

Sa'b Dhul-Qarnain, 198–201, 218, 221
Sa'b Dhu-Marathid, 198
Safa, Z., 3, 217
Sage Aristotle, *see* Aristotle
Sages of Rum, 63
Sagha, 53
Salih, 93, 211
Sassanian, 187, 217
Schlauch, M., 208
Scrope, Stephen, 216
Secretum Secretorum, 179, 216
Shahmalik (King of Taghmaj, also called King of the East), 74, 82, 114–16, 117, 118–19, 120, 122–23, 124–26, 127, 128, 134–35, 141, 147, 148–49, 150, 166, 212
Shahmalik's daughter (also referred to as Arsalankhan's daughter), 82, 83, 84–85, 86–87, 88, 98, 115, 117, 123–25, 127–30, 133–35, 211, 212
*Shahnamah*, 4, 57, 169, 185 (fig.), 189, 191, 205, 206, 208, 209, 210, 213, 216, 218, 219, 220, 222
*Sharafnamah*, 174–77, 185 (fig.), 213, 214, 215
Shattad of 'Ad, 93, 178
Shaykh Abu Sa'id Khargushi, 63, 210
Sind, 173, 201
Sindah, 91, 96, 97, 166
Sitarah, 44, 166
Siyavush, 53, 66, 208
Siyavushgard, 66
Slavs, 192
Socrates, 178, 180
Solomon, 62, 63, 64, 66, 70, 72, 76, 77, 91, 93, 142, 209, 210, 211, 221–22
Spiegel, F., 190, 217
Sudan, 192, 200
Suhayl, 41–43
Sultan Mahmud, 1, 63
Suzanna and the Elders, 210
Syria, 53, 60, 192, 195
"Syriac Legend Concerning Alexander, The," 210

al-Tabari, Muhammad ibn Jarir, 193, 194, 195, 196, 206, 207, 208, 211, 222

Tafqaj, 122–23, 124, 126, 130–33, 141, 166
Taghmaj (also Tamghaj, a country), 74, 115
Tahmuris (legendary king), 54
Tahtaj, 46–47
*Tales of Alexander the Macedonian*, 2, 221
Talmudic literature, 194, 220
Tamghaj (king of Divas), 114–15
Tamghaj (a country), *see* Taghmaj
*Tamkhisa*, see names of God
*al-Tanbih wa-al-ishraf*, 219
Tansar, 187
*Tarikh al-rusul wa-al-muluk*, 193, 194, 195, 196
*Tarikh sini muluk al-arz wa-al-anbiya'*, 220
*Tarjumah-yi tafsir-i Tabari*, 206, 207, 208, 222
*Tarjumah va taklamah-yi tarikh Tabari*, 195, 206–7, 220, 221
Tarsusi, Abu Tahir Muhammad, 2, 168, 181, 207, 213, 219
Tarzak, 147, 166
Thamud, 211
Thompson, S., 210
Tibet, 193, 194
*al-Tijan*, 198–201, 210, 211, 215, 216, 217, 218, 219, 221
Tinush, 49, 50, 51, 52, 166
Transoxania, 176
Tribal kings (muluk al-tawa'if), 187, 189, 193
Turanmalik, 127–28, 129, 131, 132, 166
Turanmalik's son, 131, 132, 166
Turanshah, 66
Turkistan, 3, 38, 54, 65, 192, 194

'Udj, 106

Valerius Maximus, 168
Valis, 178
*Vitae Prophetarum*, 167, 220

Wahb ibn Munabbih, 64, 198, 201, 209, 210, 221, 222
Warner, A. G., 213, 214

# INDEX

Water of Life, 35, 54, 55, 57–58, 64, 172, 200, 209, 215
Western Sea, 64
Wonderstone, 177, 184, 200, 217, 222

Ya'juj wa Ma'juj, see Gog and Magog
Yaqutmalik, 159, 160, 161–62, 163, 166
Yaris, 67
Yemen, 3, 40, 41, 42, 43, 173, 176, 192
Yisa', 55–56, 209

Zahhak, 33–34, 38, 55, 93, 116, 188, 207
Zamzam, 40, 208

Zangis (black Africans), 34, 78, 98, 103–5, 106–14, 119–20, 121, 131–32, 147–48, 150, 158, 174, 182, 210
*Zand Akasih, Iranian or Greater Bundahišn*, 188
Zend (translation of and commentary on Avesta), 188
Zinj, 3, 210; *see also* Zangis
al-Zirikli, 208, 210, 218
Zoroaster, 170, 188
Zoroastrianism, 175, 186, 187, 188, 189
Zubaydah, 142–44, 148, 155, 156–57, 162, 166, 211

# Persian Heritage Series

**Volumes Published**

Varavini, *The Tales of Marzuban* (No. 1), tr. Reuben Levy
  Indiana Univ. Press, 1959 (Reprint 1968)

Tusi, *The Nasirean Ethics* (No. 2), tr. G.M. Wickens
  London: George Allen & Unwin, 1964

Ferdowsi, *The Epic of the Kings* (No. 3), tr. Reuben Levy
  University of Chicago Press, 1967 (Reprint 1973)

Nezami, *Le Sette Principesse* (No. 4), tr. A. Bausani
  Rome: Leonardo da Vinci, 1967

Attar, *Muslim Saints & Mystics* (No. 5), tr. A.J. Arberry
  University of Chicago Press, 1966 (Reprint 1973)

Nezami, *Chosroès et Chîrîne* (No. 6), tr. Henri Massé
  Paris: Maisonneuve et Larose, 1970

Rumi, *Mystical Poems I* (No. 7), tr. A.J. Arberry
  University of Chicago Press, 1974

Aruzi, *Les quatre discours* (No. 8), tr. I. de Gastines
  Paris: Maisonneuve et Larose, 1968

Anon., *The Letter of Tansar* (No. 9), tr. M. Boyce
  Rome: IsMEO, 1968

Rashid al-Din, *The Successors of Genghis Khan* (No. 10)
  tr. J.A. Boyle, Columbia University Press, 1971

Mohammad ibn Ibrahim, *The Ship of Sulaiman* (No. 11)
  tr. J. O'Kane, Columbia University Press, 1972

Faramarz, *Samak-e Ayyar* (No. 12), tr. F. Razavi
  Paris: Maisonneuve et Larose, 1972

Avicenna, *Metaphysica* (No. 13), tr. P. Morewedge
  Columbia University Press, 1973

Gurgani, *Vis and Ramin* (No. 14), tr. G. Morrison
  Columbia University Press, 1972

# Persian Heritage Series

**Volumes Published**

Fasai, *History of Persia Under Qajar Rule* (No. 15)
    tr. H. Busse, Columbia University Press, 1972

Aturpat-e Emetan, *Denkart III* (No. 16), tr. J. De Menasce
    Paris: Libraire Klincksieck, 1974

Sa'di, *Bustan* (No. 17), tr. G.M. Wickens
    University of Toronto Press, 1974

Anon., *Folk Tales of Ancient Persia* (No. 18)
    tr. F. Hekmat & Y. Lovelock, Delmar, N.Y.: Caravan Books, 1974

Bighami, *Love and War* (No. 19), tr. W. Hanaway Jr.
    Delmar, N.Y., Scholars' Facsimiles & Reprints, 1974

Anon., *The History of Sistan* (No. 20), tr. M. Gold
    Rome: IsMEO, 1977

*Manichaean Literature* (An Anthology) (No. 22), tr. J. Asmussen
    Delmar, N.Y., Scholars' Facsimiles & Reprints, 1974

Rumi, *Le Livre du Dedans* (No. 25), tr. E. de Vitray-Meyerovitch
    Paris: Edition Sinbad, 1975

Rumi, *Licht und Reigen* (No. 26), tr. J. Ch. Bürgel
    Bern: Herbert Lang Verlag, 1974

Samarkandi, *Le Livre des sept vizirs* (No. 27), tr. D. Bogdanovic
    Paris: Edition Sinbad, 1975

Attar, *Ilahiname* (No. 29), tr. J.A. Boyle
    Manchester University Press, 1977

Hafez, *Divan (Hafizu-Shishu)* (No. 30), tr. T. Kuriyanagi
    Tokyo: Heibosha Ltd., 1977

Anon., *Iskandarnamah* (No. 31), tr. M. Southgate
    Columbia University Press, 1978

Nezami, *Khosrau and Shirin* (No. 33), tr. A. Okada
    Tokyo: Heibosha Ltd., 1977

# Persian Heritage Series

**In Press**

Rumi, *Mystical Poems II* (No. 23)
    tr. A.J. Arberry

Eskandar Beg Monshi, *History of Shah 'Abbas* (No. 28)
    tr. R.M. Savory

Nizam al-Molk, *The Book of Government* (No. 32)
    tr. H. Darke

Aturpat-e Emetan, *Denkart III* (No. 34)
    tr. S. Shaked

Nishapuri, *History of the Saljuqs*
    tr. A. Luther (No. 24)

**Forthcoming**

Razi, *Mersad al-Ebad*
    tr. H. Algar

Mohammad b. Monavvar, *Asrar al-Tawhid*
    tr. J. O'Kane

Naser-e Khosrow, *Safarnama*
    tr. W. Thaxton

Tabari, *Annals 774-809 A.D.*
    tr. J.A. Williams

Anon., *Myths and Legends of Ancient Iran*
    tr. E. Yarshater

Anon., *Sasanian Law Book (Matikan-i hazar datastan)*
    tr. A. Perikhanian and N. Garsoian

Ferdausi, *Anthologie du livre des rois*
    tr. J. Mohl, edit. G. Lazard

Anon., *Le livre d'Ardaviraz*
    tr. P. Gignoux

Gardizi, *History*
    tr. A. Pontecorvo

Khayyam, *The Ruba 'iyat*
    tr. P. Avery and Heath-Stubbs

# Persian Studies Series

**Published**

Reuben Levy, *Introduction to Persian Literature*
    Columbia University Press, 1969

Ali Dashti, *In Search of Omar Khayyam* (No. 1), tr. L.P. Elwell-Sutton
    London: George Allen & Unwin, 1971

James Pearson, *A Bibliography of Pre-Islamic Persia* (No. 2)
    London: Mansell Information and Publishing Ltd., 1975

M.H. Tabataba'i, *Shi'ite Islam* (No. 5), tr. S.H. Nasr
    State University of New York Press, 1975

J. Ch. Bürgel, *Drei Hafis Studien* (No. 6)
    Bern: Herbert Lang Verlag, 1975

*Biruni: A Symposium*, ed. E. Yarshater (No. 10)
    Columbia University, 1976

Christopher J. Brunner, *A Syntax of Western Middle Iranian* (No. 3)
    Delmar, New York: Caravan Books, 1977

John Yohannan, *Persian-Literature in England and America* (No. 4)
    Delmar, New York: Caravan Books, 1977

Clifford Edmund Bosworth, *The Later Ghaznavids* (No. 7)
    Edinburg University Press, 1977


**In Press**

A. Schimmel, *Rumi: A Study of His Life and Works* (No. 8)
    London: Fine Books

M.J. MacDermott, *The Theology of al-Shaikh al-Mufid* (No. 9)
    Beirut: Dar el-Machreq


All inquiries about the Persian Heritage and Persian Studies Series should be directed to Mr. Felix Weigel, Harrassowitz, P.O. Box 2929, P-6200 Weisbaden, Germany.

**OHIO UNIVERSITY LIBRARY**

Please return this book as soon as you have finished with it. In order to avoid a fine it must be returned by the latest date stamped below.